What People Are Saying About This Book

Dr Gatiss is always insightful but he is also fresh, provocative and challenging. In his exposition of particular passages, I like his repeated personal challenge to us. He draws on the riches of patristic teaching but also on his experience of the contemporary world in ways that illuminate the biblical text for us in new and helpful ways. The commentary will be a very useful aid to those preparing to read, to preach, and to hear.

Monsignor Dr Michael Nazir-Ali, Oxford Centre for Training, Research, Advocacy & Dialogue

Lee Gatiss's sparkling set of reflections on the weekly lectionary readings are crisp mini-sermons that are exegetically faithful, theologically perceptive and attentive in applying God's word to the heart as well as to the head. Highly recommended.

The Revd Dr Mark Smith, Dean of Clare College, Cambridge

At a time when biblical literacy seems to be waning, this is a timely resource that draws on wide biblical and historical sources to help make fruitful connections between the lectionary readings for each Sunday. It will provide a stimulating catalyst for further reflection to help the whole of God's word be better heard and understood in our churches.

The Rt Revd Dr Robert Munro, Bishop of Ebbsfleet

Lee Gatiss comments on the three Bible readings for the Principal Service each week over the span of three years, attempting to find a unifying theme or link between them and relating it to the season in the Church calendar. A concluding list of hymns and songs appropriate to the day is provided, as a helpful resource for those responsible for planning services with a thematic focus.

The Revd Dr David Peterson, Moore Theological College, Sydney

Those of us ministering in more liturgical, lectionary-following churches, while being committed to an expository method of preaching, occasionally feel like we're starting our sermon preparation on the back foot. How can we preach on the set readings in a way that is hermeneutically faithful, doctrinally orthodox, but also sensitive to the place within the Church year? This is where Lee's book can help. He not only gives a faithful steer on the passages themselves, but also sparks off an idea or two about how they might preach in Advent/Epiphany/Lent and so on.

The Revd Dr Tom Woolford, Vicar of New Longton and Tutor in Theology at Emmanuel Theological College

For many churches the weekly rhythm of the lectionary is both a comforting tradition and a living connection with the global church. Keeping in step with this rhythm, Lee Gatiss is poetically inspiring, lifting up our souls to glorify God, and also pastorally rooted, equipping our lives for daily service. *The Word Week by Week* is a wonderful companion for anyone who belongs to a church that follows the lectionary, and an indispensable resource for anyone who preaches from it.

The Revd George Crowder, Rector of St Mary's, Cheadle and founder of the Network of Revitalisation Ministries (NoRM).

'There can be nothing either more necessary or profitable than the knowledge of Holy Scripture.' These opening words of Thomas Cranmer's First Homily reflect the core conviction that we are primarily formed in faith as we listen carefully to God's word. Lee Gatiss helps us to do just this, and I look forward to using his book in my own preaching preparation.

The Rt Revd Paul Donison, General Secretary of the Global Anglican Futures Conference (GAFCON).

Author biography

The Revd Dr Lee Gatiss is the Director of Church Society, Fellow in Church History and Anglicanism at the Greystone Theological Institute and a lecturer in Church History at Union School of Theology. A popular speaker, he has written and edited more than thirty books on the Bible, theology, church history and Anglicanism and is the General Editor of *The Complete Works of John Owen* and *The Hodder Bible Commentary*.

The Word Week by Week

DISCOVER THE RHYTHM AND TRADITION OF THE WORLDWIDE CHURCH

LEE GATISS

HODDER & STOUGHTON

First published in Great Britain in 2025 by Hodder Faith
An imprint of John Murray Press
1

A CIP catalogue record for this title is available from the British Library

Hardback ISBN 978 1 399 82097 4
ebook ISBN 978 1 399 82099 8

Typeset in Walbaum MT Std by Manipal Technologies Limited

Printed and bound in Great Britain by Clays Ltd, Elcograf S.p.A.

John Murray Press policy is to use papers that are natural, renewable and recyclable products and made from wood grown in sustainable forests. The logging and manufacturing processes are expected to conform to the environmental regulations of the country of origin.

Carmelite House
50 Victoria Embankment
London EC4Y 0DZ

www.hodderfaith.com

John Murray Press, part of Hodder & Stoughton Limited
An Hachette UK company

The authorised representative in the EEA is Hachette Ireland,
8 Castlecourt Centre, Dublin 15, D15 XTP3, Ireland (email: info@hbgi.ie)

Contents

Introduction

There is great wisdom in following a time-honoured cycle of Bible readings in conjunction with the rhythm of the Church's traditional calendar. It gives us continuity with the past, connecting us to the same regular patterns which have punctuated the lives of our forebears over the last two millennia. It also connects us to the wider church around the world today, many of whom will be reading the same passages of Scripture each week from the *Revised Common Lectionary*.

A lectionary is a list of readings from the Bible. The name comes from the Latin word *lectio*, meaning a reading. Lectionaries are usually for use in a Sunday service at church, but there are also daily lectionaries for churches and daily Bible reading plans for individual Christians (such as that developed by the Scottish minister Robert Murray M'Cheyne in the nineteenth century).[1] Such carefully planned schedules for reading have been compiled for a very long time in the Church, and their intention is usually to ensure that over time the people of God gathered on the Lord's Day are exposed to a significant portion of Scripture. As theologian J. I. Packer once wrote, 'it is good to follow a Lectionary, because Lectionaries exist to ensure that everything of importance in the Bible is, in due course, read aloud in church'.[2] As they lay down several readings for each week, lectionaries expose us to large portions of different parts of the Bible – Old Testament Law and Prophets, New Testament Gospels and Epistles – rather than just a few short verses chosen by the preacher for their sermon that week. This can save people

---

[1] See Don Carson, 'Don Carson on the Excellencies of the M'Cheyne Bible-Reading Plan' at https://www.thegospelcoalition.org/article/mcheyne-bible-reading-plan/ (5 April 2023).

[2] J. I. Packer, 'For Truth, Unity, and Hope: Revaluing the Book of Common Prayer', *Churchman* 114.2 (2000), p. 103.

from a more narrow vision of the Bible being dictated by a pastor who only ever selects their favourite texts and subjects. It also means we expose ourselves to the manifold riches of different parts of the Bible in a regular and systematic way, which can be immensely beneficial spiritually.

Lectionaries can also enable churches to plan certain readings at particular times of the year, following the wisdom of the Church calendar through major moments in the life of Jesus: for example, at Christmas, Lent and Easter. In profound ways, we remember the birth, death and resurrection of Jesus *every* Sunday, but there is something about human nature which makes it wise to build in regular times of particular remembrance for key events like this. The Trinity is foundational to everything about the Christian life, but celebrating Trinity Sunday once a year means we regularly remind ourselves about how tremendous and astonishing this truth about God really is.

The Lectionary does not start in January, like the calendar year. In the UK, the tax year begins in April and the academic year in September, so we are used to the idea of marking time in divergent ways. For reasons too obscure to mention here, lectionary years (known as Years A, B and C) begin in Advent, in the run-up to Christmas. Outside the great festivals (such as Pentecost, where we remember the sending of the Spirit), the readings in 'Ordinary Time' (roughly June to November) cover many aspects of the Christian life. So the life of Christ and the life of the Christian are both covered in a wonderful balance throughout the year. If widely adopted, lectionaries can enable individuals and churches all over the world to be reading and studying the same texts each Sunday. This can be a joyfully unifying experience, despite all our many differences.

In my own Anglican tradition, the Church of England's classic lectionary was that found in the *Book of Common Prayer* (1662). It prescribed a healthy and robust diet of Bible reading and preaching for every Anglican church. As J. I. Packer rightly observes, 'The Anglicanism of the 1662 Prayer Book, with its hundred-verses-a-day lectionary, its monthly passage through the Psalter, its

Bible-crammed daily services, and its high valuation of expository preaching ... is a Bible-reading, Bible-loving, Bible-believing faith.'[3] If you followed all the set readings laid down in the Prayer Book, you would get through the Bible at a fairly rapid pace. So during the Reformation, the English church became the Bible-hearing church *par excellence*, because the English reformers wanted all people, not just the chosen few, to be able to ruminate and meditate on Scripture and for it to change their hearts and everyday lives.[4]

In more recent times, there have been great efforts by a number of denominations (both Protestant and Roman Catholic) to co-ordinate their Bible reading across the world. This led to the development of the *Revised Common Lectionary*, which is now used by many all over the globe. This lectionary has a three-year repeating cycle of multiple readings for several Sunday services each week. Helpfully, it focuses on one of the so-called synoptic Gospels (Matthew, Mark, or Luke) each year and covers a great deal of scriptural ground. But it is true that even if one attended three Sunday services following this lectionary every week for three years, one would not have heard *all* of the Bible read out. Yet I wonder where that would ever be true? Even in churches which pride themselves on preaching consecutively through whole books of the Bible (which is another old and honoured tradition), the amount of Scripture read and the overall coverage of it is not always as broad as might be hoped.[5] In general, what is covered here in this book and in the Lectionary itself can be seen in the Scripture Index at the end of this volume, although that also contains some of the cross-references

---

[3] Packer, *God Has Spoken* (London: Hodder and Stoughton, 1993), pp. 119–20.

[4] See Ashley Null and John W. Yates III (eds.), *Reformation Anglicanism: A Vision for Today's Global Communion* (Wheaton: Crossway, 2017), pp. 71, 76. Packer, 'For Truth, Unity, and Hope', p. 105 says 'it is plain that our Reformers meant the Anglican Church to become the greatest Bible-reading church in Christendom, and Anglican Christians to become the most knowledgeable Bible students to be found anywhere.'

[5] See Philip Keen, 'Preaching the Whole Bible? Do Conservative Evangelicals Really Mean It?', in *The Global Anglican* 135.4 (2021), pp. 347–69.

I have introduced. There is plenty of it, to feed your heart, mind and soul!

The *Revised Common Lectionary* is not perfect or exhaustive, of course, and needs complementing with our own private or group reading of the missing texts.[6] It does not have to be followed slavishly and without pastoral wisdom. But it is now widely adopted and hallowed with use to a certain extent. The Church of England suggests lengthening some of the shorter readings (and that is what I have followed in this book), and there is of course nothing to stop most of us from reading whatever we like in the comfort of our own homes and small study groups during the week. The way the Lectionary is arranged enables some consecutive reading through individual books of the Bible each Sunday. Since more than one reading is set for each week, it also ensures that no week goes by without us hearing something from the Old Testament as well as the New, whereas in many churches which don't follow a lectionary, there is such a marked preference for sermons on the New Testament and a strange desire to only read the few verses being preached on, that congregations may not even hear the Old Testament for many months, despite it being by far the largest part of the Bible. Sometimes there are various options to choose from within the Lectionary's set readings (such as between 'Continuous' Old Testament readings or ones 'Related' to the Gospel reading). I have made and indicated my own choices on those occasions.

This book contains an explanation and unfolding of the meaning of the readings in the *Revised Common Lectionary* for the Principal Service in church each week. I hope it will be a help to preachers as they prepare to enlighten and inspire their congregations. But it can be used at home in an armchair just as easily as it can in church. Just get your Bible out or open the Bible app on your phone (use whichever translation you like), read the passages allocated for each day which I've listed at the top of the page and then ponder them

---

6 For more on its imperfections, see Roger Beckwith, 'The Revised Common Lectionary' in *Churchman* 112.2 (1998), pp. 117–23.

with me as you read my reflections. Scribble in the margins, underline something that makes you think, turn a provocative thought you read into prayer back to God. You could make this book into a spiritual journal, a record of how the Spirit deals with your soul throughout the year as you hear his voice in Scripture and meditate on it. You may come back to it again and again for reminders or inspiration for prayer and action.

I have usually chosen to reflect on all three main passages as set, with the psalm for the day too, with some attempt to find a unifying theme or link between the readings. The connection of the three passages is of course a human invention, not divinely inspired in and of itself, but as long as the individual readings are not bent out of their own shape in the process, it is always illuminating to compare and contrast different parts of God's word. Scripture is its own best interpreter, since God, in the end, is the unerring author of it all.

I always find when I'm preparing to preach that it is only when I am able to crystallise the main point of the Bible passage that I can then work out how to teach and apply it. Until then it is a jumble of disconnected thoughts and ideas in my head, which would make for a messy and confusing sermon. So I have sought to find coherence and clarity as best I can, because even the great apostle Paul asked the Colossians to 'Pray that I may proclaim it *clearly*, as I should' (Colossians 4:4). Incoherent obscurity in the mind of the preacher leads to incoherent obscurity in the pulpit and incoherent obscurity in the pews – none of which is a blessing!

Eagle-eyed readers will notice that there are more than fifty-two sets of readings per year, and might be puzzled by this. It is because Easter is a 'moveable feast' with a changing date each year. The timing of it depends on the movements of the sun and the moon in the lunisolar calendar, an ancient method of dividing the year, which doesn't always line up neatly with the modern western calendar (the Hebrew and Chinese years are lunisolar too). That means the six-week period of Lent, leading up to Easter, also moves around a little each year. That creates the need for sets of readings which may not be used one year, but might be needed the next because the wait for Easter is a little longer. I have made this book as comprehensive as possible, including all possible Sundays,[7] although I have not provided a commentary for Christmas Day (which may or may not be on a Sunday) or the many midweek feast days that occur.

We are used to having certain days or times set aside in the secular calendar for certain reasons: Remembrance Day or Memorial Day, Thanksgiving, Mother's Day, Independence Day perhaps, and other days such as the International Day of Friendship. The Church year is no different in this respect, but marks events of special significance to Christians. You can see it in basic outline on the contents pages of this book. To help you work out where you should be in the Lectionary during the year, I have included some dating tips throughout the book where this is possible, but also a comprehensive table after this introduction with the key dates you need to know up to 2040. The fixed points of the lectionary year are that it starts on the First Sunday of Advent every year, and the run up to Easter starts on the Second Sunday before Lent. So-called 'Ordinary Time' is that period outside of the Christmas and Easter seasons, so there's a brief 'Ordinary' period after Christmas, and it begins again after Easter with Trinity Sunday (the Sundays during this period are labelled Propers 1, 2, 3, etc.). That's why I have provided those dates in the chart. (You may also be able to find out which week it is in the lectionary with a simple online search!)

Some special moments in the Christian story are remembered every year. The remarkable occasion where Jesus was 'transfigured' and his face shone like the sun, for example, is commemorated every year on the Sunday before Lent. There are other regular celebrations such as Epiphany (which means 'manifestation'), recalling the appearance of Christ to the Gentiles (the wise men of the Christmas story). Ascension Day (remembering Christ's ascension into heaven, in Acts 1)

---

7 The readings for the Second Sunday of Christmas are the same in Years A, B, and C, as are the readings for Epiphany, so you will only find an exposition of these in Year A.

is a midweek occasion, but there is a 'Sunday after Ascension' too. Pentecost is the celebration of the coming of the Holy Spirit (see Acts 2), and is called Whitsun or Whit Sunday in some traditions. The Feast of Christ the King was first instituted a hundred years ago, and since 1969 it has been celebrated by various denominations on the Last Sunday before Advent. You will find reference to these in the appropriate places throughout this book.

I prepared from the Greek and Hebrew, and consulted various English translations, but have tried to make this book both straightforwardly readable and nourishingly profound. I am indebted to the *NIV Proclamation Bible*, a study resource by sixty-five contributors from four continents which I had the privilege of editing some years ago, for often inspiring and helping me along the way.[8] You will also find here nuggets of gold from many other commentators and theologians who have enlightened me and illuminated the texts and their application, such as Chrysostom, Augustine, Aquinas, Luther, Calvin, Matthew Henry, George Herbert, John Owen, Charles Simeon, John Stott and Don Carson. There is an index listing these sources of wisdom at the back of the book, with a brief note about who (and when and where) these people are. I am also indebted to other modern sources such as *The Africa Bible Commentary* and *Feminist Biblical Interpretation: A Compendium of Critical Commentary on the Books of the Bible and Related Literature*, which were helpful for seeing how others summarise things or to ponder them from a different perspective to my own.[9]

I have included an appendix with suggestions for hymns and songs, both ancient and modern, which might be sung in church (or in the home) to accompany the set readings, which may also make this a useful resource for organists and musical directors. This was a feature I included in my weekly column on the lectionary in

---

[8] *The NIV Proclamation Bible* (London: Hodder and Stoughton, 2013).

[9] Tokunboh Adeyemo (ed.), *The Africa Bible Commentary* (Grand Rapids: Zondervan, 2006); Luise Schottroff and Marie-Theres Wacker (ed.), *Feminist Biblical Interpretation: A Compendium of Critical Commentary on the Books of the Bible and Related Literature* (Grand Rapids: Eerdmans, 2012).

The Church of England Newspaper (2013–19), and was well received. I acknowledge the Editor's kind permission to re-use many of those (now re-edited) columns here, as I also did in my weekly 'Lee on the Lectionary' videos on Facebook and the Church Society website (www.churchsociety.org). Some of the material in this book appears here for the first time, but it was a tremendous blessing to me to expound the lectionary readings publicly in these ways for many years – I learned a lot in doing so! I hope the fruit of my labours and the many hours of prayerful meditation on God's word which this book represents will also be a great blessing to many others.

I am very grateful to my excellent editor at Hodder, Emily Wells, for her careful attention to detail and all her many comments and suggestions which I hope have made this book much more user-friendly. I would also like to thank, and dedicate this book to, the men and women of the Junior Anglican Evangelical Conference (JAEC), hundreds of whom have attended the conference and been part of the network of which I am the Chairman over the last decade and more. They have been a terrific encouragement and a constant spur to continued fruitful engagement in the Scriptures, in theology and church history, and in the Church of England itself. May the Lord continue to bless all their endeavours for the glory of God and the good of his world!

LEE GATISS
Cambridge

A note for users of the Roman Catholic *Sunday Missal.*

A new three-volume *Sunday Missal* approved for use in the Roman Catholic Dioceses of England & Wales, and Scotland was published by Hodder & Stoughton in 2024. This contains the readings set for Roman Catholic congregations in those countries according to the English Standard Version of the Bible, Catholic Edition (ESV-CE) arranged according to the Roman Catholic edition of the Lectionary. The Missal generally has slightly shorter readings than those I have given in this volume, omitting some of the verses, though occasionally it may set a little extra. The Psalm readings do not always harmonise between this volume and the *Sunday Missal* and occasionally the epistle readings are staggered over different weeks. Roman Catholic readers will perhaps notice that I have not chosen readings from the Apocrypha in this volume, and on some occasions have elected for the 'Related' Old Testament reading over the 'Continuous' option that the *Revised Common Lectionary* offers. So there is sometimes a little difference there, but the Gospel readings almost always line up perfectly.

The *Sunday Missal* naturally contains some material absent from Protestant versions of the Lectionary, such as celebrations of 'The Most Holy Body and Blood of Christ (Corpus Christi)' and 'The Most Sacred Heart of Jesus'. The only other major difference in this respect (without touching of course on theological questions) is that the Roman Catholic celebration of the Transfiguration is on a different Sunday to the *Revised Common Lectionary*. If one bears in mind that what the *Sunday Missal* calls 'The Tenth Sunday in Ordinary Time' is here called "Proper 5' (and hence, the Eleventh Sunday is Proper 6, and so on), and that 'The Thirty-First Sunday in Ordinary Time' is therefore this volume's '4th Sunday before Advent', we can be reading from the same Bible every week even when we may not always sing from the same hymnsheet.

Despite some of these slight logistical nuances, a judicious use of the Contents page and Scripture Index in this present volume should enable readers from any denomination to find appropriate and edifying comment on any given Sunday.

Key Dates

Liturgical Year	1st Sunday of Advent	2nd Sunday before Lent	Easter Sunday	Trinity Sunday
A begins on	30 November 2025	8 February 2026	5 April 2026	31 May 2026
B begins on	29 November 2026	31 January 2027	28 March 2027	23 May 2027
C begins on	28 November 2027	20 February 2028	16 April 2028	11 June 2028
A begins on	3 December 2028	4 February 2029	1 April 2029	27 May 2029
B begins on	2 December 2029	24 February 2030	21 April 2030	16 June 2030
C begins on	1 December 2030	16 February 2031	13 April 2031	8 June 2031
A begins on	30 November 2031	1 February 2032	28 March 2032	23 May 2032
B begins on	28 November 2032	20 February 2033	17 April 2033	12 June 2033
C begins on	27 November 2033	12 February 2034	9 April 2034	4 June 2034
A begins on	3 December 2034	28 January 2035	25 March 2035	20 May 2035
B begins on	2 December 2035	17 February 2036	13 April 2036	8 June 2036
C begins on	30 November 2036	8 February 2037	5 April 2037	31 May 2037
A begins on	29 November 2037	28 February 2038	25 April 2038	20 June 2038
B begins on	28 November 2038	13 February 2039	10 April 2039	5 June 2039
C begins on	27 November 2039	5 February 2040	1 April 2040	27 May 2040

Key Dates

YEAR A

1st Sunday of Advent

30 November 2025
3 December 2028
30 November 2031
3 December 2034
29 November 2037

ADVENT

1st Sunday of Advent

Isaiah 2:1–5 · Romans 13:11–14 · Matthew 24:36–44 · Psalm 122

Let us put aside the deeds of darkness and put on the armour of light.

The beginning of a new church year comes in Advent. So we prepare to remember in our readings the humble birth of our Saviour, and look forward to his coming in glory.

Jesus tells us in Matthew 24 that his second coming will be sudden, unexpected, and overwhelming. It cannot be predicted or foreknown; even the angels do not know the day or the hour (not that this means they do know the year or the month!). He uses the great flood from Genesis as a parallel – another all-encompassing moment of cataclysmic judgment and salvation for the elect which came quickly on an unsuspecting, undisturbed world. As the waters came to sweep all away, so will the Son of Man on that day. The smaller yet devastating disasters that have come upon our world in floods, storms, tsunamis and earthquakes are a reminder to us to be ready for what is approaching. Some will survive, some will not, when the Lord returns. The illustration of the two workers in the field and the two women at work are not designed to convey to us a sense of proportion, but a sense of urgency. We must stay awake, ready and prepared for what will happen. He comes like a thief in the night: to tell us much more in advance would defeat his object.

Paul also speaks of the second coming in Romans 13 and uses it to urge us to live godly lives as we await the glorious day. We need to wake up and realise that our salvation is closer now than when we first believed. The dark ages of sin and death are gone; the daylight of glory approaches. Therefore, we must put aside the deeds of darkness. By this he means not just drunkenness and debauchery – classic sins of the night – but also things we often overlook as more respectable sins, such as quarrelling and jealousy. Gratifying the flesh, our sinful nature, shouldn't make it onto our list of priorities at all, nor be provided for in our diaries, budgets or imaginations. Interestingly, Paul uses clothing imagery twice to describe our preparation for the day: we are to put on the armour of light, and put on the Lord Jesus Christ. What we wear as we go out to meet the coming Lord will reveal how much we value and honour him.

Isaiah 2 also urges us to walk in the light of the Lord. From centuries before Christ, he looks forward to a day when the word of the Lord would emanate out from Jerusalem to Judea, and from Samaria to the ends of the earth. In his vision, that word of instruction, that *Torah*, breaks down barriers between the nations as it goes, as light comes to the world. Is this a prophecy just for the eighth century BC, or for the first century AD when the Light of the World truly did arrive and from his earliest days taught the word from his Father's house? And does it not also point forward to the day when he shall reign in glory over all the nations, who will cease their fruitless wars and in the name of the Prince of Peace begin again to plough and prune and steward God's perfect creation? The promised one has come. He will come again to judge the living and the dead, and his glorious kingdom will have no end. Are you ready for him?

2nd Sunday of Advent

Isaiah 11:1–10 · Romans 15:4–13 · Matthew 3:1–12 · Psalm 72:1–7, 18–19

Produce fruit in keeping with repentance.

The Sunday readings this week give us hope for the future in the united kingdom of the Spirit-filled Messiah, and call us to repentance in preparation for his coming.

Isaiah 11 addresses an Israel devastated by the judgment of God. Into a situation of hopelessness and despair, God speaks through the prophet to reassure his people. Yet even though all that remains of Israel is a stump, out of this shall come glorious hope and renewal. Out of the roots and stock of Jesse (the father of King David) shall come another king, great David's greater son. He is endowed with the sevenfold Spirit, the Spirit of the Lord, of wisdom, understanding, counsel, might, knowledge and fear of the Lord. He has all the characteristics of a godly and righteous king.

This messianic figure comes to judge and to save. His judgment is right and true. He is not open to corruption or manipulation by shadowy elites, but delivers a just and fair society for all. His word rules – the rod of his mouth and the breath of his lips execute judgment on the wicked. Yet all he does is clothed in righteousness and faithfulness. He not only comes to judge, but also to save. The picture in verses 6–10 is of a renewed earth, with humanity (both Jews and Gentiles, the nations) and the natural world in perfect harmony with each other and with God.

Romans 15 tells us more about God's plan to bless the nations. Christ became a servant of the Jews, to confirm the covenant promises given to the patriarchs (particularly to Abraham, Genesis 12:1–3). In turn, that means through them all the families of the earth are blessed, 'in order that the Gentiles might glorify God for his mercy'. The quotes from various parts of the Old Testament (including Isaiah 11, our previous reading) confirm that Jews and Gentiles together praise God for all he has done in Christ.

This fulfilment of God's plan brings hope to those who believe. The outlining of God's plan in the Old Testament ('all that was written in former days for our instruction') urges us on to stand firm and look to the consummation of all things. The application is to the believing community that they might live in harmony with each other, just as God has always planned for us to be united in Christ. The Scriptures give us such optimism that we may abound in hope by the power of the same Spirit who both empowers Christ and fills us. Romans 15:13 is a great Advent prayer, just as the exhortation to harmony is a crucial (and challenging) one for the whole Christmas period.

Unity with others is never easy, and so the note of repentance in the Gospel reading is both necessary and urgent. The kingdom of the Son of David is entered by turning around. Just as John the Baptiser prepared the way for Christ as he baptised those who confessed their sins, so we prepare for the coming of the glorious kingdom by bearing fruit in keeping with repentant hearts. Those who resemble the hypocritical pew-fillers of verse 7 are meant to be shocked by the jarring notes this creates amidst our seasonal joys. Whether we have Abraham for our patriarch or the Church as our mother, there is no guarantee that we are indispensable to God's vision of the future. Good fruit is required of those who have been so blessed as to hear the good news. Without it, all is lost. Either a baptism of spiritual fire or an unquenchable fire of destruction awaits us when the king walks onto the stage. So are you producing fruit in keeping with repentance?

3rd Sunday of Advent

Isaiah 35:1–10 · James 5:7–10 · Matthew 11:2–11 · Psalm 146:5–10

Be patient and stand firm, because the Lord's coming is near.

Our readings this week teach us that when the Lord comes, there will be joy for those who have waited patiently.

To those who cannot see a way out of their current impasse, Isaiah declares that a time of gladness, rejoicing, and singing is approaching. But these things are not to be found in the worldly security we often crave. Indeed, the next few chapters of the prophecy describe how all such props will be removed, and when everything is taken away only the Lord and his word can be relied upon. His grace is experienced in the midst of judgment and loss, not instead of it.

But the fearful, says Isaiah, shall see the glory of the Lord, who comes to judge his enemies and save his people. The consequences are that the blind shall see, the deaf shall hear, the lame shall walk and the mute shall sing. Even the creation shall be restored to what it once was, and ought to be: well-watered, without carnivorous animals to threaten our peace. And God's people will dwell in God's place and live under God's holy rule. This is a marvellous picture of a renewed creation, a snapshot of which was given to the people of first-century Israel when the Lord walked among them.

John the Baptist was not certain, it seemed, of whether Jesus was truly the Messiah. So he sent his friends to ask Jesus directly. And Jesus answered in terms of Isaiah's prophecy: the blind see, the deaf hear, the lame walk, and the mute sing. If that was so, then logically Jesus must be the Lord of Isaiah 35. 'Here is your God' (Isaiah 35:4) who has come to judge and to save. But Jesus goes one step further. He exalts John, and identifies him as the Messenger of Malachi 3:1, the greatest prophet of the Old Testament era. But if that is so, who comes next? To whom was John pointing? Whose way was he preparing? By identifying John as that Messenger, Jesus was implying that he himself was the divine Messiah.

In the context, this was a warning not to take offence at Jesus and the difficult things he was teaching and doing. We must take care not just to rejoice in his coming, but to walk in what Isaiah called the Way of Holiness, the way of the cross.

James therefore tells us in his epistle to be patient until the Lord comes again. His coming is near, and what a fruitful, joyful time it will be. Yet in the time we have before us, prior to his arrival in glory to bring the new creation to its full consummation, we must act in a certain way. James says, 'Do not grumble against one another' because that would only lead to the Last Day being one of sorrow for us, of judgment rather than joy. James says to set before us, as a model of patience, the prophets of old who spoke God's word. Men like Isaiah, who were warned beforehand that people may not listen to them, that their hearts would be hard and their ears clogged up, but who preached and proclaimed the word they were given, trusting in God to do his work through it. He knew he was announcing judgment, but also hoped for salvation. What courage and patience he must have needed! So as the Church of England's set prayer (or collect) for this week says, 'give us courage to speak the truth, to hunger for justice, and to suffer for the cause of right, with Jesus Christ our Lord'. Let's pray for this steadfast patience.

4th Sunday of Advent

Isaiah 7:10–16 · Romans 1:1–7 · Matthew 1:18–25 · Psalm 80:1–7, 17–19

You are to give him the name Jesus, because he will save his people from their sins.

This week's readings celebrate the fulfilment of prophecy in the birth of great David's greater Son – Jesus, who comes to save his people from their sins.

Isaiah's prophecy is a warning sign to a corrupt and wicked king. He has just been told that if he does not stand firm in faith, he will not stand at all (Isaiah 7:9), a key verse for the whole book. Yet even when offered, he will not ask for a sign from God to aid his faith. Isaiah gives him one anyway: a virgin will be with child. He will be called Immanuel – God with us. And before he reaches the age of discernment, Ahaz's enemies (Syria and the Northern Kingdom of Israel) will have been destroyed by a bigger threat (Assyria). This is the good news which Ahaz is called to believe and trust in.

Much ink has been spilled over the precise shade of meaning of the Hebrew word *almah* in Isaiah 7:14. Whether in the eighth century BC it unambiguously meant virgin, or just a young maiden, the Greek of Matthew's Gospel makes it crystal clear that in the ultimate fulfilment of the prophecy, Jesus the Messiah *was* born of a virgin. Matthew tells us that not only is Jesus the Christ, and Immanuel (God with us), but he is 'from the Holy Spirit' and will rescue his people from their sins. Joseph's relationship to the ancient kingship is also made clear when the angel addresses him as 'Joseph, son of David' (see also Matthew 1:16), so we know that this child has impeccable human and divine claims to be the King of the Jews and Saviour of his people. It is also clear that he will be a far greater king than Ahaz ever was.

Just how much greater, Paul outlines in the magnificent opening of his letter to the Romans. The good news which Paul preaches is a gospel 'promised long ago through his prophets in the holy scriptures'. It is centred on God's Son. Paul tells us two things about this virgin-born Son: in flesh he is descended from David, the royal line from which the Messiah was expected to come and which God promised would provide a king for ever. Paul's gospel is rooted in Old Testament expectations, even when he is sent to the Gentiles, who probably had not heard of Isaiah's prophecy. Yet Jesus is also the Son of God, a title which Paul links to the Lord's resurrection from the dead – a powerful demonstration that he is the long-awaited, death-crushing, everlasting King. 'The hopes and fears of all the years are met in thee tonight', in the little town of Bethlehem, the city of David.

Paul goes on to link his own mission to that of the Messiah. He is an apostle 'set apart for the gospel of God', but he received this grace and apostleship through Jesus, that the Gentiles might believe in him. His calling is to bring about 'the obedience of faith among all the Gentiles for the sake of his name', which includes the Romans, and those of us in the (predominantly Gentile) rest of the world.

We too can be part of the Messiah's people, the ones he came to save from their sins. The question we are faced with is, as always, will we trust and obey? Or will we, like King Ahaz, refuse to believe the good news proclaimed to us and look to the God who has promised to save?

CHRISTMAS

1st Sunday of Christmas

Isaiah 63:7–9 · Hebrews 2:10–18 · Matthew 2:13–23 · Psalm 148

He said, 'Surely they are my people, children who will be true to me'; and so he became their Saviour.

Christmas is about God himself graciously coming among us, not just to identify with us or bless us in the abstract, but to die, as planned. Our merciful Saviour suffered in our place.

Isaiah rejoices in the presence of God with his people, and in all his gracious and mighty works for them. His steadfast love to his people meant that he could not remain at a distance or refuse to get involved in their sufferings and struggles. He shows them favour, not because they deserve it, but 'according to his mercy'. They are his people, his children, and so sending a mere messenger or angel to help them would not be entirely sufficient. He must come himself.

As astonishing as that is, God goes further. He 'lifted them up and carried them' – a sustaining love and care which shows an ongoing concern for those he aspires to lift up, out of their sin and sorrow. The plans of this covenant-keeping God are not thwarted by either his enemies' strength or his people's transgressions. Isaiah has already announced that one is coming who will bear the iniquities of his people, and be punished in their place, and yet triumph over death to see the light of life (Isaiah 52–53).

Right on cue, the shadow of death falls over the nativity in Matthew 2, but it proves no obstacle to the fulfilment of God's purposes. The devil planned to strike the heel of Immanuel and kill him. Yet the time had not yet come for him to serve through suffering. A baby is too passive to be a willing sacrifice for sin, so if the Christ-child had died it would not be so clear that God was at work to save. Yet Herod did all he could to destroy the baby who threatened his power. A messenger or angel was sent to warn Joseph, and a timely escape was executed instead, fulfilling Scripture in the process, which cannot help but point to this child.

The devil does not give up so easily. Herod is incensed by the failure of his plan, and so unleashes all the forces at his disposal. The innocent children – innocent, at the very least, because they are not guilty of being the Messiah! – are slaughtered. Yet none of this falls outside the providence of God, whose prophet Jeremiah foresaw what would happen (Jeremiah 31:15). When the threat from Herod is over, the path seems clear for a homecoming; but even then, Herod's son might have threatened the return from Egypt. Yet God knows, and God provides: he warns Joseph in a dream, and again fulfils the prophets.

Hebrews 2 reflects on the work of the covenant-keeping God from the other side of the cross and resurrection. The author sees clearly that God's plan was to lift up his children and to bring them to glory. The necessity of the crucifixion is brought out in verse 14: the pioneer of salvation would have to go through death in order to destroy the one who brought down that veil upon the world. And so the immortal, invisible God – who alone can save, as Isaiah said – needed to become blood and flesh so he might die for his children. He became flesh to taste death, that his people, his family, might be atoned for and live.

Through his suffering, they are sanctified. Through his death they are released from the fear of death which held them in slavery all their lives and caused them to resort to religious and superstitious protectionism. Now they have a saviour God who gets his hands dirty, and out of mercy acts as both faithful high priest and willing victim.

In the distress of temptation and testing, there is only one who has been perfected through suffering himself who is adequate to lift us up and carry us home. If we are his children, and true to him, he will be our Saviour.

2nd Sunday of Christmas

Jeremiah 31:7–14 · Ephesians 1:3–14 · John 1:1–18 · Psalm 147:12–20

Praise be to the God and Father of our Lord Jesus Christ!

The focus of our readings this week is the joy that comes from God's cosmic plan to save his undeserving people and make them his children by his grace alone.

Jeremiah's prophecy (which comes just before his oft-quoted prophecy of the new covenant, later in this chapter), begins with a command to 'sing aloud with gladness!' God has come to save his people, and not just out of Babylon. Those who are scattered over all the earth will hear his call. Whether they are blind or lame or in labour, he will gather them all. He will keep them as a shepherd keeps his flock, but also, it says, he will be a father to them and they shall be his firstborn. The glory and credit for this salvation goes entirely to God – Jacob is redeemed 'from hands too strong for him', and the people are 'radiant over the goodness of the Lord'. He does not share his glory with another, or merely augment Israel's own efforts to free herself. And so young and old, men and women, rejoice and dance and flourish, satisfied with the good gifts that God has freely given them.

The apostle Paul likewise calls for rejoicing as he blesses God for blessing us in Christ. God's strategy, which he outlines in this magnificent and joyfully breathless single sentence in Ephesians 1:3–14, centres on verse 10: God's plan to unite all things in heaven and on earth under one head, Jesus Christ. The plan stretches backwards to our unconditional election in eternity; brings us redemption in the present through irresistible grace; and reaches out into eternity again with an unwavering, promised hope. We *were* destined for adoption as sons, according to God's eternal pleasure; we *have* forgiveness of our sins according to the riches of his grace; and we are *destined* to obtain an inheritance, having set our hope on Christ when we heard the gospel of our salvation. No wonder Paul peppers this paragraph with the language of praise directed to God alone: it is all 'to the praise of his glorious grace, that he freely bestowed on us'.

John also lays out God's plan from eternity, beginning his Gospel where Moses began his Genesis. In the beginning was the Word: not just any old Word but one which was with God in the beginning, and who – wonderfully – *was* God. When the world was created, it was he who made it. Where there was light, it was light because of him. Darkness, even the darkness of our sin, could not hold out against this light, which came as a beacon for all. Yet because of our rebellious nature, we did not accept this, but like Adam and Eve we hide from the searching light of the world. John says only some were given the power to become children of God, and this not from any exercise of the will, but by God's power and grace alone. Christ has made him known, and in this revelation, he has focused on divine grace. Through this glorious Son, we too can become children of God, who like John the Baptiser point to the light before us and ahead of us as our only hope and salvation.

People give gifts at Christmas for all kinds of reasons: out of love, out of custom, out of habit, out of fear, out of hope, out of a desire to win friends and influence people. God gave his own Son out of pure grace and mercy, to make us his children. Don't you think his priceless gift should elicit more than a mere thank you card? Let's give him the deepest songs of everlasting, heartfelt praise.

EPIPHANY

Epiphany

Isaiah 60:1–6 · Ephesians 3:1–12 · Matthew 2:1–12 · Psalm 72:1–15

May all kings bow down to him and all nations serve him.

These readings should make us rejoice in the good news that Jesus is truly light for the world, including Gentiles.

The traditional story for Epiphany is Matthew 2:1–12, although strangely we had verses 13–23 as the Gospel reading two weeks ago! Matthew's narrative is of course somewhat different to our standard nativity play version: we are not told how many wise men from the East came to find the new born 'King of the Jews', although we often assume it was three because they gave three gifts (though some in the East today believe it was as many as a dozen); we are not told they came on camels (or 'one in a taxi, one in a car, one on his scooter' as the sacrilegious hymn I learned in childhood has it!); we are not told their names (medieval inventions); they probably came up to two years after Jesus's birth (see verse 16), rather than two minutes after the shepherds; and we are not told here that they were 'kings' (though see Psalm 72:10–11).

What is important, however, is the significance of this episode. For Matthew (the only Evangelist to report on the visit of the Magi) this revolves, as always, around the fulfilment of the Scriptures. Herod is afraid when he hears they have come to find a new king, and all Jerusalem with him, because they realise there is now a threat to their corrupt regime. They ascertain from the prophecy of Micah that the Messiah (for who else could command his own star? Numbers 24:17) would be born in David's birthplace, in Bethlehem (Micah 5:2). No longer in a manger but a house (verse 11), they meet the Lord and his blessed mother and hand over their precious gifts. There is no end of speculation about *their* significance, but they may point to the kingly (gold), and priestly (frankincense) ministry of the child, while myrrh is sometimes thought to be the kind of sap or ointment which would have been used to anoint a dead body – a foreshadowing of Christ's saving death.

With Isaiah 60 in mind, Matthew's story can be seen with even more colour. When the light of Israel comes, the Lord and his glory will shine on the whole world, even those who dwell in the darkness of the Gentile world. The nations shall come to that light, even 'kings to the brightness of your dawn'. This may be a prophetic indication that the tradition of *royal* Magi is not so fictitious after all. Or it may project a longer-term view of how far the gospel will penetrate in its centuries' long expansion, from Emperor Constantine to King Charles II and other monarchs who profess to follow the Servant King. Camels from the East appear in verse 6 along with gold and frankincense, so it is not hard to see the appropriateness of this reading alongside Matthew 2, which also features the note of thrilling joy and wonder at what the Lord has done, as unbelief is turned to worship of the one true God.

Paul too reflects on this theme with excitement, with a view to our encouragement (Ephesians 3:13). The key is in Ephesians 3:6 where we hear that through the gospel the Gentiles share the inheritance, the body, and the promise in Christ. All the nations of the world were promised blessing through Abraham (Genesis 12), and in Christ that hope of the ages is fulfilled. But Paul sees this achievement against an even bigger canvas in verse 10, where he tells us that through the Church united in Christ, God's multi-faceted wisdom is declared in the heavenly places to the angelic rulers and authorities. This expansive, cosmic vision is intended to strengthen the hearts of believers, even in the midst of the suffering and persecution which always seem to accompany the fulfilment of God's purposes in history. But have *you* come to bow down before him, and serve him?

1st Sunday of Epiphany

Isaiah 42:1–9 · Acts 10:34–43 · Matthew 3:13–17 · Psalm 29

All the prophets testify about him that everyone who believes in him receives forgiveness of sins through his name.

The readings this week proclaim the glorious truth that the Spirit--anointed Saviour has come, to bring God's forgiveness to all the nations of his world.

Isaiah 42 prophesies that God's chosen servant will bring justice and truth to the nations. Because the Father delights in him, he is anointed with his Spirit. That anointing often led to works of mighty power in the Old Testament from the judges and kings of Israel, but this servant is anointed for gentleness. Those who are damaged and bruised will not be hurt; those whose spiritual fervour is growing dim will not be put out; he will not shout above the noise of the public square but influence it and change it for good all the same. The redemption he brings is extended to the nations, all of whom are created and sustained by God. The light of the covenant is opened to them, so that even the coastlands which wait for his teaching, the farthest flung islands, will hear the truth of his word and have their eyes opened to its glory.

In Matthew 3, that long-awaited servant comes. To fulfil all righteousness he submits to baptism because all Israel were doing so in response to the call of God's prophet, John. Identifying wholly with them, though having no sin of his own to repent of, he is baptised by his cousin, who senses what a profound and serious moment this is. The Spirit comes upon the servant, in the form of a dove, and the Father speaks from heaven to repeat what he said in Isaiah 42 – this is the one in whom I delight! This servant is my own true Son. The Trinitarian-ness of God is exposed to full view, as the plan and work of God to save his people begins in earnest.

Peter begins to spread that same word to the waiting nations in Acts 10, as he preaches to Cornelius and his family. He recounts the story of Jesus, the Lord of all, sent first to the Jews to preach peace to them. He narrates how Jesus was baptised, and how the message of the good news spread, and how he was anointed with the Holy Spirit. He retells the story of Christ's good works, his healings and miracles, and defeat of the devil. Supremely, as a first-hand witness, he marvels in the death and resurrection of this Messiah, and testifies to its truth: 'we ate and drank with him – he was no ghost or phantom!'

After this gospel outline, we might expect an altar call, so to speak. And Peter does not disappoint. But the way he presents the message he has been called to preach is startling when looked at closely. We are often told that the Old Testament God is supremely a God of judgment and wrath, but that Jesus is gentle and meek and wouldn't exclude anyone. Yet look how Peter sums it up: we, the New Testament apostles, preach that Jesus has been ordained by God to bring justice to the nations: he is judge of the living and the dead. That is the New Testament gospel. Yet Christ is also the fulfilment of the Old Testament hope: the prophets testify that he is the one who brings forgiveness of sins to all who believe in him. Forgiveness preached in the Old; judgment in the New. How surprising the message of the Bible can be, undercutting our preconceptions or lazy formulas with its precision and depth!

2nd Sunday of Epiphany

Isaiah 49:1–7 · 1 Corinthians 1:1–9 · John 1:29–42 · Psalm 40:1–11

What do you want?

This Sunday's readings are about calling: the calling of God's servant, Jesus, and the calling of God's saints. Do you want to call on him, and be in their number? Or are you looking for something else?

In Isaiah, we again hear more about the servant of God who will draw God's people back to himself and gather them together. He himself calls to the nations, to announce that he has been called by God, in two ways. First, he was *named* by the Lord himself, but second, he was called and given the *vocation* of a servant. That vocation involves him in speaking God's powerful word, but only at the right time: he is kept like a polished arrow ready to be revealed in due course (as Galatians 4 puts it, 'when the fullness of time had come', or Romans 5, 'at just the right time').

This vocation will be ultimately for God's own glory and fame, but the servant himself confesses that it seems from a human perspective to be weak and empty: has he laboured in vain and spent his strength for no earthly gain? His work might appear a failure to some eyes, but he is confident too, that his reward is ultimately secure with God. He is called to be a light and the salvation of the nations, though this final victory only comes to one who is deeply despised and abhorred for a time.

John, called the Baptiser, names Jesus in the Gospel reading. Jesus is 'the Lamb of God' who takes away the sin of the world. He is the pre-existent and supreme one, who baptises with the Holy Spirit (as the Father told John when he sent him), and is himself the Son of God. The Trinity is seen acting together not just in the baptism of Christ but in the Baptiser's calling and understanding too. These names not only mark out our Saviour as the long-awaited King, but also as the Suffering Servant, called and destined to bear sin on our behalf, to suck in all its fatal poison then carry it away in his sacrificial death.

Identified as such, Christ calls his followers. But those who began to follow him when pointed in his direction by John are asked, as are all his disciples, 'What are you looking for? What do you want?' They call him 'Rabbi', a teacher, and that he most certainly is, but how much more will their understanding grow as the Gospel progresses! 'Come and see,' he tells them, beckoning them into a lifelong calling as followers and learners. Andrew in turn calls his brother, Simon, to be a follower too. And as he begins his new life, Jesus calls him by a new name: Peter, the Rock. Being called and regenerated by Jesus can change you at the most fundamental level of your identity.

Paul shared in Peter's calling to be a foundation, an apostle of Jesus Christ by the will of God. In 1 Corinthians he writes to an errant, somewhat wild, arrogant and disobedient church. Yet nonetheless, they are 'called to be saints, together with those who in every place call on the name of our Lord Jesus Christ.' Their identity is in him, and most fundamentally they are saints, holy ones, because they call on the name of Jesus. It is interesting that Paul twice mentions that this calling is not a solitary one (in verses 2 and 9), because some of the Corinthians thought that the word of God (practically!) originated with them, and that they in their idiosyncrasies were the only truly spiritual Christians (see 1 Corinthians 14:36). Yet Paul reminds them that despite their great grace and strength, they relied upon God for their gifts and calling, and to keep them in the worldwide fellowship of his Son. The question for us is: is that what we want, or do we have a different identity and plan?

3rd Sunday of Epiphany

Isaiah 9:1–4 · 1 Corinthians 1:10–18 · Matthew 4:12–23 · Psalm 27:1, 4–9

The Lord is my light and my salvation – whom shall I fear?

These readings unfold the power of the gospel to bring light and healing to those who believe.

There was gloom, anguish, and deep darkness for the people of Zebulun and Naphtali in the northern regions of Israel's Promised Land. Conquest and exile had brought the land into contempt, says the prophet Isaiah. And even as the glory the prophet foresaw was beginning to dawn in that area, many centuries later, people would still be saying of one of its towns, 'Can anything good come from Nazareth?' (John 1:46).

Yet it was precisely in that lowly, mixed-up place, Galilee, overrun by the Gentiles, that God's light would shine. God's plan to bring together a people for himself would begin to bear fruit here, in the very place where hope seemed lost when the Assyrians ravaged the land. This region was favoured by the first preaching of our Saviour, which brought life and joy to those who heard it after so many years of tumult and tension. Their rejoicing was like that of labourers who finally enjoy the harvest they have longed for and arduously reaped, or like that of a victorious army after long and wearisome battles. Their chains fell off, their hearts were free.

Matthew 4 narrates how Christ made his home among the people of Galilee and proclaimed to them the good news that the kingdom of heaven had come near. His call to repentance was addressed first to the ordinary working people of a neglected northern backwater. The Lord began looking for his people not in the palace of Herod or the temple offices of Caiaphas but in the smelly, sweaty harbours of Simon and Andrew, James and John. He chooses the weak things of the world, to shame the strong. It may seem foolish to some, but there is unfathomable wisdom in the divine plan.

The old Bible commentator Matthew Henry (1662–1714) comments that 'Diligence in an honest calling is pleasing to Christ, and no hindrance to a holy life ... Idle people lie more open to the temptations of Satan than to the calls of God.'[1] These fishermen certainly proved open to Christ's call as they left their nets and followed him. And though God's call is always solely by grace, quite apart from any supposed merit foreseen in us, their actions on that day perhaps suggested their future usefulness. Peter and Andrew cast a net into the lake, so the Lord called them to be fishers of men. James and John were 'mending their nets', and though the text here is not explicit about it, one wonders if Matthew is alerting us to the healing, uniting vocation of the apostles, whose words would be the foundation of the church and its unity in him (Ephesians 2:20; 4:11–12). Jesus's ministry, in any case, was one of literal healing, we're told, as he travelled the area curing every disease and sickness.

Paul's appeal to the divided Gentile church in Corinth certainly is an example of applying the gospel to heal the divisions within God's people. In the face of person-centred factionalism – 'I follow Apollos', 'I follow Cephas', 'I just follow Christ' (how very sanctimonious!) – Paul urges them to be of one mind and purpose. That unity should focus on 'the message of the cross' and its power to save all those who believe, and their purpose should be to bring light to their city by proclaiming that glorious truth. So Paul calls on the Corinthians to be united, to mend their tearing nets (using the same Greek verb in verse 10 as in Matthew 4:21, above). Those who agree on the apostolic preaching of the cross can put aside their other differences by a unity of affection and purpose; though without such foundational consensus, of course, both unity of purpose and affection remain perilously weakened and resist being knit together.

Let us pray for light and healing to come to the church, as well as to the world. What is there to be afraid of?

---

[1] Matthew Henry, *Matthew Henry's Commentary on the Whole Bible: Complete and Unabridged in One Volume* (Peabody: Hendrickson, 1994), p. 1626.

4th Sunday of Epiphany

1 Kings 17:8–16 · 1 Corinthians 1:18–31 · John 2:1–11 · Psalm 36:5–10

The message of the cross is foolishness to those who are perishing.

With the feast of the conversion of St Paul coming in late January, it is fitting to consider the reading today from his first letter to the Corinthians. Let's focus just on that this week. Here, the apostle reminds the church that appearance isn't everything.

Like Elijah in 1 Kings 17, Paul was sent to places outside his comfort zone, outside the nation of Israel. The biggest issue in the church at Corinth in ancient Greece, where Paul had once evangelised, was that there was too much Corinth in the Corinthians. That is, the church was corrupted and infected and infused with the worldliness of its surrounding culture. Corinth was a big, successful and strategic city, a port at the centre of some vitally important trade routes, and with multitudes of wealthy and important people passing through all the time.

It was a place steeped in power and wealth – a glitzy, glamorous place of entertainment, including all those types of entertainment one usually finds in port cities. It was full of temples and temple prostitution, and sexual promiscuity of every conceivable kind, heterosexual and homosexual. It was New York, Amsterdam, London. It also had something of the Las Vegas or Hollywood about it. A city of bright lights and big dreams and money and celebrity. And the church? The church had all those things too, sadly. Too interested in looking good, in what's impressive, in sex, in knowledge and in power.

Every church has to fight against its surrounding culture, of course. But none more so than the church encircled by rampant immorality and greed and glamour and power. It is true that it was a spiritual church, not lacking in any spiritual gift (1:7). It was full of gifted, talented people. But it was also a split church, divided between various factions (1:10–12). And that sectarian spirit can only have been strengthened by the supercilious arrogance of those who thought they were so discerning and wise that they could look down upon the others.

Paul's answer to this is to stress how weak and foolish God's ways appear to sinful human minds. His salvation comes through weakness and foolishness. Jews demanded signs (like the turning of water into wine perhaps, from John 2) and Greeks looked for wisdom; but Paul preached Christ crucified (verse 22)! To the world's eyes, and to worldly Christian eyes, the cross of Christ is frankly stupid. It appears weak and pathetic and a little bit embarrassing. Especially in that culture where crucifixion was something you just didn't talk about; it was so disgusting and barbaric and low. The 'utterly vile death of the cross' as the Corinthian chatterati might have called it, was God's unique way of rescuing dying humanity. To paraphrase one modern celebrity atheist, 'it's so petty, it's so trivial, it's so local, it's so earth-bound, so unworthy' – and yet it turned the world upside down and destroyed its much-vaunted wisdom.

Sometimes as Christians, although we know somehow that it is the power of God and the wisdom of God, we don't really like God's foolish way. We don't want it to be weak and stupid. We don't want people to think *we* are weak and stupid. Imagine the PR men in Corinth chatting it over with Paul: 'Not a good marketing strategy for your product, old boy, this dying on a cross business. Need a better logo. Might work with some weak-minded folks who need a crutch and an inspiring example of suffering. But not here in Corinth. Gotta be more upbeat, old chap. Go for the glory rather than the gory. That'll work better here.'

If our idea of success is measured in terms of numbers, style, popularity, money, church plants, social media followers or some other worldly indicator, Paul deconstructs and disarms us here. No one can boast, except in the Lord – for his foolishness and feebleness is greater than all that we take pride in.[2]

---

[2] See my exposition of 1 Corinthians 1–2 in Lee Gatiss, *The Forgotten Cross: Some Neglected Aspects of the Cross of Christ* (Darlington: Evangelical Press, 2014), pp. 13–26.

Presentation of Christ in the Temple (Candlemas)

Malachi 3:1–5 · Hebrews 2:14–18 · Luke 2:22–40 · Psalm 24:1–10

But who can endure the day of his coming?
Who can stand when he appears?

This week, our readings present to us Christ in the Temple, the glorious Saviour and judge of all.

Malachi's prophecy reveals that God will send his Messenger (in the Hebrew, *malachi*) to prepare the way for him to return to his Temple in Jerusalem. The Temple of Solomon had been filled with God's glory, just as Moses's Tabernacle had been, so the exiles of Malachi's day hoped and expected God to show himself and his glory in the rebuilt ruins after their return from Babylon. Indeed, Haggai prophesied greater glory for that place than ever before (Haggai 2:9). So the Lord (*Yahweh*) reveals that the Lord (*Adon*) will come, as they desired and anticipated, after the Messenger. Yet that divine coming would not herald glory and salvation immediately, but a winnowing, a division, a purifying judgment. When the Lord appears, he will save his God-fearing people and purify their hearts and offerings, but swiftly judge those who long not for his arrival but for their own pleasure and gain.

When, many centuries later, the righteous old man Simeon sees the Lord Jesus arrive at the Temple for the purification ritual, he declares him to be a light for revelation to the Gentiles and for the glory of God's people in that place. He has come, a few months after his older cousin, John the Baptiser, to fulfil all righteousness according to the Law of Moses. Mary and Joseph (called in Luke 2:33 'the child's father', though we already know that is an honorary title), are amazed at the things they hear. The prophetess Anna has been waiting for just this moment, never leaving the Temple but longing for the coming of the Lord. When she sees him she rejoices in the dawn of redemption.

But Simeon, led by the Spirit, also has words of warning. Jesus will bring not only salvation but also divisive judgment. He is a sign that will be opposed, the rising and falling of many – either the fall and restoration of the same people, or the rise of some and the fall of others. That will be true not least for his own mother, whose heart will be pierced with pain as she one day watches her son die in that very same city. News of his subsequent resurrection would divide the inhabitants of Jerusalem, just as his teaching in the Temple had persuaded many to oppose and crucify him.

Yet this was why he came, according to Hebrews 2. He took on our nature, our blood and flesh, precisely that he might be able to die. The incarnation made possible his defeat of the devil on the cross, as through death he destroyed the one with the power of death. Through death he redeems those who were slaves to fear and achieves the salvation of his children, those who share the faith of Abraham. He grasps hold of humanity (our nature, and us) 'so that' he might sacrifice himself as a wrath-bearing sacrifice of atonement for the sins of his people. He was coming to purify the priests that they might 'present offerings to the LORD in righteousness' (NRSV), said Malachi. Yet he himself is our merciful and faithful high priest, presenting his own tested and genuine perfection to God as a pure and holy offering in our place.

Here is a Saviour who understands our weaknesses and struggles from the inside, no distant God who remains aloof but one who bares his holy arm, rolls up his sleeves and gets his hands dirty, with blood, to help us. Here too, then, is a God, before whom none can make excuses when he draws near to us for judgment; a Lord to be both adored and feared – but most of all to be trusted, eagerly awaited and embraced.

ORDINARY TIME

Proper 1

Sunday between 3 and 9 February inclusive
(if earlier than the Second Sunday before Lent)

Isaiah 58:1–12 · 1 Corinthians 2:1–16 · Matthew 5:13–20 ·
Psalm 112:1–10

Blessed are those who fear the Lord,
who find great delight in his commands.

All three readings this week bring an unexpected change of perspective to surprise their worldly audiences and jolt them into a change of heart and life. Will they move you and delight you in a similar way?

Isaiah 58 exposes a supposedly religious people, who claim to delight in God's ways and seek after him, but whose outward righteousness hides a quarrelsome spirit. While fasting, they fight. Their focus is on their own interests, not those of others. The fasting which God, on the other hand, requires, is more than orthodox religious conformity. It involves freeing the oppressed and taking care of the vulnerable. God refuses to hear the prayers of those who point the finger at others but do nothing for the cause of true freedom. Light, healing, vindication, guidance and satisfaction are all promised here but only to those who reorientate their lives around God's revealed priorities. Those who persist in self-seeking, self-serving and worldly piety will have no access to the inextinguishable fountain of divine strength. God cannot be manipulated into blessing and restoring those whose eyes are only on themselves.

The shock in the Gospel reading is that true righteousness is still to be public. The salt of the earth and the light of the world must do their thing in the public square. The response to the condemnation of public hypocrisy, such as in Isaiah 58, is not to hide away and do nothing but to be more clearly what God made us to be. We must not shrink but shine. Yet the focus is not on 'to thine own self be true', a gospel of self-realisation through which I can attain fame and celebrity; but 'let them see your good works and glorify *God*'.

Yet again Jesus shocks by not lowering the standard, as he is often thought by many to do. He did not come to abolish the Ten Commandments, or to lighten the impact of Isaiah's critique of our merely outward godliness. If we wish to be great, the Law and the Prophets point the way to advancement in the kingdom of heaven. Indeed, only righteousness that exceeds the meticulous legalism of pharisaic expectations is good enough to open the gates of that dominion. An intolerable burden for us sinners to bear, were it not for the one who spoke these words becoming sin for us, so that in him we might become the righteousness of God (2 Corinthians 5:21).

Paul's bolt from the blue in the epistle reading is to undercut the Corinthians' expectations of a great preacher. He had no lofty words, no oratorical skill. In his letters he was weighty and forceful, but in person he was weak and pathetic, they said (2 Corinthians 10:10). Yet just such a man demonstrated the power of the Spirit as they – even they! – put their faith in the crucified God he proclaimed. This is unworldly wisdom, which the rulers and philosophers of every age have struggled to comprehend without a spiritual paradigm shift that makes them appear foolish in the eyes of social media. Rather than lose face, lose position, we prefer to crucify the Lord of Glory. We avoid his weakness, to avoid looking weak.

Paul wants this divided church to appreciate this true spirituality: not an expansion or enhancement of worldly ideas, the baptism of our cultural ideals; but a Spirit-revealed secret only grasped by the truly mature. No other eye, no other ear, no other human heart can even conceive of it. So let us delight to rest our faith in God alone, not our own feeble efforts and strategies.

Proper 2

Sunday between 10 and 16 February inclusive
(if earlier than the Second Sunday before Lent)

Deuteronomy 30:15–20 · 1 Corinthians 3:1–9 · Matthew 5:21–37 ·
Psalm 119:1–8

Oh, that my ways were steadfast in obeying your decrees!

Our readings this week present to us three stark contrasts, calling for three different responses. Listen carefully and consider your own response.

Moses sets before us the starkest contrast of all, between life and death, prosperity and adversity. Under the Mosaic covenant, there was no hidden mystery about how to live well in God's eyes. It was written for all to know. Obedience would lead to blessing, including a numerical increase in the Israelites' numbers. Yet if their hearts turned away from God's word and they refused to listen to his voice, they would inevitably begin to worship and serve other gods, which would lead to their destruction and exile. Blessings and curses are clearly set forth, and Moses exhorts the people to choose life, not just for themselves but for the sake of their descendants. Under this old constitution, long life and long tenure in the land were conditional. Heaven and earth are called to witness that the choice is clear and the warnings have been given. Though through it all, God's overarching promise to Abraham would remain firm and unchangeable.

However much some would like to draw the equation between faithfulness and numerical increase in churches today, we are no longer under that Mosaic constitution. So it is hard to be so dogmatic about these metrics without a prophetic insight into individual situations. It remains true, however, that obedience to God's word is always the way of blessing and enrichment, and leads to a harvest of righteousness for those who sow bountifully and cheerfully to the Spirit (2 Corinthians 9:6–11; Galatians 6:8). That harvest may be in depth and maturity as much as in numbers, though it has been granted to us to suffer like Christ and for Christ in this world, not only to prosper outwardly (Philippians 1:29).

Paul excoriates the Corinthians for their immaturity in his epistle, exposing the worldly nature of their thinking and behaviour. They are of the flesh, not of the Spirit. They are infants, not mature as they arrogantly thought. The jealousy, strife and factiousness between them was a sure sign that they had not grown up into spiritual people through the meat of God's word but were behaving in a human, worldly way with secular norms dictating their ecclesiastical policies. They should have understood that human leaders are unable to grow churches: one plants, another waters, but God alone gives the growth (and for his own glory too, not the growing celebrity of the planters or the smugness of the water-bearers). That being said, where these servants do well, they can expect a reward on the Last Day, in proportion to their labour, from the God who is no man's debtor. But their churches belong to God, and have his name stamped upon them, not anybody else's.

The contrast the Lord Jesus outlines in the Gospel reading between two ways of interpreting God's Law could easily provoke despair, until we realise that it is intended to demonstrate that only Jesus can perfectly keep and fulfil the Law of the all-seeing, all-knowing God. If the Israelites failed to keep the external observance of the Mosaic dispensation, how much less could they fulfil its more penetrating meanings? Where the heart goes astray, sin is not absent, even in the outwardly moralistic life. As the specific examples given by the Lord here show, our true ethical standard as Christians must not be based on legal loopholes or gymnastics of interpretation, but on the positive life-giving purpose of God in creation.

Choose life. Get a proper perspective on who you are. Live as God intended. But when we fail, when we fall, we must flee – to the perfection and beauty of a forgiving Saviour who graciously helps us up to start again.

Proper 3

Sunday between 17 and 23 February inclusive
(if earlier than the Second Sunday before Lent)

Leviticus 19:1–2, 9–18 · 1 Corinthians 3:10–11, 16–23 ·
Matthew 5:38–48 · Psalm 119:33–40

Be holy because I, the Lord your God, am holy.

The theme of our readings this week is holy, counterintuitive generosity to others. God is far more generous and kind than we could ever imagine, which challenges us to be like him.

In Leviticus 19, we are told to be 'Be holy because I, the Lord your God, am holy.' This passage refers particularly to holiness in relationships with our neighbours, especially those who are disadvantaged in some way. The poor and the foreigner should be considered at harvest time. We are not to take out all the profit we can from our fields, but leave some for others to glean. It doesn't all belong to us, even if we think it does. God means to generously provide for others out of what he blesses us with. We should not slander those who are susceptible to it, however much we savour juicy gossip, and we must not seek revenge and bear a grudge, even if people seem to deserve it. Truth, not falsehood should mark our lives, and a contentment that speaks volumes about our trust in God to provide.

In 1 Corinthians, Paul is speaking about the different ministries which people can have in God's field, God's building and God's temple. The Corinthians are divided because they follow various prominent leaders to the exclusion of others. Some follow Paul, but some follow Apollos or Cephas. But each one is only a servant, assigned their respective tasks by the Lord of the harvest himself. Paul planted the seed of God's word among them, and Apollos watered it, but the point is that God is the one who makes it grow, and who owns the field, which is his Church. By grace (not because of his own merit or competency),

Paul laid a foundation for the Church that others can build on. But the foundation itself is Christ, whose Spirit lives among us.

The temple which the Spirit is building out of us is precious to God, and must not be torn apart by rivalry and contentiousness. The wisdom of the world says that we must build our empires and look after our own reputation, but this is foolishness in God's eyes. He sees such craftiness and will not bless the chancer who takes liberties with his own property, the Church. We don't need to pit one leader against another, because all those who build on the foundation of Christ in a way that honours him belong to us and can bless us. All are ours in Christ. In a polarised world and a Church which is fractured by in-fighting and party spirit, this is a counterintuitive, culturally startling assertion.

In the Gospel reading, Jesus corrects a false understanding of the Old Testament Law. It does indeed say 'an eye for an eye' (Exodus 21:24; Leviticus 24:20; Deuteronomy 19:21). In context, that was an instruction to the judges of Israel, an injunction to be rigorously fair in the application of justice (just as our reading from Leviticus states that we should not show partiality to the poor or favouritism to the great). This law, as John Stott says, 'had the double effect of defining justice and restraining revenge'.[3] But it was not meant to apply in the realm of personal relationships, in the sense of enabling people to foster grudges and mete out personal vengeance for any affront to their dignity (as even the Law itself in Leviticus 19:18 makes clear).

Holiness, as Jesus sees it, is remarkably generous and kind towards others who harm us. Turn the other cheek, and go the extra mile – even for what he calls 'an evil person'. This is certainly counterintuitive! Love for our friends – this is easy. But love for our *enemies* – who could possibly see this as anything but naive in the world that we live in? Yet that is precisely what Jesus encourages us to have, so that we will be like our Father in heaven, who makes the sun rise on the evil and the good, and loved us so much that he gave his one and only Son for us and for our salvation. Be holy and perfect as he is holy and perfect, and you will stand out a mile.

---

[3] John Stott, *The Message of the Sermon on the Mount: Christian counter-culture* (Leicester: IVP, 1978), p. 104.

2nd Sunday before Lent

Genesis 1:1–2:3 · Romans 8:18–25 · Matthew 6:25–34 · Psalm 136

But seek first his kingdom and his righteousness.

This Sunday's readings preach the good news that God works to provide for both creation and new creation, so that we may patiently strive to please him. The question is: is that what we do?

The opening chapter of the Bible is a magnificent exposition of creation, and perhaps the most commented-on chapter in the whole Bible. There is a stately rhythm to its majestic poetry which demonstrates the power of God's word: God *said*, and it was. God shaped and filled, the master craftsman, before resting from his completed work on the seventh day. He laboured to provide a hallowed creation, pronounced 'very good', which was fully stocked with every good thing for his glory and our good. Of his human image-bearers it is said that he assigned them a task and gave them what they needed to thrive and fulfil it. His gracious initiative created, commissioned and equipped.

In Romans 8, by contrast, we hear about the eager expectations of this creation after the devastation of the Fall and its subjection to futility. If the first creation was glorious, how much more will be the glory to come. The creation itself will share in the unmerited but unsurpassed freedom of God's children, set free from the decay unleashed on it by Adam's sin. Their inward groaning is shared by the world, which looks forward to physical redemption. Our adoption is our hope, and so we are exhorted to put our present sufferings into this redemptive perspective, and wait with patience and perseverance for what God has prepared by his grace for us.

Yet Christian hope is not just a longing for the distant future. God graciously supplies 'strength for today' as well as 'bright hope for tomorrow'. Jesus told his disciples not to devote themselves to the pressing concerns of this present world alone as the Gentiles, who do not know God, do. But knowing God, the gracious giver who himself works for our good, will release us from inordinately striving for worldly wealth and security. Our Father feeds the birds, who eat what he has sown and grown. We are more valuable in his sight, the pinnacle of his creation; we can trust that he will lavish no less care on our daily well-being, though he provides for our need, not our greed.

Jesus calls us not to worry or stress, but to daily look to God. The flowers of the field do not go shopping for their decoration, and yet Solomon's famously glamorous glory pales next to their abundant testimony to the beauty and generosity of their maker. They are temporary, fragile and fleeting, while we are endued with the inestimable benefit of an immortal soul and a divine commission – surely he will not leave us without what is requisite and necessary to fulfil our calling? These things will not be withheld from those who, regardless of how tiny their faith is, strive to please God and seek after his kingdom and righteousness.

Do not worry about tomorrow, but to look to the future – a glorious hope that our Father has prepared through the suffering of his Son for our glorification and ultimate satisfaction.'Give thanks to the LORD, for he is good. His love endures for ever', redeeming and leading his people and providing for all creatures (Psalm 136).

Sunday next before Lent (Transfiguration Sunday)

Exodus 24:12–18 · 2 Peter 1:16–21 · Matthew 17:1–9 · Psalm 2

This is my Son, whom I love; with him I am well pleased. Listen to him!

Our readings this week focus on the glory of the Lord and the consequent necessity of listening carefully to his word. Consider the awesomeness of the one who speaks to you through these passages of Scripture, and do what he says!

In Exodus 24, Moses goes up to Mount Sinai in response to God's command, while others worship the Lord from afar. They have agreed to obey the Law of the Lord, and have made sacrifices to him. The elders of Israel have actually seen the God of Israel and the pavement of sapphire beneath his feet, and eaten with him in peace. Now Moses goes to receive the Law on tablets of stone and be instructed about the building of the tabernacle. It is not just the magnificent and awe-inspiring appearance of God's glory, but the delivery of God's word to his people in this context that is key here. How often we simply consider that word to be a familiar background part of our lives, and forget the graciousness of its revelation to us, and the height from which it comes. Yet a word whose arrival is so majestically trumpeted is worthy of our weightiest consideration.

In the Gospel reading, Peter, James, and John also see the glory of God, in the face of a transfigured Jesus Christ. His face shone like the sun and his clothes became dazzling white. Moses himself, the bringer of the Law, and Elijah, the chief of the prophets, appear to testify to the significance of this new revelation. Peter wants to enjoy the moment, but again, that is not the point. The point is made clear to us by the word from above. A bright cloud overshadows them and the voice of the Father is heard. 'This is my Son, the Beloved, with whom I am well pleased.'

Although the disciples may have started to doubt, because he had spoken of going to Jerusalem to die, Jesus is identified as the Son of God that they hoped and longed for, just as he had been at his baptism. Despite his seemingly depressing announcements, which Peter had satanically attempted to counter, the Father was pleased with Jesus so his disciples should not be displeased. Moses and Elijah had both suffered rejection, and this new revelation, this Word, would fare no better in himself when he went to the cross. The command from on high is startlingly clear and simple: 'Listen to him!' Listen to his teaching. Listen to his prophecies of the future. Listen to his hint of a new day soon to dawn on the far side of death and betrayal.

Peter clearly got the message, though his thick skull took some time to penetrate (as ours often do as well). In his second letter he speaks of being an eyewitness of Christ's majesty (as Luke spoke of those who were 'eyewitnesses of the Word', Luke 1:2). He recalls the voice of the 'Majestic Glory' and the great honour and glory it conveyed upon Christ. This was, he says, 'the prophetic message more fully confirmed'. Jesus is the fulfilment of all prophecy, and his power and coming is the hope of all. And his application? Listen to the prophetic word. 'You will do well to be attentive to this, as a lamp shining in a dark place.' Men and women moved by the Holy Spirit spoke from God in the self-interpreting pages of Scripture. This is sufficient to guide and lead us until we no longer live by faith but by sight. This is no 'cleverly devised myth' but a sure and certain hope, a precious unerring word that equips us with all things for life and godliness. So, let us listen.

LENT

1st Sunday of Lent

Genesis 2:15–17, 3:1–7 · Romans 5:12–19 · Matthew 4:1–11 · Psalm 32

Man shall not live on bread alone, but on every word that comes from the mouth of God.

This Sunday's readings compare and contrast Jesus Christ with Adam and with Israel, to show us that he is our obedient Saviour and righteous Lord. How much better he is than anyone else who tries to lead us!

The narrative of the Fall in Genesis demonstrates the culpability of Adam and Eve in turning away from God's goodness and truth to follow the subtle, corrupting lies of the devil. God's command is clear and kind. His generosity is abundant and the warning obvious. Yet that ancient, crafty serpent opens the conversation with the insinuation of disbelief and ambiguity to facilitate Eve's downfall. She adds to God's word by fencing it (adding 'you shall not touch it' to what God had said about not eating), though this is not what the sneaky snake latches onto. His outright denial of the spiritually dangerous implications of this eating are followed up immediately by the promise of great fulfilment, and the false accusation that she is being deceived by someone who only wants to keep her in her place.

Having manipulated the conversation thus far, the satanic creature may even (as some conjecture) have eaten the fruit himself before her; for how else would Eve see that 'the tree was good for food'?[4] Either way, having disobeyed God and listened to the Siren voice of the serpent instead, she leads Adam into sin, persuading him in word and deed to join her in seeking what looks good, feels right, seems harmless and promises satisfaction. He foolishly follows, and when the eyes of both are opened, it is too late. No fig leaf can cover the stain of sin; they have fallen from grace and only a bloody death can save and clothe them now (Genesis 3:15, 21).

Faced by the same adversary, Jesus's response is very different to Adam's. It is part of our salvation, and a pattern for our sanctification. The Spirit leads him in the way he needs to go to fulfil his destiny as the second Adam. 'O wisest love! that flesh and blood, which did in Adam fail, should strive afresh against the foe, should strive, and should prevail' as John Henry Newman's hymn 'Praise to the Holiest in the height' puts it. The tempter comes to him, not when he has all the lavish trees of Eden to provide for him, but at a point of weakness and human frailty. After forty days of fasting in the desert, he was famished (perhaps one of the greatest understatements in Scripture!). Yet when it is implied that he can assert his identity and satisfy his desires at the same time ('*If* you are the Son of God, command these stones to become bread'), he chooses a different way. Three times he chooses the path that Moses taught the Israelites that they should walk in: trusting in God alone and the satisfying food of his word. When devilish Bible interpretations were wheeled out to muddy the waters (verse 6), a trusting 'it is written' convinced and sustained our Lord.

Romans tells us that Adam is a 'type' of Christ, a picture to teach us; and it is a point of contrast between them which undergirds Paul's teaching, as well as a point of similarity. Sin came into the world through one man and death, through him, came to all. (Adam was clearly a real-time historical figure for Paul.) In the

---

[4] See for example, Lee Gatiss (ed.), *The Sermons of George Whitefield* (Wheaton: Crossway, 2012), 1:49.

same way, the righteous obedience of another man has brought world-changing implications too. Christ's obedience has overcome Adam's sin. But the free gift through Jesus is not like the trespass of Adam, says Paul. His 'abundance of grace and the free gift of righteousness' bring enjoyment of life and freedom from condemnation, much more surely, to those who trust in God. All who belong to Adam die; but all who belong to Christ shall live.

So who will you listen to? Who will be your leader? Whose word will be your bread and butter?

2nd Sunday of Lent

Genesis 12:1–4a · Romans 4:1–5, 13–17 · John 3:1–17 · Psalm 121

No one can see the kingdom of God unless they are born again.

The subject of our readings this week is the gracious blessing of a new start with God, however old one might be. It's never too late to listen to what God says and learn from it.

Abram is called by God, aged seventy-five, to leave everything he is familiar and comfortable with to go to an unspecified new location. Leaving his family and friends, he is promised a great nation in return. Forsaking the comforts of hearth and home, he is assured of fame and a blessing so magnificent it will be proverbial. It can be dangerous to wander the vast tracts of the ancient world alone, but the Lord promises to prosper Abram's allies and curse his enemies. But more than all this, he promises to faithful Abram that the world that came of age in the shadow of the Fall will be redeemed from its bondage to decay through him. If the families of the world are to be saved from their enslavement to sin East of Eden, it will be solely through a divine plan in which Abram will play a crucial part.

Abram obeys, and goes as God has told him, despite his great age. He trusts the promise and is greatly blessed. Another old man, in our Gospel reading, finds following the path that the Lord shows him more difficult to accept. Nicodemus approaches Jesus under cover of night, with self-assured, flattering words. 'We know God sent you,' he kindly assures Jesus, 'we can see God's power and presence in the miracles'. Who is this 'we'? Jesus cuts through the proud human attempt to validate his ministry and have it accredited by this experienced professor: 'you can't even see the kingdom of God unless you're born again'. So why should I care what you think of me?

Nicodemus is surely startled by this abrupt and unwelcome opener from Jesus. His face no doubt is a picture! He thought he knew a few things already and could build on his knowledge by asking some questions of this prophetic newcomer; perhaps they could work together? But Jesus tells him that he knows nothing, sees nothing, and he makes attainment of the sought-after wisdom seem impossible. 'How can anyone be born after having grown old?!'

Nicodemus must do more than turn over a new leaf. He requires new life. This is not an easy message for one so long in the tooth and one so respected for his learning. 'Are you the teacher of Israel, and yet you do not understand these things?' Jesus turns the professor's own rhetoric around: 'Very truly, I tell you, *we* speak of what *we* know and testify to what *we* have seen; yet *you* do not receive our testimony.' Nicodemus hasn't been listening carefully enough to the words of Jesus, too dazzled by the miracles and his own agenda. Yet Jesus offers the blessing of eternal life to everyone who believes in him. He has administered a rebuke, a humiliation even, yet he came not to condemn but to save. Jesus doesn't want to be talent-spotted, but trusted.

Nicodemus and Abram both learned that the blessings of God are given graciously and freely, quite apart from our merits or good works. This liberating truth calls us to move forward in faith, not trusting our own cleverness or human wisdom but the guarantees of God. It is those lessons which the apostle Paul draws from the Genesis narratives as he dwells on them in Romans 4. The promise of divine blessing rests solely on undeserved grace, and is only for those who imitate the faith of Abraham. It brings justification and peace to the ungodly, and life to the dead (and the old!). Have you learned this yet, or are you still clinging to your old, comforting ways?

3rd Sunday of Lent

Exodus 17:1–7 · Romans 5:1–11 · John 4:5–42 · Psalm 95

Whoever drinks the water I give them will never thirst.

As is appropriate for Lent, the readings this week use physical hunger and thirst to point us towards our true spiritual needs and satisfaction. Only Jesus can give us water which will satisfy us for ever. All we have to do is ask for it.

The narratives in Exodus between the Red Sea and Sinai focus on God's good provision for his people. The bitter waters of Marah are made sweet; the Lord our healer keeps them healthy; bread rains down from heaven; quail covers the camp. The defeat of Amalek and the organisation of delegated civil government will follow. But in the episode we read this week, the people cry out for water. Bitter or sweet, they may not care, such is their thirst. Instead of turning to the gracious Lord, as they should, their anger and frustrated hopes are focused intensely onto a mere mortal, Moses. He does the right thing, seeking wisdom and help from God. The divine answer is merciful and kind, but also enigmatic. Moses is to strike the rock, from which, miraculously, water will then pour out. Yet the Lord himself stands on the rock: must Moses's staff fall on him first before the water flows? That rock is Christ, the New Testament tells us (1 Corinthians 10:4). Punishment for sin is foreshadowed and provision for sinners is accomplished in one act.

The Samaritan woman at the well discovers true satisfaction and the quenching of her physical thirst too. But the episode is primarily about Jesus, not the woman. When he first answers her, he begins to lead her to a fuller understanding. 'If you knew who I was…' he says. All she hears is the line about the living water. He leads her gently through the intricacies of the conversation to the final conclusion: 'I am the Messiah!' What she needed all along was not just water, but Jesus; not a husband, but Jesus; not answers to her theological questions, but Jesus; not prophetic insight into her life, but Jesus.

And as he draws her to himself, Jesus draws others through her. The disciples, arriving late to the party, think he must need some food. But he is more than content with the fruit of his mission in the conversion of this Samaritan woman. He teaches them to see the harvest right in front of them, and then stays for two days, reaping and rejoicing. The Saviour of the World has brought salvation to the worldly.

In Romans 5, Paul thoughtfully reflects on the story of salvation. The deepest need of human sinners is peace with a righteous God. That is our ultimate desire and satisfaction. Our gracious justification by faith gives us all we truly need, including the eternal hope of glory, so that in this present age where physical and emotional suffering is common, disappointment need not be our lot. God pours into our hearts his living love through the Holy Spirit so that even our afflictions are turned to our good, producing endurance, character and hope. His love is demonstrated by the unconditional grace he has shown us in sending his Son to die in our place. There is no longer war between us, but peace. We are saved through Christ's sacrifice from the wrath of God we deserve. So as the psalm says, 'Come, let us sing for joy to the LORD; let us shout aloud to the Rock of our salvation.'

4th Sunday of Lent

1 Samuel 16:1–13 · Ephesians 5:8–14 · John 9:1–41 · Psalm 23

People look at the outward appearance, but the LORD looks at the heart.

Light and sight. Day and night. These two metaphors recur in this week's readings, suggesting how distinctive the power of God is in our lives.

The key to 1 Samuel 16 is the crucial word from God to Samuel concerning his choice of the new king of Israel: 'The LORD does not look at the things people look at. People look at the outward appearance, but the LORD looks at the heart.' The Lord has rejected Saul as king, and now looks for a man after his own heart, but Samuel has not quite understood the proper criteria for a king. He sees the tall, handsome Eliab and immediately thinks that he must be 'the one'. Each of Jesse's sons parades before the prophet, yet the Lord has not chosen but rejected them. Only one is left, the youngest, but thrones do not usually pass to youngest sons. David just so happens to be handsome (unlike his glorious descendent Jesus, of whom it is said, 'he had no form or majesty that we should look at him, and no beauty that we should desire him', Isaiah 53:2). But the vital thing is that the Lord has chosen him, and the Spirit comes upon him to empower and enlighten.

John chapter 9 is a crucial passage in the Gospel, a key moment that John will allude to again (see John 10:21, 11:37). This clearly made an impact on people at the time. Jesus says that the man was born blind for a reason; he has been chosen so that God's works might be revealed in him. 'While it is day,' says Jesus, we must do God's works, because 'night is coming, when no one can work'. The difference between the night and the day is Jesus himself, 'the light of the world'. As if to illustrate what this means, he immediately goes on to heal the blind man, who sees for the very first time.

We then see, as clear as day, what it means that God has blinded the eyes and hardened the hearts of many (John 12:40), as the Pharisees and others dispute what has happened and doubt Jesus's power and calling. Jesus makes a teaching point of this, and clarifies why he has come: 'I came into this world for judgment,' he says, 'so that those who do not see may see, and those who do see may become blind.' He has come to reverse the judgment of the world.

Paul also takes up the theme of darkness and light in the application section of his letter to the Ephesians. From Ephesians 4 onwards he urges them to live a life worthy of their calling, as those who are now one in Christ. In the Lord they have changed from darkness to light, and so they must live differently to those around them. As 'people of distinction', their overarching aim must be to find out what is pleasing to God, rather than pursuing the age-old chimera of their own personal happiness. To pursue 'all that is good and right and true' means distancing themselves from 'the unfruitful works of darkness', the secret, shameful self-absorption of their past and the surrounding culture. As they are brought into the light of Christ, his searching gaze exposes the true nature of such things. As they see them for what they are, their repentance and faith bring them back from the sleepy death of sin, as Christ shines his glorious light into their darkened hearts.

The challenge is: do we see the world in the light of Christ, or are we looking at it all wrong, as if its darkness was attractive and not pitiable?

5th Sunday of Lent

Ezekiel 37:1–14 · Romans 8:6–11 · John 11:1–45 · Psalm 130

In his word I put my hope.

This week's readings proclaim to us the glorious new life of the Spirit that is ours in Christ through his powerful word.

Ezekiel's vision of a valley of dry bones is a vision of the people of God without the Spirit. Though chosen by God, they are dead and lifeless before he speaks to regenerate and enliven them. The deathly, hopeless scene is transformed by the noise of rattling bones as the breath of God, carried on the prophet's words, enters the valley. Though originally a picture of a nation restored to their land after the Babylonian exile, this has often been seen as paradigmatic, a suggestive model of how the sovereign Lord works to bring life to his people. The purpose of God's actions and words here, as with all his acts of self-revelation, is to make friends with us: 'then they shall know that I am the LORD, [and know that I have spoken]' (NRSV).

Jesus demonstrates the symbolic truth of Ezekiel 37 in the life of one particular Israelite. Just as last week we met a man who had been born blind 'so that the works of God might be displayed in him', so this week we see a man who is allowed to die and a corpse that is permitted to fester 'so that the Son of God might be glorified' in his new life. Through the faith displayed in the intimate interactions between Jesus and Lazarus's sisters, we discover that Jesus is not only a powerful healer but '*the*' resurrection and the life. The dead will rise at the Last Day, as Martha confesses, but to prove his power over death even now, the living Lord speaks the word and out the beloved man comes from what was thought to be his final resting place. He is raised to (eventually) die again, but this points to the stupendous reality of Jesus's own resurrection from the dead, a once-and-for-all-time resurrection to a new world, not just a temporary restoration (Romans 6:9).

Romans 8:11 begins with an awesome idea linking this all together: 'If the Spirit of him who raised Jesus from the dead dwells in you…' The very thought that that Spirit could dwell in us, a Spirit of such immense power, is surely a magnificently humbling one. Not only that, but 'he who raised Christ from the dead will give life to your mortal bodies also through his Spirit that dwells in you.' Strength for today, and bright hope for tomorrow! And along with the ten thousand blessings that accompany this, there is a new impulse to live for him.

Paul says that 'those who are in the flesh cannot please God'. Without the Spirit, even their seemingly good works only ever have the nature of sin, and are without merit in his eyes, however stunning their quality may appear to us.[5] Yet those who by faith are possessed by the Spirit can, and must, please him who died, rose, and lives for them. This is a privilege and a duty that is ours in Christ alone. So will we put our hope in his powerful word so that we might see his Spirit at work in us today?

---

[5] I have explored this strikingly unfamiliar thought further in Lee Gatiss, *Living to Please God: Life for a Higher Purpose and Pleasure* (Nottingham: IVP, 2025), chapter 3.

Palm Sunday

Matthew 21:1–11 · Psalm 118:1–2, 19–29

See, your king comes to you, gentle and riding on a donkey.

On Palm Sunday we have two readings: Matthew 21 and one of the Old Testament passages Matthew quotes, Psalm 118. They present to us the King who comes in the name of the Lord, but who will shortly be rejected. Are you drawn to him as your King, or merely curious and cold towards him?

Jesus sends two disciples ahead of him to collect not one, but two donkeys (the mother and her foal), in fulfilment of Zechariah 9. The other Gospels mention Jesus riding only one donkey, and there are perhaps various reasons for that (such as the fact that he may have only ridden one donkey *at a time*, or that the 'them' in verse 7 on which he rode in fact refers to the cloaks, not the donkeys together). We never hear of him travelling in such style at any other time, so this was a carefully choreographed and deliberately prepared entry into the capital, designed to make an impact.

Jesus rode into Jerusalem and he was certainly noticed. Crowds of pilgrims flocking to the holy city from round about recognised the King, and perhaps believed the biblical prophecy was being fulfilled. They transformed his arrival into a triumphal procession, spreading their own cloaks of cloth and branches on the road, much as we might lay out the red carpet for the arrival of an honoured dignitary. Matthew says most or many used their own cloaks, and only some used branches – something that may be harder to persuade congregations to re-enact on Sunday! All around him, the sweet hosannas ring. The songs of the crowd recognise the arrival of one born to be king, in the line of David, and one who comes in the name of the Lord himself, as his beloved Son. They recognise, as the word 'Hosanna' ('Save! Help!') implies, that he is their long-awaited

Saviour. Saviour from the Romans, or from their sins? What a mixture of emotions and motives and understandings there must have been on that day. Yet with the eye of faith and hindsight, we can look back on the scene and see that many must have spoken better than they actually knew.

The inquisitive people of the city itself did not all immediately join the pilgrims from the villages and towns in proclaiming him the Messiah. 'Who is this?' could equally well mean 'Who does this chap think he is? What on earth is all this fuss about?' City-dwellers are not so easily convinced! The Northern lad is feted by some of his own, 'He's one of us, from Nazareth in Galilee!' they cry. But not everyone is persuaded he is the one to watch. He has come to his capital as much to divide as to rule. One crowd sings 'Hosanna' but by the end of the week another would be bellowing 'Crucify him!' As Samuel Crossman so eloquently rendered it:

> Sometimes they strew his way,
> and his sweet praises sing;
> resounding all the day
> hosannas to their king:
> then 'Crucify!' is all their breath,
> And for his death they thirst and cry.

Yet this strange irony was also prophesied by Psalm 118. The same song which declares 'Hosannas' to the King, and blesses the one who comes in the name of the Lord, also prophesied, 'The stone which the builders rejected...' Little did they know at that point something too marvellous for their eyes to see – that he would not be triumphantly enthroned on their premature praises, but that it was in his very rejection that he would prove to be their salvation and chief cornerstone. The stage is set for the drama of Holy Week.

EASTER

Easter Sunday

Acts 10:34–43 · Colossians 3:1–4 · John 20:1–18 · Psalm 118:1–2, 14–24

Since, then, you have been raised with Christ,
set your hearts on things above.

Easter Sunday is about the resurrection of our Lord and Saviour Jesus Christ. These readings chosen from the various options in the lectionary put that glorious event into the perspective of his life, death and second coming. They urge us to believe he is risen indeed, and to live in the light of the glory to come.

In Acts 10, Peter evangelises Cornelius, a God-fearing Gentile. Finally understanding that the gospel is a message for all people, not just the Jews, he tells Cornelius and his household the story of Jesus, his message and miracles and his death. In essence, it is the message of all his speeches in the book of Acts: they killed him but God raised him; we are witnesses of that fact, so repent and believe. Peter tells the attentive family that he ate and drank with the risen Christ, who commanded him and the other apostles to preach this message. When examined closely, the summary of that message in verses 42 and 43 may surprise many. It is sometimes said that the Old Testament is about judgment and the New Testament is about forgiveness. But look at what Jesus told Peter to say: Christ is the one ordained to be *judge*, the risen judge of all. That's the message of the New Testament – the resurrection shows us who our judge will be 'on that day'. The Old Testament pointed to the other side of the message: all the prophets show that forgiveness of sins is received through believing in this risen Messiah. Peter's apostolic message from Jesus emphasises forgiveness in the Old, and judgment in the New! A similar pattern is found in other speeches in Acts (e.g. Paul in Athens, Acts 17:30–31).

In his letter to the Colossians, Paul shows how once we are believers, we are united to Christ in his death and resurrection. We are raised with him, because we died with him: that faith-union is unbreakable. Since we died with him, our life is hidden with him and is not to be worldly in its orientation. Since we were raised with him, we are to set our minds, thoughts and affections, on 'things that are above' – Christ himself at the right hand of the Father, the glory to come, the end of sin and death and tears. But verse 4 also reminds us of the future hope this brings us too, the eschatological (end times) perspective. When Christ, who *is* our life, is revealed to all at the Last Day, then we too can expect to be revealed as his, and to stand before him in glory. The resurrection transforms life in the here and now, and re-orientates everything about it around Christ. It does this in the here and now, in anticipation of the everlasting focus of eternity to come which is riveted on Jesus, the dying and living Lord.

John 20 narrates the sheer wonder and amazement of the first Easter morning, which is recreated in all those who receive the message of Acts 10 and Colossians 3 with faith. Mary Magdalene is the first to see the empty tomb; bewildered, she runs to Peter and John with her grave-robber theory. They run to see for themselves. Though John is quicker, he is more hesitant to enter the tomb and properly look than the typically bold Peter. But when he sees, he believes what the Old Testament should have persuaded him of already. The Christ must rise; the Christ has risen! Mary is not quite there yet. Even the angels she sees in the tomb can't quite convince her that the body has not been stolen. Even when she sees him, she isn't yet awake to the new day that has dawned. It is only when he calls her by name, 'Mary!' that the eyes of her heart are opened and she cries out '*Rabbouni*! My teacher!' And so it is with us. He is not with us now, but has ascended, as he told Mary he would. Yet we may stare these truths in the face each year, and hear them questioning us many times, before we are given the ability to embrace them. Can you see it yet? Do you believe it? Do you want to?

2nd Sunday of Easter

Acts 2:14a, 22–32 · 1 Peter 1:3–9 · John 20:19–31 · Psalm 16

Even though you do not see him now, you believe in him and are filled with an inexpressible and glorious joy.

This Sunday's readings naturally focus again on the resurrection of Christ, and particularly on the deep inexpressible joy it brings to believers who have not seen Jesus in the flesh. Do you have this joy?

Acts 2 is a Pentecost reading, but Peter's speech to the crowd gathered in Jerusalem focuses very clearly on the resurrection of Jesus. His message sets the pattern for the rest of Acts: Jesus was the divine Saviour; you killed him; God raised him; and we are witnesses of that. The usual response is 'therefore, repent and believe!' The reading this week zeroes in on Peter's use of Psalm 16 and the glad rejoicing of the Messiah whose body has been raised to the right hand of God. The psalm speaks of the path of life, which Jesus has opened up. The psalm cannot be about David, who wrote it, argues Peter. He is still dead! Instead, he prophesied through this psalm what Jesus would do. Or rather, he prophesied what God would do for Jesus: he would not abandon him to Hades for ever, or let death have the final word. Jesus would be the promised King in David's line, for ever. The solid reality of Jesus's own resurrection from the dead, and his joy, is the basis for our joy, our gladness, both now and after death 'in his presence'.

Peter continues that same theme in his epistle to the dispersed believers of Asia Minor. The letter begins with blessing and praise – he has given us new birth into a living hope through the resurrection. The things we own in this world, especially as exiles or strangers in it, are fragile and precarious. Our spiritual (but nonetheless real!) inheritance is kept safely in heaven, protected by God. The resurrection blasted a hole into the new world, for all who cling to Jesus with true faith. The genuineness of our faith is tested by trials and temptations which come our way in this sinful world. Those who love him, though they do not see him, will receive the salvation of their souls from the risen Lord Jesus. Who could hold back from expressing the inexpressible and glorious joy which comes from such assurance?

There is an element of Pentecost in the reading from the Gospel this week too, just as there is in the reading from Acts. The Johannine Pentecost, as it is called, is briefer and more enigmatic perhaps, and focuses on the disciples' mission to go out into the world in the power of the Spirit, to live and work to his praise and glory. That is to come, once the doors are opened, but the drama in that locked house is all about Jesus: when they saw the Lord, they rejoiced. Except Thomas did not see, and so he did not rejoice because he did not first believe. What a puzzling time it must have been for him – 'Why, if he is risen, has he left me out?' he may have wondered. But one look at the holy hands and pierced side of the Lord convinced the doubter. His exclamation is best understood as a confession of Christ's sovereignty and divinity, 'My Lord and my God!'

John completes his narrative with a blessing on all those who believe without having to see the risen Lord for themselves. We rely on the eyewitnesses. Much more could be written, he says, but what we have in his Gospel is sufficient to convince us that the Messiah is this Jesus – the one who gives us joy, when we gain life through faith in him. Moods may ebb and flow, but the joy of knowing the risen Jesus is something we all can know if we trust in him today.

3rd Sunday of Easter

Acts 2:14a, 36–41 · 1 Peter 1:17–23 · Luke 24:13–35 ·
Psalm 116:1–4, 12–19

God has made this Jesus, whom you crucified, both Lord and Messiah.

You need to engage your heart, respond to Jesus's resurrection from the dead, and change direction. That's the message of today's readings.

Two disciples on their way to Emmaus meet the risen Christ on the road. Their eyes are kept from recognising their travel companion, who has plans of his own as he steers their conversation. They recognise that Jesus was 'a prophet mighty in deed and word', but dismiss the idea that he could be the Christ, the redeeming Messiah, because he was condemned and crucified. 'How can he redeem us, if he's dead?', they must have reasoned.

Yet Jesus confounds their reasoning, and jolts them out of their foolish unbelief. He shows them all that the Scripture foretold about the suffering and subsequent glory of the Christ, and their hearts burn within them. Though they do not yet realise why, they insist he stays with them at the end of the day. They need more than newly kindled hearts before they will change direction. They need their eyes opened, to see that the prophesied Messiah is Jesus himself, the one who walks with them and breaks bread with them. Once they see it, they turn around and run to share the news.

The crowd in Jerusalem during the Pentecost festival must deal with the sudden reversal of their expectations and thoughts about Jesus too. He was not a crucified failure, another in a long line of disappointing messianic pretenders. They had judged him badly, and written him off, but God had appointed him both Lord and Messiah (titles which Mary and the shepherds knew right from the start of Luke's Gospel). They are cut to the heart by Peter's preaching, stabbed by a sudden realisation.

Like a car screeching to a halt, the smell of burning rubber rising from the tyres, they are arrested in their tracks and forced to reconsider. They are not just affected emotionally, but volitionally too, asking the apostles, 'What shall we *do*?' The only course of action open to them must be to repent and do a U-turn. They will find, if they do so, says Peter, more than adequate reasons to pursue a different course: the gift of the Holy Spirit is for all who believe and are baptised as a sign of that change of heart. This is also an offer for their children (quite normal for those who thought so easily in terms of family solidarity), and for those who are far off (that is, in context, the Jewish Diaspora, though it perhaps hints at a wider ultimate concern). About three thousand souls were saved from a corrupt generation that day. So many that they were not necessarily all baptised by immersion, as some suggest must be normative, since there was no river near to the Temple.

Reflecting on these events some years later, Peter writes to the dispersed exiles of far off Asia Minor about their trust in God, 'who raised Jesus from the dead and gave him glory'. They too have been redeemed, ransomed from the futility of their former ways and that of their ancestors, by the blood of the true Passover lamb. This had always been the eternal plan of God for our redemption, yet only now had this way of salvation been revealed with the coming of Christ. They now knew for themselves the purification which only comes through obedience to the truth, and so they must 'love one another deeply, from the *heart*'. The living word of God gives us new life – a fresh start, a new direction, a new family. Heartfelt engagement in reverent fear of God is the only true response. Pray for the Lord to open your heart and move you in this way today.

4th Sunday of Easter

Acts 2:42–47 · 1 Peter 2:19–25 · John 10:1–10 · Psalm 23

I have come that they may have life, and have it to the full.

These readings remind us that Jesus calls and gathers his sheep, who hear his voice and follow his example. If we follow him, he promises us life in full abundance.

Three thousand newly baptised converts in Jerusalem, who responded to the word of the Lord through Peter at Pentecost, devoted themselves to hearing more and obeying. Their wholehearted commitment to that word made them unreserved members of the new fellowship, which met for teaching, prayer and the breaking of bread. As a sign that a new age had dawned, signs that pointed to something greater and wonders which grabbed the attention were performed by the apostles in the power of the Spirit. Equally miraculously, there was a widespread sharing (not renunciation) of possessions and wealth among this fledgling church as they gathered daily in the Temple and were filled with much joy. External opposition seemed to melt away and internal disharmony was nowhere to be seen for this all-too-brief moment in the church's history.

Not everything about that special time is normative for today, of course. The apostles are not personally with us to perform signs and wonders, and nor can every Christian believer fit into the space once occupied by the Jerusalem Temple! But we are still urged to be liberal (relationally and financially that is), and devoted to the teaching of the apostles with all our hearts.[6] Prayer

[6] Article 38 of the Church of England's *Thirty-nine Articles* says, 'The Riches and Goods of Christians are not common, as touching the right, title, and possession of the same; as certain Anabaptists do falsely boast. Notwithstanding, every man ought, of such things as he possesseth, liberally to give alms to the poor, according to his ability.'

and the breaking of bread can still be our comfort and joy as we gather with Jesus's family. But pressures within and without are hard to escape.

That point is very clear in the epistle reading this week, as Peter addresses the growing and suffering churches of Asia Minor. Speaking especially to those who were slaves at that time, he reminds them that it is no credit to them if they are disobedient to their masters and punished accordingly. Yet if they do right, act properly and endure suffering for that, God is with them throughout their ordeal and will reward them accordingly. By quietly persisting they will silence the ignorance of foolish people, as the Lord Jesus himself did when he went like a lamb to the slaughter and did not open his mouth to retaliate (harder for us in the age of social media than it might seem). The picture of the cross which Peter paints for us here is *substitutionary* ('he bore our sins in his body on the tree ... by his wounds you have been healed'), as Jesus takes the punishment we deserved and objectively achieves our reconciliation with God. It is also *exemplary* ('leaving you an example, so that you should follow in his steps'). Any unjust suffering we might face from a harsh and unbelieving world is not divine punishment, paying for our sins or purging us of them; rather, it is a following in the steps of the suffering Shepherd. He calls us and gathers us as his sheep, as we take up our crosses 'to tread the sacred way that Jesus watered with his blood' (as the eighteenth-century hymnwriter Augustus Toplady so beautifully put it).[7]

This pastoral imagery, which Peter borrows from Isaiah 53:6, is dominant in the Gospel reading from John chapter 10. The sheep hear their master's voice. He knows them, and calls them by name. They are his. He laid down his life for his own, so that they can enjoy life in all its fullness. The threat in the first half

---

[7] See his hymn, 'Contempt of the World' in Augustus M. Toplady, *The Works of Augustus M. Toplady* (London: Edinburgh: William Baynes and Son; H. S. Baynes, 1825), 6:390–91.

of the chapter is not from wolves, or even from mercenaries who watch the sheep but flee at the first sign of trouble beyond their pay grade (though wolves and hired hands abound). The threat is from those who seek to steal the sheep for themselves, taking them away from the Shepherd and guardian of their souls. Their strangely seductive voices seek to entice the flock to death and destruction outside the safety of the sheepfold. Do not listen to them or join their fellowship. Stick with Jesus.

5th Sunday of Easter

Acts 7:55–60 · 1 Peter 2:2–10 · John 14:1–14 · Psalm 31:1–5, 15–16

I am the way and the truth and the life.
No one comes to the Father except through me.

'The way that leads to glory lies through ill-report, contempt, and loss', the great hymn-writer Augustus Montague Toplady once wrote.[8] Our readings today focus on the road to glory and the suffering and rejection which accompany believers on that path. Will you keep on this way to true glory, or be seduced away from it by something that seems easier?

Jesus outlines the way to his Father's house in our Gospel reading, as a comfort to his anxious disciples. For him, preparation of that destination for his people lay in dying for them. He goes to prepare a place for them, and indeed his going, his death, *is* that preparation, opening up the new and living way by his blood (Hebrews 10:20). He himself, he tells Thomas, is *the* way, and *the* truth, and *the* life. And just in case the firm positive statement isn't sufficient, he adds a negative: no one can arrive safely at this hallowed destination by any alternative route. No one comes to the Father, the centre of heaven and the reason for its glory, in any other way. Conscious trust in the Father and the Son, and leaning on their words and works, is the path. Asking explicitly 'in Jesus's name' (no other), is the key.

This is, of course, a controversial, even contemptible, truth in a commercial world which has elevated consumer choice almost to the status of a human right. In a fractious world where we want to get along and not make exclusive truth claims, it is counterintuitive and hard to stomach. Yet Jesus is the authority on such matters, and

[8] 'Contempt of the World' in Toplady, *The Works of Augustus M. Toplady*, 6:390–91.

to him we must defer. He would know, after all, what the way to the Father is, and if there is only one.

The way to truth and life is through suffering, but there is triumph and solace after humiliation. The martyr Stephen discovers this first in the wake of Christ's resurrection and ascension. After a provocative and penetrating speech outlining the work of God beyond the boundaries of the establishment, piercing through the bigotry and bile of those who confined God to *their* holy structures, Stephen sees the Lord Jesus at the right hand of the Father in glory. He had opened the heavens and shown the way! But the Sanhedrin cover their ears and shout at Stephen, so as not to hear his testimony to that truth. Dragged beyond the city walls, where 'Jesus also suffered outside the gate in order to sanctify the people through his own blood' (Hebrews 13:12), he ends his earthly pilgrimage, rejected and alone, praying for the forgiveness of his persecutors by God. The apostle Paul, as yet unconvinced but surely attentive, stands by, watching.

In his epistle, the apostle Peter also speaks of Christ as 'rejected by mortals yet chosen and precious in God's sight'. God's purposes and plans cannot be equated with mere worldly success. Neither can worldly lack of power, privilege or patronage be equated with lack of God's approval. Some people stumble, says Peter, and reject those upon whom God smiles – those royal priests, that holy nation, whose task and joy it is to declare the grace of the one who has saved them. If some don't believe, they disobey as they were destined to do, while the chosen proclaim not their own worthiness, but the mighty acts of the merciful one. So will you stumble at what Jesus says today, or will you joyfully embrace him, whatever comes your way?

6th Sunday of Easter

Acts 17:22–31 · 1 Peter 3:13–22 · John 14:15–21 · Psalm 66:8–20

Come and hear, all you who fear God;
let me tell you what he has done for me.

Our readings this week are about giving an account of the hope that is in us because of the risen Christ's authority and his loving gift. How can we keep this to ourselves?

In the Gospel reading, following on from last week, Jesus reassures his disciples that his imminent departure is not the end of their friendship. He continues to love them, and they must continue to obey his commandments, even in his physical absence. To help them with this, he will ask the Father to send them another Advocate, a counsellor and friend like him. This Spirit of truth will abide with them, and be *in* them, he says. The world will not enjoy this privilege and will not know, love, or obey him, who remains their Lord and Master even beyond the grave. They do not understand it, but after his resurrection and the giving of the Spirit, these things become clearer to them.

The apostles look to Christ's resurrection power and authority in their ministries both to believers and unbelievers. Paul, addressing the sophisticated metropolitan elite of cultured, unbelieving Athens, explains in Acts 17 about Jesus and the resurrection (which they thought might be two new gods). They confessed in their altar 'to the unknown God' that they were ignorant of God, so he sets about proclaiming to them the truth revealed in Jesus. Beginning with first principles for those with little understanding of the Old Testament narrative and background, he leads the different philosophical parties in the Areopagus council to his impromptu speech's stunning climax: Jesus is going to judge us all, so repent and believe before it's too late. God has given proof of this final, personal judgment to come by raising Jesus the Judge from the dead.

On the way to this conclusion, Paul affirms God's creation of the universe, his creation of all the nations of the world through one man (Adam), and yet his independence from creation (his 'aseity' as the theologians call it – he doesn't *need* anything from us). This God does not live in temples made by human hands – a provocative thing to say while standing on Mars's Hill with the glorious and expensive Parthenon right behind him! This transcendent and almighty God is, however, not a distant deity like Athena, closeted away in her temple at the top of the Acropolis, but close to us. Paul's quotation of the pagan poet Aratus ('For we are indeed his offspring') shows he is adept at using cultural allusions which the Athenians would have appreciated as testimony to the fact that humanity gropes after God and feels its indebtedness to him, yet perceives only very dimly without divine revelation.

Peter, addressing believers in his letter, tells them to similarly 'always be ready to make your defence to anyone who demands from you an account of the hope that is in you'. This hope, despite suffering, is that through the substitutionary death and powerful resurrection of Christ, they are brought to God with a clean conscience. The tricky verses on the spirits in prison and Noah and baptism are related to the main purpose of the letter. They proclaim that the risen Christ is victorious and supreme over evil and that believers can be assured of their salvation – precisely what suffering Christians need to hear. Interpretations vary wildly, and certain readings must surely be ruled out (such as those which build whole industries of superstition on speculative reconstructions of what's happening in these verses). Peter's main point, however, is to strengthen the hope of those who are called on to give hope to a persecuting, and ignorant, world. That hope lies solely in the risen Lord Jesus, at the right hand of God, to whom every power and authority is ultimately accountable. Those who trust in him and speak of him will never be put to shame.

7th Sunday of Easter (Sunday after Ascension Day)

Acts 1:6–14 · 1 Peter 4:12–14, 5:6–11 · John 17:1–11 · Psalm 68:1–10, 32–35

The God of all grace, who called you to his eternal glory in Christ, after you have suffered a little while, will himself restore you and make you strong.

The days after Ascension Day until Pentecost are days of prayer and preparation for the celebration of the outpouring of the Holy Spirit. The readings this week focus on the power and the glory to come for those who are united to Christ by faith. We can trust him whatever happens in this life.

Acts 1 retells the story of the disciples waiting for the Spirit. Someone once said that the question they ask Jesus ('Is this the time when you will restore the kingdom to Israel?') contains as many errors and misunderstandings as it does words![9] They are looking for power and glory in the here and now, and they will receive it. But it will not be as they expect. They will receive power from on high when the Holy Spirit comes, and they will be blessed with the awesome privilege of witnessing to Jesus's resurrection. For many, this will end in their deaths, as the gospel spreads inexorably from Jerusalem to Judea, and (beyond Israel) to Samaria, and then to the ends of the earth.

They watch as Jesus disappears from sight, only to be told that he will come again in the same way one day. They return to Jerusalem from Olivet and immediately devote themselves to prayer as they wait for the things they have been told about to happen. The names of the eleven foundational apostles are again given (as they were

[9] John Calvin, *Commentary upon the Acts of the Apostles* (Bellingham, WA: Logos Bible Software, 2010), p. 43.

earlier in Luke's Gospel account), but minus Judas Iscariot. Jesus's mother and his brothers also believe and pray with them, with some other unnamed women. The gift that Jesus promised will come, and then, at some unknown future point, the Lord himself will return again in glory.

The Gospel reading goes back to just before the crucifixion, when Jesus prayed his high priestly prayer in John 17. He prayed that he might be glorified, as he was glorified before the foundation of the world, so that he might glorify the Father and give eternal life to all those who had been given to him – the past glory, the future glory and the present glory. In a wonderful one-liner (verse 3) he tells us that eternal life is knowing God and the glorified Son. He prays, not for the world, but for those given to him by the Father out of that world, that they would go on believing his word, even when he has returned to the Father's side. He asks that they might enjoy the closest, most intimate spiritual unity with God. This is his present prayer for us – right now! – as he intercedes with the Father on our behalf before his return.

Peter reminds his readers that in this time of waiting we must suffer before the glory to come is revealed. We must not be surprised by this, because it has been prophesied and is inevitable for those who follow a crucified Messiah. Sharing his sufferings means sharing in the glory to come, because of our union with him by faith. The Spirit of God rests on those who confess his name under pressure and endure to the edge of glory with his divine assistance. In this period of waiting, we entrust ourselves to him and cast all our burdens and sorrows upon him, along with all those who likewise are joined to him by bonds that are deeper than blood and stronger than death. The God of grace and eternal power equips us for the glory to come, with all that we need in Christ, by his Spirit. So hold on, by his strength; because the suffering is just 'for a little while'. Eternal glory is on the way.

PENTECOST

Whit Sunday (Pentecost)

Acts 2:1–21 · 1 Corinthians 12:3b–13 · John 20:19–23 · Psalm 104:24–34, 35b

And everyone who calls on the name of the Lord will be saved.

The readings for Whit Sunday naturally have at their heart the coming of the Holy Spirit at Pentecost and the outworking of that crucial moment in salvation history for the life of the Church. The emphasis falls on the impact it has on the outward-looking mission of the Church. We must get out there with this good news!

Acts 2 narrates what happens as the Spirit comes on the day of Pentecost, just as Jesus had promised he would. The disciples are all together in one place, waiting. And suddenly the Spirit arrives, not quietly and gently, but 'like the rush of a violent wind' and with tongues of fire. In an awe-inspiring experience, Babel is undone (Genesis 11) and the Spirit gives them the ability to speak in other languages. They proclaim to the Jews in Jerusalem, from all over the world, God's mighty deeds.

It puzzles and perplexes the crowd. Yet, as always when God is at work, others sneer and draw the wrong conclusion. But this is not 'new wine' as those dismissive critics understand it, inebriating the disciples so that they lose control, but *the* new wine, spiritual refreshment, which Jesus had foretold. Peter explains it to the crowd as a fulfilment of Scripture. It is not drunkenness but prophecy they are witnessing – the great and glorious day of the Lord. It calls not for mere astonishment or derision, but comes with an implicit challenge for the whole world: 'everyone who calls on the name of the Lord shall be saved'. Will you?

The Gospel reading takes us back a little in time before Pentecost, to a different moment, prior to Jesus's ascension. Fear is turned to joy when the risen Lord appears. There can be no doubt about who he is and what he has done when he shows them his hands and his side, where the cruel nails and vicious spear had pierced him as he hung on our behalf from a cross. The breathing of the Spirit upon the disciples at this point is different from the more dramatic filling with the Spirit narrated in Acts 2, but it is again linked to them being sent out to proclaim the gospel. As Jesus had come at the Father's bidding to live, die, and rise for our salvation, so they would also be sent to bring news of that salvation to others. Only through faith in that joyful proclamation will people have their sins forgiven; without it, their sins are retained, unforgiven. This is a reminder for us of the obligation not to hoard the gospel, and that it comes with a commission to pass it on.

Paul reflects on the giving of the Spirit in 1 Corinthians 12, for the edification of a church which argued over who was most spiritual. No one confesses Jesus as Lord without the aid of the Spirit, and that same Spirit cannot lead people to curse Christ. He is the common possession of all who profess. Our relationship to him is begun and directed by him. The Father empowers us in all spiritual activities; the Lord Jesus enables us in varieties of service; and the Spirit endows us with diverse spiritual gifts – but none of this is for ourselves alone, but for others. Those who have come to know God in Christ are baptised in one Spirit into one undivided body. Christ cannot be torn in pieces, and his Spirit is the inexhaustible fountain of all good things for all people, whether Jews or Greeks, slaves or free. Those worldly identity markers are no longer basic or primary for those who drink of the Spirit. Our relationship to Christ is all, and it impels us outward, to serve others as he did, not to rate or rank ourselves above them any more.

ORDINARY TIME

Trinity Sunday

Isaiah 40:12–17, 27–31 · 2 Corinthians 13:11–13 · Matthew 28:16–20 · Psalm 8

May the grace of the Lord Jesus Christ, and the love of God, and the fellowship of the Holy Spirit be with you all.

Trinity Sunday is the day we realise that God is not some incomprehensible philosophical construct that is difficult to get our minds around, but that his Trinitarian-ness is something familiar to all Christians from our new life's first cry. Don't be confused by the Trinity – revel in it!

Matthew's Gospel, famous for the Sermon on the Mount, also ends on a mountain, with the disciples worshipping Jesus. The word 'worshipping' is of course natural and correct, and the disciples have had cause to fall down before his divine power more than once before this. In a programmatic statement, Jesus explains why they feel the urge to bow the knee to him. All authority in the created realm has been given to him, both in heaven and on earth: as legions of angels bow to him, so must we, that his will may be done in both these realms. The fact that he is now Lord and Christ, our priest and King, compels us to go out into his world and bring about the obedience of faith among the nations. We do not share some good advice that others may take or leave, or present a lifestyle option for consumers' consideration; we bring the authoritative word from the universal king to his rebellious world; and as we do so, Jesus is with us in divine power.

Response to that word is twofold: one must be baptised and one must become a disciple, and the first should naturally lead to the second. Discipleship involves learning all that Christ has taught. Making disciples means teaching people to obey that, not just presenting a dotted outline, but marking in the lines and colouring in the picture so people know how it is meant to look in practice. According to Jesus, disciples need to be taught how to obey what they read, not just told the stories and left to draw their own conclusions. One with such authority demands obedience.

And one specific command we are to obey is the command to be baptised. We are to be baptised (we should note) not into three names, but into *the* one name of the Father, of the Son, and of the Holy Spirit. This is not just to be immersed in his teaching, but to receive what the Church of England calls the 'sign of profession and mark of difference, whereby Christian men are discerned from others that be not christened', which is also 'a sign of Regeneration or new birth, whereby, as by an instrument, they that receive Baptism rightly are grafted into the Church'.[10] We begin our faltering new life of obedience with the gracious promise of forgiveness signed and sealed upon us, in the name of the holy Trinity.

Our continuance in the obedience of faith is energised and enabled by that same blessed Trinity. Born again into the kingdom of God, as brothers and sisters we are to live in love and peace together, as Paul urges the Corinthians at the end of 2 Corinthians. As we reflect his goodness to the world, the God of love and peace will be with us. Note that for a second time in these readings we are assured of God's presence – and they say the doctrine of the Trinity makes God distant and cold! This is not so in the New Testament. Paul moves effortlessly from the oneness of 'the God of love and peace' to the threefold blessing we know as 'the grace'. The unmerited favour we enjoy through the work of the Son, stemming from the redeeming love of the Father, enables us to enjoy the communion and the fellowship of the Holy Spirit which they themselves enjoy together. That Spirit of the Lord, as Isaiah had already prophesied, is the everlasting God of covenant and creation, who lifts up the weary on wings like eagles and instructs us in the way we should go. The God who was, and is, and always shall be Trinity, is with us from beginning to end.

---

[10] Article 27 of *The Thirty-nine Articles.*

Proper 4

Sunday between 29 May and 4 June inclusive
(if after Trinity Sunday)

Genesis 6:9–22, 7:24, 8:14–19 · Romans 1:16–17, 3:22b–31 ·
Matthew 7:21–29 · Psalm 46

I am not ashamed of the gospel, because it is the power of God that brings salvation to everyone who believes.

The theme of our readings today is God's gracious provision of salvation in Jesus Christ from his righteous judgment on the universality of sin. If you believe in him, you are saved and do not need to fear Judgment Day.

Sin continued to spread in the wake of Adam and Eve's disastrous fall in Genesis 3. By Genesis 6, God could see 'how great the wickedness of the human race had become on the earth, and that every inclination of the thoughts of the human heart were only evil all the time' (Genesis 6:5). He was deeply troubled by this, and could with perfect justice have wiped us all out and started again. But 'Noah found favour in the eyes of the LORD.' Grace found Noah, but not because he was immune from sin, for as we see later, he certainly was not; he is not exempt from the sentence of Genesis 6:5 or that in Genesis 6:11–12 that says '*all* the people on earth had corrupted their ways'. Yet God determined to save a remnant of humanity (and the animal kingdom), and provided a way for Noah and his family to be preserved from the righteous, cleansing judgment which was about to sweep the earth. When they emerge after the great flood, the creation mandate to be fruitful and multiply is repeated and the covenant in renewed.

Our reading from Paul's letter to the Romans has the same basic shape. The gospel of Jesus Christ is 'the power of God for the salvation of everyone who believes'. It reveals 'a righteousness that is by faith from first to last'. The gospel is needed because of the universality of sin: 'for all have sinned and fall short of the glory of God' he says (Romans 3:23). So if anyone is to be acquitted before God it can only be because grace finds them in their lostness just as grace found Noah. God may have left countless sins unpunished for now, but one day everyone will be brought to account. On that day, God will be a just judge, but also the one who justifies those who trust in Jesus. Either we pay for our own sin then, or we hide ourselves in him, covered by his blood which acts as an atoning sacrifice to turn away God's wrath.

This means of course that there can be no boasting that we are saved while others are not. We are not saved by or because of anything within us, or anything we have done. We are only saved by believing in God's promise that if we hide ourselves in Christ, we will be safe from the flood waters. It doesn't matter if we are Jews or Gentiles, circumcised or uncircumcised, male or female, religious or profane, educated or uneducated, white or black, posh or pleb, or somewhere in between. We can only be justified by faith in Christ, whoever we are, whatever we've done.

Hebrews 11:7 comments that 'By faith Noah, when warned about things not yet seen, in holy fear built an ark to save his family. By his faith he condemned the world and became heir of the righteousness that is in keeping with faith.' Jesus makes a similar point in the Gospel reading. He starts with the thought of judgment 'on that day' which is coming. He himself will be the judge (see also John 5:22). The judgment is pictured like a great flood: 'the rain came down, the streams rose, and the wind blew and beat against that house'. That cleansing judgment will reveal whether we have built the house of our lives on the words of Jesus by faith, or not. 'In a word,' says the sixteenth-century Reformer John Calvin on this passage, 'he declares that, so soon as the doctrine of the Gospel shall have begun to bear fruit by obtaining many disciples, there will not only be very many of the common people who falsely and hypocritically submit to it, but even in the rank of pastors there will be the same treachery, so that they will deny by their actions and life what they profess with the mouth'.[11] Some will call him Lord, who never submit to his Lordship. Don't let that be you!

[11] John Calvin, *Commentary on a Harmony of the Evangelists Matthew, Mark, and Luke* (Bellingham, WA: Logos Bible Software, 2010), p. 367.

Proper 5

Sunday between 5 and 11 June inclusive
(if after Trinity Sunday)

Genesis 12:1–9 · Romans 4:13–25 · Matthew 9:9–13, 18–26 ·
Psalm 33:1–12

Let all the earth fear the LORD*;*
let all the people of the world revere him.

The common thread in our readings today is the spread of life-giving blessing which comes when people obediently trust in God's promise. When you are blessed, you become a blessing.

The spread of blessing is a key theme in Genesis 12, as God starts to turn around the doleful spread of sin. After the rebellion of Babel came confusion and the scattering, but God reaches down to one man in the midst of that world. In marriage, a man leaves his father and mother and is united to his wife (Genesis 2:24), but Abram is called to go, to leave his own father and land and people for the sake of an unnamed place that God promises to show him at some point. That is quite a leap of faith, to move so far in response to such a call, without clarity on all the details. What would persuade *you* to do this? The promise with which God allures Abram is world-changingly huge, a charter for the salvation of fallen humanity. God promises that he will become a great and blessed nation, a great and blessed name and a blessing to all the peoples of the earth. And so obediently he sets out in faith, taking his wife and nephew with him.

In the Gospel, Jesus confronts Matthew, sitting at the tax collector's booth. As with Abram, he commands him simply, 'Follow me.' And Matthew obediently gets up and follows Jesus. Many tax collectors and 'sinners' also then come to have dinner with Jesus at

Matthew's house, because the one who is blessed has become a blessing to others. Obviously there are religious grumblers who don't like this influx of chaotic life into their nicely ordered (dead) piety, but Jesus says he has come for the unhealthy, the sinners, as their doctor to heal and bless them. We get a further illustration of what this will mean when, in response to the submissive faith of a synagogue leader, Jesus goes to raise a dead girl to life again. On the way he also heals a woman who has suffered a very long time. She reaches out in faith and trust to Jesus, who brings healing. How could news of all this not spread through the entire region?

In Romans 4, Paul reflects on the life of Abraham. The whole chapter seems to make three points, related to what he has already demonstrated in the previous three chapters. He says getting right with God has *never* been about what you do (verses 1–8); it's *never* been about who you are (verses 9–16); and it *always* brings life-from-the-dead hope (verses 17–25). Abraham did not receive the great promise of Genesis 12 because he had been circumcised (which he hadn't been yet) or *because* he was so obedient. The promise came first and he obediently trusted God in response to it. Which teaches us that the promise is fulfilled by faith 'so that it may be by grace and may be guaranteed to all Abraham's offspring – not only to those who are of the law but also to those who have the faith of Abraham' (Romans 4:16). The question is, do we have the same faith as Abraham – faith in God who clothes himself with promises?

For Abraham that would later mean trusting a promise that at the age of 100, he and his aged wife would have a child of their own who would continue the line of promise. Because God said so. Humanly, it seemed impossible. But he reasoned that God could bring life from the seemingly dead, and had the power to do what he had promised. In the same way, says Paul, we trust in God 'who raised Jesus our Lord from the dead'. And obediently stepping out in faith with him is something which brings life to people of every tribe and nation and tongue even today. Even for you.

Proper 6

Sunday between 12 and 18 June inclusive
(if after Trinity Sunday)

Genesis 18:1–15, 21:1–7 · Romans 5:1–8 · Matthew 9:35–10:23 · Psalm 116:1–2, 12–19

God has brought me laughter, and everyone who hears about this will laugh with me.

This week we learn that what God compassionately does for his suffering friends will make them laugh and rejoice.

In Romans 5, Paul says that those who have faith can also have hope because of God's love. He breaks that down by saying that Christians have hope because God's love transforms our suffering; and also that we have hope because God's love is so different to ours.

Our suffering in this life is not a meaningless tragedy to be avoided, but a means of gaining resilience, character and hope in the providence of God. 'We rejoice in our sufferings, knowing that suffering produces endurance, and endurance produces character, and character produces hope, and hope does not disappoint us' (Romans 5:3–5). Suffering is not the end. It is not the final answer. It is not the ultimate thing. If God is your friend, although it doesn't mean you won't suffer in the here and now, because even Jesus suffered in this world and we're simply following in his footsteps.

The early Church Father Basil of Caesarea said that for us who know Christ, 'tribulations are like certain foods and exercises for athletes which lead the contestant on to the inheritance of glory'.[12]

---

[12] Gerald Bray (ed.), *Romans (Revised)*, Ancient Christian Commentary on Scripture (Downers Grove, IL: InterVarsity Press, 1998), p. 124.

So drink that protein shake and take those vitamins for now. One day you won't need them, but for now they help to develop our hope. No pressure, no resilience. No suffering, no depth of hope. And hope, like a muscle, needs to be exercised and flexed or it will wither. But it leads us on to the hope of glory. As Christopher Ash puts it in his helpful recent book on teaching Romans: 'the Christian life is not a miserable one, crawling along in pain but happy to have an entrance ticket to the new creation safely in our pockets; it is a tough life, but one in which God is daily at work in us to change us and prepare us for glory'.[13]

God's self-giving love is not like our human love – and this is cause for hope. Sometimes there is heroic self-sacrifice in this world. People do occasionally dare to give their lives for others. Usually their friends or their family. Sometimes for duty. Occasionally even for strangers or foreigners they do not know. We rightly remember and celebrate their heroism, courage and sacrifice. But we have hope as Christians because God's love is not like our love. 'God shows his love for us in that *while we were still sinners*, Christ died for us.' While we were his enemies, Christ died for us. When we were ungodly, undeserving, unworthy and unlovable, God loved us and gave his only Son for us. While we were shaking our puny fists in his loving face, sticking two fingers up to his kindness and care – while we were running rampant through his world without a thought for our Creator, dismissing him with a casual grunt or sneer or hypocritical nominal religion – God showed his love in this: Christ died for us.

Now think about this: 'if Christ died for his enemies, just think what he will do for his friends!'[14] (I love this comment from the early Church Father Ambrosiaster.) The picture in Genesis 18 is of God dropping in unannounced on his friends. It's an intimate household scene. He promises so much that it makes Sarah laugh with shocked

---

[13] Christopher Ash, *Teaching Romans: Volume One – Unlocking Romans 1–8 for the Bible Teacher* (Fearn: Ross-shire: Christian Focus, 2009), p. 215.

[14] Gerald Bray (ed.), *Romans (Revised)*, p. 126.

surprise. By Genesis 21, the blessing has been given, and she concludes, 'God has brought me laughter, and everyone who hears about this will laugh with me'. Good news has to spread. God's compassionate love, which we also see in Matthew 9:36 as Jesus looks on the harassed and helpless crowd, cannot help but try to spread the joy. The kingdom of heaven has come near, and its powerful positive presence will inevitably be felt, even when the human response to it might sometimes be to persecute the messengers. Faith should not waver in the face of such reactions, but continue to trust in the one who brings joy.

Proper 7

Sunday between 19 and 25 June inclusive
(if after Trinity Sunday)

Matthew 10:24–39 · Romans 6:1b–11 · Jeremiah 20:7–13 · Psalm 69:7–18

Count yourselves dead to sin but alive to God in Christ Jesus

The readings this week are about identity and identification, how our new life in union with Christ cuts us off from the world, the flesh and the devil, and how painful that disconnect can be. Is that something you feel?

The Gospel reading emphasises that being disciples of Jesus is a radical calling which takes priority over all our other relationships and commitments. A disciple and their teacher will be identified together, even as the one imitates the other. To get our prepositions straight, we are not above our Master, but in him, and if in him then like him as far as others are concerned. We will be maligned along with him because of our close association. Yet that is not something of which to be afraid, for our Master is a loving and caring Father and we should not censor ourselves nor keep quiet about him for fear of others.

As a military friend of mine said to me once, hurt and fear are minefields in which the enemy spiritually eviscerates many believers. Since he had just surveyed the D-Day battlefields in Normandy, the image had some resonance and power. Realistically, there will be division on earth if our primary focus is on our Father in heaven: it will even set members of the same family against each other, Jesus said. But a Christian's primary identity is no longer their earthly family; the one we are to love above all others, and acknowledge before all, is the one who took up his cross for our sake, to show us the way to life, a path out of the minefield.

In Romans 6, Paul's basic point is that if we are Christians, we are cut off from sin because of our new identification with the one who died to sin. God's grace, his undeserved favour towards us, does not give us an excuse to wallow in our sin. We have been baptised into Christ, completely identified with him. That outward physical sign points us to an inward and spiritual reality: as far as sin is concerned we are as dead as Jesus was on Good Friday as they laid him in a tomb. He died to take the punishment that we deserve for our sin. He lived the life we could not live, and died the death that we deserve but he didn't. There are times when we may doubt it, when walking in newness of life with Jesus day by day isn't going as well as we'd like it to, and when troubles come in battalions to knock us off course. But if we are with Christ, in him, immersed in him, he is not going to let us go. We are bound together, and so must consider ourselves dead to sin and alive to God. He is our new King, so sin does not reign over our bodies in the here and now and in the life to come it will have no dominion over us. Sin will not win. It is not the final victor, and so we resist its claims of sovereignty over us because of the prior claims of another.

Jeremiah reflects some of this alluring power of grace. When the Lord overpowers and entices us, drawing us to himself, others may mock and heap scorn upon us. But something like a burning fire deep within our bones compels us to go on speaking and identifying ourselves with his word. Amidst denunciation and attempts to charm us away, we can sing of his deliverance and know that persecution will not in the end succeed.

Proper 8

Sunday between 26 June and 2 July inclusive

Jeremiah 28:5–9 · Romans 6:12–23 · Matthew 10:40–42 ·
Psalm 89:1–4, 15–18

Now that you have been set free from sin and have become slaves of God, the benefit you reap leads to holiness, and the result is eternal life.

Our readings this week urge us diligently to do good for Jesus's sake and look forward to the reward of those who obey his word. This is a great encouragement as we face a new day as his disciples.

Matthew 10 ends with a reminder that those who trust in the Lord have an eternal reward. We will not lose it, guaranteed as it is by Jesus's word and righteousness and not our own. Good works don't earn our salvation, but they flow naturally out of a living faith. So Jesus says whoever welcomes his disciples because they are disciples of Jesus are blessed. Whoever welcomes those who speak God's word or who are righteous because they are speaking for and following Christ will be rewarded. Serving Jesus's people, however lowly they are and however basic the service, will not prove pointless on the Last Day. The key is to do it for Jesus, and not for the reward. Rewards, like joy, disappear if we focus on them to the exclusion of their giver.

Jeremiah's warning to a rival prophet in the public arena of the Temple offers a clear test of authenticity to those who wonder which word to trust. Hananiah has prophesied peace and restoration to the downtrodden exiles, the desire of all their hearts. At one level, Jeremiah would like this vision of a flourishing future to prove true, 'Amen! So be it!' Yet he knows that God is sovereign, not our feeble, self-centred hopes and self-serving pretences. There will be no peace for that generation. It will be clear to all when his word, not

Hananiah's, is fulfilled and enacted in accordance with God's sure covenant. The people standing by should know who to trust and prepare themselves accordingly.

Paul continues in Romans 6 to speak to those who have indeed trusted in God. He draws out the implications of our faith union with Christ. Our ongoing walk in response to grace is not to wallow in sin because Jesus is gracious, but to count ourselves as dead to sin. We now obey a new master, and present ourselves to him, standing to attention at his presence and listening to his words of life. We are 'obedient from the heart to the form of teaching to which we are entrusted', slaves to righteousness because united to the Righteous One.

Our former master, sin, was a heavy taskmaster and never took us anywhere but down, into the joyless decay of death's cold unrelenting grip. The perfect freedom of enslavement to God, however, brings sanctification and the gift of never-ending, incorruptible glory. Eternal life in Christ Jesus our Lord is the destiny for which we were made and the destination of the faithful; but the fate of those who choose to embrace the disordered desires of their mortal bodies is the merciless dole queue of death. Show in your life today which destination is yours.

Proper 9

Sunday between 3 and 9 July inclusive

Zechariah 9:9–12 · Romans 7:15–25a · Matthew 11:16–19, 25–30 · Psalm 145:8–14

The L*ORD* *is gracious and compassionate, slow to anger and rich in love.*

Our readings this week are about the joy of following the one who graciously saves us from our sin. Let us rejoice in his compassionate love for us.

Zechariah urges us to rejoice greatly at the arrival of our triumphant, victorious King. Yet he is not, like so many conquerors and leaders, an arrogant narcissist. He is humble. He rides a donkey. And he commands peace to all the nations, over whom he exercises dominion. He does not follow his own arbitrary will, ruling on a whim, but he covenants with his people. They know where they stand with him, and the blood of the covenant is shed to save them and bless them in abundance. It is difficult not to read these words as a prophecy of the life, death, and triumph of the Lord Jesus Christ, and to sing for joy at their fulfilment.

Yet we are living in the transition between his victory and its final consummation. Romans 7 takes up the tensions and angst of that situation in the overlap of the ages. There is debate about who is speaking in this section. Is the 'wretched man' (the 'I'), the apostle, Israel, or the pre-conversion Saul? Is the struggle here a reflection of birth pangs leading to the joy of conversion and the assurance of Romans 8? Or is it the everyday experience of the imperfect believer, wrestling with the forces of sin which will pound and pester us to the end? Sin remains our constant companion even once we are born again and follow Jesus wholeheartedly. So whichever way we read the chapter, the glad conclusion of verses 24–25, that God through Christ has rescued us from death, is appropriate and fitting.

Christ has broken the tyranny of sin and sent his Spirit into our hearts. Our freedom is for his service. Yet it is no burden to serve and follow him but a privilege and a joy to take his gentle yoke. The rest he brings to weary souls is joyous and liberating. But it is not understood by the worldly who, like children, want Jesus to dance to their tune and fit in with their ideas and plans. They will carp and criticise when he does not, but Jesus shows us here in the Gospel reading that such reactions to his teaching only expose the fact that many so-called worldly wise and letter-learned commentators have had the truth hidden from their eyes. The thought that Jesus has not chosen to reveal the truth to them is shocking. But he with the Father is sovereign and exercises his gracious will as he pleases. If we have caught a glimpse of his goodness, it is cause not for applauding our own cleverness, but for exulting in his merciful kindness.

Proper 10

Sunday between 10 and 16 July inclusive

Isaiah 55:10–13 · Romans 8:1–11 · Matthew 13:1–9, 18–23 ·
Psalm 65:1–13

My word will not return to me empty, but accomplish what I desire.

The great and grand theme of our readings this week is the power of God's word of grace to accomplish God's saving purposes in us. Be assured that he is powerful, and will do what he has promised.

The passage from Matthew 13 is the first Gospel's account of the Parable of the Soils. The focus is not on the Sower, as often implied, but on his activity and its reception by various people. He sows the word indiscriminately – on the path, the rocky ground, the thorns, and on good soil. As the famous international gathering of theologians called the Synod of Dort (1618–19) put it many centuries ago, the gospel is to be 'declared and published to all nations, and to all persons *promiscuously* and without distinction'.[15]

God is the one who makes it grow (as Paul also reminds us in 1 Corinthians 3:6, again taking the focus away from any human sower). The fruit comes variously as thirtyfold, sixtyfold or a hundredfold (a huge and bountiful harvest) when the word falls on good soil. But those with ears to hear can also discern that many hearers will not bear fruit. That may be because the evil one snatches away the word, as the gospel bounces like a pebble on a lake then disappears from sight and consciousness. It may be down to the superficial rootlessness of those who hear but do not persevere in persecution or trouble. It may be because the thorns of worldly care and comfort choke the

[15] Canon 2:5. See Philip Schaff (ed.), *The Creeds of Christendom, with a History and Critical Notes. 3 vols*. (New York: Harper & Brothers, 1882), 3:561.

life out of the seed, which is given no space to germinate. There is a warning here about how we listen and how we respond to the Bible.

But there is also an assurance to those who sow that God will accomplish his productive purposes in some, however unpromising a particular patch might seem. Isaiah makes the same point, not in a parable but more poetically. The rain and snow come down from heaven, like the word in Jesus's parable. The water helps in the process of producing bread to eat and seed for continuing the cycle of life (though in other places, all it generates is puddles). Thus God's word will produce an effect, and succeed in its purpose, though it can appear to be wasted in wanton, excessive provision. Yet somewhere it will bring joy and peace, as it did eventually for the returning exiles of Judah when the highway home from Babylonian captivity was opened to them at last. All creation sings when the people of God are freed: the mountains and hills, the trees clapping their hands, the productive, fruitful trees replacing the dreadful signs of God's curse. An everlasting sign, not just for one generation, but for all who long for the final transformation of our fallen, suffering planet.

In similarly joyful mood, Paul declares that there is no longer any condemnation for those who are united to Christ by faith. They are justified, acquitted, declared not guilty (and the righteous requirements of the Law are met) by virtue of what God has done in Christ. Sin (and the condemnation it deserves) is dealt with by Christ so that we might walk in a new direction, according to the Spirit, which previously we were unable to do. The sinful mind not just *will* not, but *cannot* please God, says Romans 8. Without God we can do no good. Salvation is entirely of the Lord, to whom we belong and without whom we are lifeless and lost. Yet since we belong to him, his Spirit (like his word showered upon us) gives fruitful resurrection life to our otherwise mortal bodies. Thanks be to God.

Proper 11

Sunday between 17 and 23 July inclusive

Isaiah 44:6–8 · Romans 8:12–25 · Matthew 13:24–30, 36–43 ·
Psalm 86:11–17

The creation waits in eager expectation for the children of God to be revealed.

Our theme this week is the release of tensions and fears that will come at the end of the age. Are you looking forward to it?

Isaiah 44 presents to us a God who knows no beginning and no end, the King. He is the first and the last, with no equals, an incomparable God who alone knows what is to come even before it has happened. His eternal nature might terrify mortal, temporal beings such as ourselves, and yet Isaiah's God says 'Do not fear, or be afraid'. He has revealed himself and his ways, and is a rock to those who trust in him. There is no vacillation or indecisiveness in him. He will constantly remain our God and King throughout the changing seasons and circumstances of life. 'There is no shadow of turning with thee.'

Humanity, on the other hand, is very different. We are a tense and complex mixture of good and evil. In Romans 8, Paul presents the strain within us as a conflict between the flesh and the Spirit. There are two ways for us to live: by the flesh or by the Spirit. One way leads to death and destruction; the other to life and glory. One is a way of slavery to fear; the other a way of adoption and glory but with suffering thrown into the mix between the two. Suffering, however, is put into perspective by the glory to be revealed when this present evil age is over. It is not insubstantial, but it is light and momentary when compared with what is to come.

This hope, for which we wait patiently yet longingly, is ours in Christ alone. But it is also shared by the world he created. We groan inwardly, but with the first fruits of the Spirit to comfort us, for the full revelation of the Last Day, when our decaying bodies will be redeemed. The rest of creation groans with us, since our redemption will be its liberation day, as the curse by which it was subjected to futility in Genesis 3 is finally lifted. There will be labour pains for the whole creation until that day of new birth and regeneration. On that day the sinful flesh with its fears, strains and sufferings will be purged and done away with for ever.

Until that day evil is always mixed in with the good. Jesus's parable of the wheat and the weeds in Matthew 13 likewise reminds us that the tensions we experience before the end of the age are not just within us as believers, but between the righteous and those who do or cause evil in the world. Like the slaves in the parable, we might long for the weeds to be uprooted immediately, gathered together and prevented from causing any further damage or trouble. But the Lord in his wisdom has, rather, set a day on which he will judge the world in righteousness by a man he has appointed (Acts 17:31).

The tension is acute when we find evil even within the church. In such a situation there must be discipline and deposition, according to the inheritance of faith we have built on. Yet however careful and rigorous that might be, it can never be perfect until the Son of Man sends his angels to throw evil, and the causes of evil, into the furnace of fire on the Last Day. This is not an excuse for laxity or a licence for *laissez-faire*, but an encouragement to persevere in hope when the odds seem stacked against the godly and a time of great difficulty draws near. However bleak things may seem today, we will shine like the sun in the kingdom of our Father.

Proper 12

Sunday between 24 and 30 July inclusive

1 Kings 3:5–12 · Romans 8:26–39 · Matthew 13:31–33, 44–52 · Psalm 119:129–136

In all these things we are more than conquerors through him who loved us.

Our common theme this week is the abundant steadfast love of the Lord to the multitude of his people. What a joy it is to have him as our King.

When God appeared to Solomon at Gibeon, the new and inexperienced king recounts the steadfast covenant love of the Lord to his father, David. God blessed David in many and varied ways, but not least by giving him a son to inherit the throne of Israel securely. Though Solomon pledges to be the Lord's servant in his new role, he confesses his youth and inability to govern such a large and abundantly numerous people. Given not 'Sophie's Choice' but 'Solomon's Choice', a gift from God of whatever he asked for, the wise youngster asks for more wisdom. To those who have, more will be given (Matthew 13:12). God is delighted to grant greater wisdom, even superlative wisdom, and an abundance of other blessings too. His steadfast love endures to David's son and heir, since ultimately his purpose to bless the whole world will be focused and fulfilled through Jesus, great David's greater Son.

Paul also celebrates the steadfast love of God which brings with it a multitude of blessings for all who trust in Christ. The Spirit helps in our weakness, inexpressibly interceding for us. Those who love God (because he first loved us and is 'for us') are blessed with a golden chain of glorious gifts. We are known by God, predestined to be like his son and part of the innumerable multitude of his people.

This eternal knowledge and divine choice enters time as we are called by the gospel, drawn to Christ to be justified in union with him, and finally glorified when he returns. Nothing can effectively obstruct the infallible procession of this train of salvation. Satan tempts us to despair; hardship and persecution throw themselves onto the tracks. But nothing can derail God's loving plan for his people since his love binds us to him in a bond that is stronger than any other force in the universe. To meditate on this is full of sweet, pleasant, and unspeakable comfort.

Jesus continues to teach about the kingdom of heaven through parables in Matthew 13. The key to each image is the abundant blessing that it brings, though it appears at first to be small and insignificant. The mustard seed is tiny yet flourishes, to the benefit of all. Yeast leavens the loaf and brings growth beyond expectation. The hidden treasure of the kingdom brings joy to those who enlist all their resources in pursuit of it, like the pearl of great price for which all else is gladly surrendered. Though there's also a note of the judgment to come in the parable concerned with fishing; all kinds of fish fill the kingdom's net until it is full. Some separation is inevitable, for not all are chosen, but the general picture is one of abundance. Let those who understand these things present the treasures of the word to God's people this Sunday.

Proper 13

Sunday between 31 July and 6 August inclusive

Isaiah 55:1–5 · Romans 9:1–5 · Matthew 14:13–21 ·
Psalm 145:8–9, 14–21

Come, all you who are thirsty, come to the waters!

Each of our readings this week focuses on God's compassion for the lost, and the provision he has made for us in Christ. We are urged to seek the Lord while he is near.

Isaiah 55 is a rousing marketplace call to respond to the free offer of life in the gospel. 'Hey! Come!' grabs the attention of the passerby. But more striking still is the deal on offer: satisfaction for no cost! Eat and drink without money, without price! People spend their hard-earned cash on all sorts of things which will not satisfy them, whether at a spiritual or merely physical level. We are often left disappointed by the shoddiness of workmanship or inbuilt obsolescence of the items raved about by today's retailers. But Isaiah claims to offer something rich and delightful at less than a bargain basement price. Is it a literally unbelievable deal, or a trusty old promise backed up by divine guarantee? The prophet claims the latter, an everlasting covenant, the one that has stood for hundreds of years in David and his dynasty and will endure the purging of the exile. Israel is glorified and nations shall run to it for blessing because of the work of the Suffering Servant, despite current appearances or despondency. Who will listen carefully and come?

In Romans 9 we barge in on an emotionally unpleasant truth: many in Israel would not only reject Isaiah's offer, but they would reject the Messiah himself when he appeared. Moses offered himself as a substitute, to be punished in Israel's place in Exodus 32, when they rejected God in favour of a golden calf. 'Blot me out of your book!' he suggested, but forgive their sin. Likewise, Paul feels so strongly and deeply for his people that he has great sorrow and unceasing anguish in his heart for them. If it were possible, he would be willing to be accursed and cut off from Christ in their stead, placed back under the wrath of God he spoke so eloquently about in chapter 1. The privileges Israel enjoyed were so immense and numerous that their current rejection of the fulfilment of all their hopes and longings was doubly tragic and lamentable. The glory of the old covenant with its temple worship and future promises was theirs, and they were humanly related to the patriarchs of old and to Jesus Christ himself. Yet they had not embraced the one to whom all things pointed, when God in flesh had appeared. No wonder Paul was so deeply troubled by this, when in Romans 8 he had just praised the unbreakable love of God to sinners. If Israel turned aside, had God's word failed? The answer must come back – 'by no means!' But the agony of heart is real even as we wrestle to the ultimate conclusion.

Jesus too felt gut-wrenching compassion for Israel, even when they gathered together in a worldly fashion to try and compel him into political action. But he is greater than an earthly king, and more glorious than any prophet. His free offer of satisfying food and bodies made whole is like manna in the desert under Moses, or Elisha's multiplying of the loaves in a time of need (2 Kings 4:42–44). But will they respond with merely temporary gratitude for needs met, or see in these things a sign of something greater – the fulfilment of all in the person of the self-sacrificing God-man? We, and our congregations too need to face this question: are we here to satisfy our felt needs, or to meet the One who feels our need and took our place to give us eternal life?

Proper 14

Sunday between 7 and 13 August inclusive

1 Kings 19:9–18 · Romans 10:5–15 · Matthew 14:22–33 ·
Psalm 85:8–13

I will listen to what God the LORD says; he promises peace to his people, his faithful servants – but let them not turn to folly.

Faith and doubt are the twin themes of our Bible passages this week, together with the power of God's word, which brings true perspective on the world. Will we have faith in his word, or turn to folly as the Psalmist fears?

As often happens, Elijah experiences a deep low after a great spiritual victory. Fresh from exposing the prophets of Baal as phoneys and crooks, he is alone and beset by frailty and a form of depression. The visible church seems to have entirely departed from the written word of God's covenant with it. They have replaced true worship with something more culturally acceptable in the context, and persecuted those who stood against the tide, silencing and marginalising the prophetic word and prophetic leaders. Elijah laments this, and fears that he is next. He complains to God, wondering what is going on. He is ready to give up and die.

God's answer comes not in further works of earth-shattering power from the mountain where he commissioned Moses and appeared in fire and smoke to deliver the commandments, but in silence followed by a still, small voice. The word of God comes to comfort and challenge the prophet of God. He is not at work merely in dramatic and public demonstrations of power. Sometimes he is there and he is silent – but even when silent he is living and active, despite the inability of his people to discern it. The Almighty gives instructions for moving on his work among the nations, appointing kings and a prophet. But, rebuking Elijah's arrogant narcissism, he also informs him he has 7,000 loyal followers. Elijah is not the only one left and neither is he indispensable. With this corrected perspective, he can press on and do his part.

In the Gospel reading, Jesus is also alone on a mountain, praying to God. When he comes down, the disciples' boat is lashed by waves, far from safety, and with the wind against it. They are terrified by the apparition of him walking on the water itself towards them. Fear takes hold, but his word reassures them in the midst of the surging waves. It heartens the impetuous Peter so much that he proposes joining the Lord in his act of dominance over nature. He succeeds – quite a miracle! – but only while he looks to Jesus. He begins to sink when the howling wind distracts his attention. It makes him turn, and he becomes fearful and doubtful.

When we are battered, alienated and opposed, we recall from this that the wind and waves still know the one that mastered them so effortlessly on the sea that night. We look to him for help, and think less of the terrors and threats that surround us. 'Lord, save me!' will always be answered in the end, though our feet may get wet before the Lord takes hold.

In Romans 10, Paul exults in this power of faith in the revealed word of God. God's righteousness is available through faith, as opposed to our own faulty righteousness through the Law. The gospel word is near to save those who trust in its truth and power. A living faith to grasp hold of it, is all that is needed; it can't be earned or deserved by us.

Those who fail to believe will sink and fall, but this is by no means a failure on God's part. He will save those whom he has chosen, not just 7,000 in Israel, but a larger multitude of elect believers from all nations than narrow-minded bigots could ever conceive of or imagine. Paul delights to praise this God and urges us to proclaim his good news to all who have not heard. Everyone who calls on the name of the Lord will be saved.

Proper 15

Sunday between 14 and 20 August inclusive

Isaiah 56:1, 6–8 · Romans 11:1–2a, 29–32 · Matthew 15:10–28 · Psalm 67

May God be gracious to us and bless us and make his face shine on us – so that your ways may be known on earth, your salvation among all nations.

The theme of our readings this week is that God's mercy extends to those from all nations who come to Jesus in faith. It is not just for us and our group, but for everyone.

In a section of his prophecy which will focus on the work of the coming anointed conqueror, Isaiah speaks of 'foreigners who join themselves to the Lord'. They serve the Lord, love his name, and hold fast to his covenant. He in return will bring them joyfully into his house of prayer, accepting their sacrifices. He is a God who not only gathers the outcasts and downhearted from his own sinful people, but joins them to others from elsewhere who also believe and trust in the God of the covenant. This is a passage Jesus himself used to refer to the Jerusalem Temple as 'a house of prayer for all nations' (Matthew 21:13). That Temple had turned into a convenient hideout for bandits and exploitation, but God always intends the gatherings of his people to attract and draw in outsiders, not repel or hinder them.

Jesus teaches on defilement and sin (a subject of universal fascination and importance, not one to be avoided). Naturally he offends the Pharisees, who are overly concerned by outward cleanliness and ritualistic rules. He clarifies for his disciples that even with clean hands and a strict kosher diet one can still be defiled in God's sight by the state of one's heart. Interestingly, by including the word *porneia* among the things that defile, he does actually speak into our modern debates about sexuality (whereas it is commonly asserted that he is silent on the issue). *Porneia* does not mean pornography, though we derive our modern English word for that from this ancient Greek term. It does not narrowly mean 'fornication' either, as some translations have it. It is the word used in the ancient world for all kinds of transgressive and illicit sexual encounters, whether heterosexual or homosexual, male or female, marital or extra-marital, consensual or otherwise. Alongside evil intentions, murder and slander, Jesus says that these behaviours which cross the creation boundaries set by God are what defile a person in his sight. No amount of whitewash can cover that up.

The Lord is then confronted by someone whom many pious Jews would have considered defiled by nature: a Canaanite woman. And he shows by his interaction with this woman that, even though it was not yet time in his plan of salvation to bring grace in all its fullness to the Gentiles, what would count with them ultimately is faith. If they trust in his word and his power, and turn to him as Lord – whoever they are, whatever they have done, they can experience the joy of healing forgiveness.

Paul wrestles in Romans 11 with the nagging implications of this divine mercy extended to the Gentiles. Does it mean that God has once and for all rejected Israel, the ethnically Jewish people? The answer must be a resounding no. He himself is a Jew, descended from Abraham, of the tribe of Benjamin. There is a remnant, chosen by grace, even though many have been hardened to the alluring call of the Messiah's word. That is what 'the Scripture says to Elijah' (noting *en passant* that Paul equates the words of Scripture with the very words of God himself) – there is a remnant that has not bowed the knee to the convenient god of this comfortable age. So God's mercy comes to both Jews and Gentiles in Christ, as each one turns to the Lord in faith. He gathers the outcasts of Israel, and he gathers others to them. Peace for Jews and Canaanites will only come as they turn to Christ together, for he alone is our peace.

Proper 16

Sunday between 21 and 27 August inclusive

Isaiah 51:1–6 · Romans 12:1–8 · Matthew 16:13–20 · Psalm 138

Though I walk in the midst of trouble, you preserve my life.

This week's readings rest upon a rock. The Old Testament reading instils hope. The Gospel inculcates faith. And the epistle inspires love. Will you base your life on the rock that is the trustworthy word of Christ?

Isaiah urges the people to 'look to the rock from which you were hewn!' He goes on to explain that by this he means look to your ancestors, Abraham and Sarah, the old and childless couple who trusted God's promise and walked in its light. When Abraham was called he was but one man, and yet God blessed him and his family grew. In the same way, Isaiah intimates, God will comfort his people when it seems all that's left is waste places and wildernesses. The desert will become like Eden, and the people will shout for joy. If you doubt that such a turnaround can happen, look to the rock, the faithful man of old, and see what God can make from unpromising raw materials. His teaching will be broadcast around the world, as a light to the nations, salvation and justice. Heaven and earth will pass away, and people will perish like gnats, but those who are saved and delivered from the wrath to come will endure for ever in a renewed and re-beautified creation. Just as Abraham was assured when he was called, all the nations of the earth will be blessed through him (Genesis 12:3). So look to the rock, and the promise made to him. And however bleak life may appear today, seek the Lord and wait hopefully for the life to come.

Trusting God's promise was a turning point for Abraham, and in a turning point moment in the Gospel story, Jesus gathers his disciples to ask them a crucial question – 'Who do people say I am?' It's a question with many different answers, even today; answers which reveal more about the questioned than the questioner. Jesus expects a varied response, but he then confronts his closest followers with the question that demands an immediate, personal engagement: 'Who do *you* say that I am?' Simon Peter replied with clarity and conviction: you are the Messiah, God's Son. Jesus does not congratulate (or reward) him for working it out. He says Peter is fortunate to have been *given* such clarity by God. 'Flesh and blood has not revealed this to you, but my Father in heaven.'

Peter, just like Abraham is blessed. His name, Peter, means 'rock', and on the solidity of his divinely gifted confession, Christ the cornerstone will build his undying Church. The church is constructed on the foundation of the apostles and prophets (Ephesians 2:20). Just as the house built on a rock would survive the wind and waves in Jesus's memorable ending to the Sermon on the Mount (Matthew 7:24–27), so the Church which begins with one man seeing Christ as the divine Messiah will endure beyond the gates of Hades and multiply. As the Baptist commentator Don Carson says, 'This claim is ridiculous if Jesus is nothing but an overconfident popular preacher in an unimportant vassal state of first-century Rome.'[16] But who do *you* think he is?

Paul's appeal in Romans 12 is that we build on the foundation of God's mercy and grace with lives that are wholly given over to pleasing him. Those who will live on beyond the tottering doors of death must be transformed in this world, not conformed to its fatal patterns of self-worship and self-love. That renewing of our minds which comes with the paradigm shift of faith causes us to see ourselves in a humbler light. It also causes us to see ourselves as part of a body, a people, a church. Abraham was *one* when he was called. Peter was *one* when he confessed. We are now many. And that multiplication of blessing continues despite suffering, persecution and death, as we build one another up in love.

---

[16] D. A. Carson, *Matthew: Chapters 13 through 28* (Grand Rapids; Zondervan, 1995), p. 370.

Proper 17

Sunday between 28 August and 3 September inclusive

Jeremiah 15:15–21 · Romans 12:9–21 · Matthew 16:21–28 ·
Psalm 26:1–8

Lord, you understand; remember me and care for me.

Our readings show us the biblical way to respond to persecution. It is not by running away or by seeking revenge, but by overcoming evil with good, as we trust God to vindicate his people.

Jeremiah speaks for many believers under pressure. 'Lord, you know', is an ominous, pithy phrase pregnant with feeling and unspoken hurt. The Lord understands. 'Remember me', don't forget me in the midst of this strife, discord and injustice. But he also adds 'don't let them get away with it. Bring down retribution for me on my persecutors.' He is suffering insult on account of God, and his unflinching faithfulness to God's difficult word. It is ungodly to avenge, but not to pray for justice from the God who sees and knows. Jeremiah's pain is unceasing and his wounds seemingly incurable as he sits alone under the weight of God's hand, far from the merrymakers who do not know the true joy and delight of God's word. The particular promise to this prophet, at this time in the Middle East, was of deliverance from the hand of the wicked and redemption from the grasp of the ruthless. Many others have not been saved from their enemies in this life. Sometimes evil appears to prevail over the followers of Jesus of Nazareth. But not for ever, not over those who believe and trust in the crucified, risen, and ascended King.

Jesus taught his disciples that he must undergo great suffering, be killed and then rise again. Only after tasting death would he then return in the glory of his Father to 'repay everyone for what has been done'. This was not the timetable Peter was expecting or hoping for.

'God forbid it!' he says. And yet God had planned it. 'This must not happen to you,' he said, perhaps betraying his own fears about what it meant for him too. He could understand glory and putting right the wrongs of the world. But no one ever won a crown via a cross. To be indicted by the elders, chief priests, and scribes and bear the curse and penalty of the Law did not seem the way to Paradise.

Yet Peter was suggesting the same strategic approach as Satan, who offered the Nazarene all the kingdoms of the world if only he would bow to him in worship. This was a scandal, a stumbling-block, to deflect the Suffering Servant from his God-appointed destiny in the God-appointed way. Let the vain world applaud or frown, Jesus must pursue heaven's path. And so must all who follow him. They must follow the trail of his precious blood, for the way that leads to glory lies through the thorny briers of contempt and loss in the here and now. Yet profit in abundance is assured in the coming new age.

Paul banks on this being true when he lays out the path in more detail for the Romans. They could both rejoice in hope and be patient in suffering because of the pattern set before them by Christ himself. Like him, they should bless those who persecuted them, and not be tempted to curse them. Repaying evil for evil in this life is the human-style mindset for which Peter was rebuked. Christians are to try to live at peace with all, with that important proviso 'as far as it depends on you'. It is not always possible to live peaceably with some. But even then, says the apostle, leave room for God to act. Vengeance belongs to him, not us. He will repay. We can pray for that, but not take matters into our own hands by presuming to be his instruments to right the wrongs against us personally. Be quick to advocate for others who suffer injustice; but when our pride or our power are involved, let it go. Rather, overcome evil with good by blessing those who oppose us. It may show them a better way. Or increase their ultimate liability. That choice is theirs. Ours is to follow the narrow way, in the steps of our Master and Saviour, however foolish the world may think that is.

Proper 18

Sunday between 4 and 10 September inclusive

Ezekiel 33:7–11 · Romans 13:8–14 · Matthew 18:15–20 · Psalm 119:33–40

Turn my heart towards your statutes and not towards selfish gain.

The thread which unites the three readings this Sunday is loving our neighbour, even when that is inconvenient, awkward or difficult.

Ezekiel must warn his neighbours to turn from their evil ways. Only then can they be forgiven and live. If they do not turn and repent, they will die in their sins and be condemned by God to face the punishment due to those sins. The problem, it seems, is not primarily the damage which sin does to their lives (Ezekiel is not offering self-improvement advice), but that God will judge us all and is justly angry about sin (as we sometimes are too, but usually about other people's). However, the prophet can help his neighbours and hence show love to them by warning them about this impending judgment, spelling out the correct response. It is loving and kind for us to do that, though socially and personally uncomfortable perhaps, for the Judgment Day is still approaching and only Jesus can 'deliver us from the wrath to come' (1 Thessalonians 1:10) which we deserve. At the same time, if Ezekiel does not do his job and warn his neighbours of this, then he will be guilty of a serious crime himself and be brought to account for it. If Jesus wants people to turn from their sin and live, has done everything necessary to deliver us, and can save completely those who come to God through him, then why would we be negligent of this duty? Why would we refuse to pass on this good news of his love for the world?

Paul continues this theme in Romans 13. In the light of God's love for us, we are indebted to love others. Our love for God is revealed in our love of neighbour. If we profess to keep the commandments relating to God, we must demonstrate that by obeying those which relate to others, in costly love and service to them. Why? Because the day is near. The time is approaching. The moment is coming – the moment of destiny, when what we truly are shall finally be revealed. Darkness will be replaced by light on that day. St Augustine (354–430) read this passage one day when he was struggling. 'Take up and read!', he heard someone say, and took it as a message from God himself. Later he confessed, 'I had no wish to read more and no need to do so. For in an instant, as I came to the end of the sentence, it was as though the light of confidence flooded into my heart and all the darkness of doubt was dispelled.'[17] He could put his life of self-centred gratification and jealousy behind him, and embracing Christ be enfolded in him. If he had not, the darkness would have won, and enwrapped him for ever in its soul-destroying works.

Jesus also speaks of the love that believers in churches must show to each other, in the Gospel reading. If we are sinned against unnoticed, in a persistent way that endangers the soul of the offending other, we don't need to harbour resentment or fear but can have that awkward conversation with our sibling and get it into the open if necessary. If they repent they are regained: like Ezekiel you have saved both yourself and your hearer. If they do not, and the salvation of their soul remains in doubt because of their excommunicatable error or failing, take others to help persuade them and to testify to the hurt. Ultimately, if they refuse to listen or respond to appropriate ecclesiastical discipline, it needs to be clear that their salvation is at stake – unless they turn they will die in their sins, outside the church and outside Christ, and fall into the hands of God as hardened, unrepentant sinners.

---

[17] Augustine, *Confessions*, Book 8, Chapter 12.

Jesus cares how these earthly relationships between his disciples work out. Whether the world is looking on or not, he is watching to see how we love one another. And he is listening to hear if we will talk to him about it, or simply to others and our seething selves as if he himself was not in our midst, as our mediator with the Father and Lord of the Church. Turn your heart to him and not to the seeming comfort of silence.

Proper 19

Sunday between 11 and 17 September inclusive

Genesis 50:15–21 · Romans 14:1–12 · Matthew 18:21–35 · Psalm 103:1–13

He does not treat us as our sins deserve or repay us according to our iniquities.

The theme of our readings this week is living as those who have been forgiven by God and serve him alone. Forgiving others is sometimes hard. Why do we find it so easy to pass judgment on one another?

In any community, especially a Christian community, which is by definition full of sinful people who know they are not perfect, we need to work out a way of coexisting with those who have different convictions and who sometimes hurt and offend us. In our Gospel reading, Peter asks the Lord how this is meant to work. Perhaps he thought himself rather admirable and gracious for suggesting he might forgive his brother or sister up to seven times for such a sin. But Jesus soon pricks that bubble and raises the stakes much higher: forgive not seven times, but seventy-seven times. By which he means that we should actually stop counting and just get on with forgiving, habitually.

The story Jesus tells illustrates this proposition. The kingdom of heaven is ruled by a king who is gracious and forgiving. We owe him, big time, and a day of reckoning is coming where we will have to settle accounts. Those who cannot repay what they owe can be pardoned by his sheer mercy and released. Yet the emancipated slave in Jesus's parable does not react to grace as he should. He seizes by the throat those who owe him and extracts by force what he is due. These small debts should pale into insignificance alongside the incalculable debt that he himself has been forgiven. But he imitates neither his master's patience nor his pity, and continues to live for himself alone. Yet we are to pray, 'forgive us our debts *as* we forgive our debtors.'

Joseph in Genesis 50 is an example of how to forgive. His brothers are worried about what he might do to them now Jacob is dead and no longer around to restrain his son from vengeance. They dare not even identify themselves as Joseph's brothers, referring to themselves, rather, as 'servants of the God of your father' and as Joseph's slaves. Yet he is so far from paying them back in full for the wrong they did to him (which they know they deserve), that he promises to provide for them and their families. His eyes are not on retribution (which belongs to God alone) but on the guiding hand of divine providence which transformed their evil intentions into a blessed result, and on fulfilling (as they never did) his brotherly responsibilities.

Familial responsibilities is also the theme of our Romans 14 reading. Paul reminds us not to pass judgment on our brothers and sisters, since we are ultimately accountable to God alone. We stand or fall, particularly in our opinions on secondary issues, before the Lord. We cannot pass judgment on someone else's servant. Paul warns us elsewhere that living in persistent sin excludes us from God's kingdom altogether (1 Corinthians 6). But God welcomes all who walk uprightly with the Lord whatever their 'opinions' on more debatable matters, so we too are not to despise or pass judgment on those who are our brothers and sisters in the kingdom. If people find it hard to follow this teaching, let us forgive them (of course) but also demonstrate in our response what we understand these passages to be commanding us.

Proper 20

Sunday between 18 and 24 September inclusive

Jonah 3:10–4:11 · Philippians 1:21–30 · Matthew 20:1–16 · Psalm 145:1–8

Whatever happens, conduct yourselves in a manner worthy of the gospel of Christ.

This week we are confronted in the readings with two reactions to the long-awaited kingdom of our gracious God. We can be compassionate and gracious like he is, or we can be angry with him for his mercy.

The Gospel reading and the Old Testament reading both illustrate the sin of envy. Jonah is none too pleased with the repentance of the Gentiles in Nineveh. In response to his preaching, they turned from their evil ways. In response to their repentance, God turned away from the calamity of judgment with which he had threatened them. There is no need to posit a contradiction between Jonah 3:10 and the doctrine of God's unchangeableness, it seems to me. He only 'changed his mind' in the sense that the original threat of destruction had within it the inherent offer of an alternative future if only the Ninevites heeded the warning God sent via his prophet. Why else would he go to such trouble to send a messenger in the first place? Numbers 23:19 is not a lie: 'God is not human, that he should lie, not a human being, that he should change his mind.'

God is compassionate and gracious. Jonah, however, is not. He envies the care God has for his enemies – he feels about the Assyrian capital as we may feel about the most brutal regimes in our world. His first thought was not forgiveness but vengeance – God should repay them for what they had done and were threatening to do to 'the good guys'. He should not pardon them, or let them off. That seemed all wrong to the ancient prophet. 'Forget Iraq,' he says, 'I'm off to Benidorm instead!' God's grace is just as incomprehensible to most people today but we don't usually run away to Tarshish to escape the call of the loving God, as he did. We have other ways of avoiding it. Jonah's anger with God's slowness to anger was unwarranted: he should, like God, have been deeply concerned for the city of 120,000 souls who persistently failed to discern right from wrong and not only rejected God's plan for human flourishing but actively opposed it. Instead, his dominant emotion was anger, despite being forcibly reminded of his own frailty and need of salvation. They didn't deserve grace, but they got it. Jonah felt hard done by.

The parable of the labourers in the vineyard hits a similar raw nerve. Several groups of workers agree a fair wage and get down to business. They wouldn't have complained at all, except the master of the vineyard decides to reward the latecomers with exactly the same pay as those who have toiled all day in the scorching heat. The landowner rejects the petition of their union – they agreed on wages and he'd stuck to the bargain. But they are envious because he is generous. They don't like grace being given to those they consider undeserving. But just as in the story of Jonah, God gets to decide what to do with the things he has made and owns: in Nineveh, the people and animals; in the vineyard, his money.

In Philippians 1, Paul is also wrestling with the themes of 'fruitful labour' and his reward. He longs to be with Christ, for that is far better, but for the sake of these Gentiles he is content to delay that glorious moment (and even to lose his salvation for others, Romans 9:3), despite what it might mean for him. How different to the attitude of Jonah! What a contrast to the labourers in Jesus's parable! The Philippians are urged to imitate Paul by living a life that is worthy of the gospel of a compassionate and gracious God. Like Paul, they need to be unintimidated by the opposition and unfazed by the suffering they may have to endure. Let us strive, side by side, for the same goal and the same prize, rejoicing that we serve a merciful Father.

Proper 21

Sunday between 25 September and 1 October inclusive

Ezekiel 18:1–4, 25–32 · Philippians 2:1–13 · Matthew 21:23–32 · Psalm 25:1–9

Do not remember the sins of my youth and my rebellious ways.

Our readings this week proclaim the liberating and challenging truth that it is not where you start but where you finish that matters to God.

Ezekiel's message is that everyone belongs to God. The life of the parent and the life of the child are both mine, says the Lord. People who belong to God have to give an account for their lives to their maker and owner. But some people were saying to Ezekiel that God is not fair in his judgments. Children are punished for the sins of their parents, languishing in Babylonian exile not for their own sins but for some previous generation's. Ezekiel puts them straight on these things, by reiterating the doctrine of individual responsibility. If a righteous person turns away from righteousness, they will be judged. If a wicked person turns away from wickedness, they will be saved. The privileges of youth and upbringing and opportunity mean nothing if we do not pursue the path of justice and peace.

There is a hint here, however, that even the best of us cannot escape a just sentence. The only way to save our lives is to repent and turn around: but merely exhorting us to get a life, get a new heart and spirit, cannot accomplish the deed. We have no power in ourselves to change, to have faith, and live a new life. God must act to regenerate us, and help us at every step.

In Jesus's parable of the eventually obedient and disobedient sons, we again see that to make a good beginning is never enough. Those who had risen to high positions within the religious leadership of

God's people at the time stumble over the authority of Jesus. They do not hear his word and obey it, but stop to question and examine it with a view to disobedience. Their shared conversations in verses 25–26 are predicated on an unwillingness to embrace the politically difficult Christ. So Jesus points out that not only is starting off well not sufficient, but starting off badly is no impediment to entering the kingdom of God. One can refuse at first but later repent and do the will of the Father – sexual sinners and economic sinners are ready to do just that when they truly meet Jesus. But the once keen hearts of the high religious leaders have grown cold with advancing status, so they are no longer sensitive to the authoritative voice of their master. It's not where you start, but where you finish.

The Lord Jesus himself both started and finished in glory, Paul tells the Philippians. His path from glory to glory, however, was through obedience and suffering, through the emptiness of death itself. What is the 'therefore' in verse 9 there for? It tells us that it was precisely because of his obedience that God exalted Jesus. That was the agreement between Father and Son in eternity, a covenant for our redemption: Christ took it on himself to die for those given to him by the Father, who promised in return to raise and exalt him.

In the same way, we are to love those whom the Father has given to us as brothers and sisters in spiritual fellowship. We pursue unity with them and Christ-like love for them, not out of selfish ambition (though there is great reward in obeying the Father), but with fear and trembling. In this we tread the sacred way that Jesus watered with his blood, walking to the end the path of salvation he has set before us, in his strength and for his good pleasure.

Proper 22

Sunday between 2 and 8 October inclusive

Isaiah 5:1–7 · Philippians 3:4b–14 · Matthew 21:33–46 · Psalm 80:7–15

Whatever were gains to me I now consider loss for the sake of Christ.

The theme of this week's collection of readings is that faith in Christ, with its fruits, is more important to God than the flesh and its privileges.

In our Gospel reading, Jesus startles the Pharisees and chief priests with a parable aimed squarely at them. The vineyard in the parable is clearly Israel, a point established by Isaiah's use of the image some seven or eight centuries before. In Isaiah 5, the Lord blesses and provides for his people, who are his 'pleasant planting' and his 'beloved'. Everything that needs doing for them, he does, building a winepress, watchtower, and wall. And yet when he comes looking for fruit from these precious vines, what does he find? 'He looked for a crop of good grapes, but it yielded only bad fruit' (Isaiah 5:2). The vintage was no good, useless and only fit for recycling and pruning. The fruit he longs to see, it turns out, is justice and righteousness, and yet instead he is confronted only by bloodshed and violence. Every privilege had been squandered and lost.

This would be in the back of the minds of those 'biblical' Pharisees as they hear Jesus tell his vineyard parable, a not-so-subtle recasting of the familiar story from Isaiah. The vineyard owner sends for fruit, but is rebuffed – but the new element in Matthew's Gospel is the agency of the tenants themselves. Their culpable negligence and violent greed is all too clear in the way they treat the prophets; and, Jesus hints, they will treat the glorious Son no differently, but throw him out and kill him. Just as in Isaiah 5, where the inhabitants of the land are asked to judge between God and his vineyard, so here, Jesus's listeners are asked to form their own judgment on the situation, and to enter into the story: 'what will the owner of the vineyard do to those tenants who abuse his son?' Answer: he will both punish and dispossess, giving their privileges to others. The final obstacle for them had been the Son, and yet (Psalm 118 should have warned those Scripture-searchers!) the cornerstone will be the cornerstone, whether they accept it or not.

Paul the apostle has every reason to boast in his earthly privileges too. A Hebrew of the Hebrews he calls himself (i.e. a quintessential Jew of impeccable lineage), and a blameless Pharisee to boot; he was so zealous to be a good Jew that he persecuted the early Christian church. Yet these fleshly boasts are far from the spiritual fruit that God expected, and Paul has come to see them in a new light. Everything he thought he was doing well, he now realises was rubbish (literally, a more crude term than it would be polite to print here!). Compared to knowing Jesus, the once rejected cornerstone, everything else pales into insignificance.

Indeed, Paul goes further and embraces the rejection and suffering of the cornerstone himself. He wants to know Christ, the power of his resurrection, and to share in his sufferings. Becoming like Jesus in his death, the death to which he was pursued by pharisaical sticklers, Paul hopes to also attain to the glorious resurrection. He realises he has not yet reached perfection, but is making progress towards the prize as he strains and presses forward with his mission to take the good news beyond the borders of Israel. The gospel comes to those outside as a result of its rejection by the leaders and people of God's precious vineyard. They had no right, and no righteousness of their own, to present as fruit to their Creator and sustainer; yet through Christ they can obtain a righteousness from God by faith alone. So the justice of God, and his mercy embrace each other, to fulfil the mystery of our salvation.[18]

---

[18] See Lee Gatiss (ed.), *The First Book of Homilies: The Official Sermons of the Church of England in Modern English* (London: Lost Coin, 2021), pp. 54–5.

Proper 23

Sunday between 9 and 15 October inclusive

Isaiah 25:1–9 · Philippians 4:1–9 · Matthew 22:1–14 · Psalm 23

I will dwell in the house of the Lord for ever.

This week, our readings teach us that destruction will come to the city which opposes God, as the world rejoices in the feast of salvation. We are confronted with a question: Will you be part of the city that is destroyed or part of the wedding feast in God's house?

Isaiah's 'little apocalypse' focuses on the downfall of God's enemies and the promise of a restored and renewed creation which breaks forth in joy. Chapter 25 is particularly concerned with the demise of the ruthless who tyrannise God's people. The destruction of their city, their fortified way of life, has been planned from long ages past and will last into eternity. But God will be a refuge and shelter for the poor and needy who have been assaulted on every side by these terrifying, alien oppressors. Instead of the biting winter storm and the stabbing summer heat, they will enjoy calm and rest on God's holy mountain, and a feast of the richest fare. Death itself will evaporate, its dark shroud and shadow removed from the world as forgiveness descends in its place, and every tear is wiped away with joy.

Jesus's parable of the wedding banquet conjures up a similar scene. A king throws a party for his son's wedding and sends out messengers to call the guests to come (a reference, of course, to 'the wedding supper of the lamb' as Revelation 19:9 calls it, and the proclamation of the gospel which commands all people to repent and turn to Christ). But those who are called are negligent, dismissive or downright abusive in response. The king destroys those who murder his messengers, and burns their city to the ground in just and righteous indignation (echoes of Isaiah 25:2 but applied more shockingly to Jerusalem).

Yet the king in the parable still wants to celebrate for his son. So, many more are called from elsewhere and the church is filled. However, some of those later invitees are also negligent and contemptuous of the privilege they have been given. The man without his wedding suit on is thrown into the outer darkness, where those who rejected the Lord earlier are crying and gnashing their teeth in frustrated regret. Notably, Jesus doesn't conclude that many are called but few respond well. Rather, he says: Many are called; few are chosen.

Philippians 4 takes us back to the joy of those whose names *are* in the book of life. They stand firm in the Lord, struggling together in the work of the gospel, but must also takes steps to end their struggles with each other. Euodia and Syntyche in verse 2 are especially in mind. As the Anglican Homily on strife and contention says, 'Quarrels are often between two people (for no one commonly criticises themselves), and involve two most detestable vices: one is picking quarrels, with sharp and contentious words; the other is giving argumentative replies and multiplying evil words in return.'[19] So Paul urges those who have fallen out with fellow believers to rejoice and be reasonable, because Jesus is near (whether attentively or chronologically is perhaps deliberately ambiguous). Rather than speaking crossly to one another, they should speak instead to God in peacemaking prayer. God's peace protects those who pray.

Paul also urges them to fill their minds with good things: whatever is true, noble, right, pure – whether 'spiritual' or not. It is good to dwell on things which are worthy of praise in the sight of God, rather than on the faults of others or more ignoble thoughts. He also exhorts them to continue in the path which he laid out for them. Some may baulk at the idea of sticking to what *Paul* taught and how he embodied the gospel in his lifestyle. But the God of peace is with those (and those only) who follow Paul's example in word and deed.

---

[19] Gatiss (ed.), *The First Book of Homilies*, p. 180.

Proper 24

Sunday between 16 and 22 October inclusive

Isaiah 45:1–7 · 1 Thessalonians 1:1–10 · Matthew 22:15–22 · Psalm 96:1–13

So give back to Caesar what is Caesar's, and to God what is God's.

The common theme of this week's readings is not easy to discern. When crowd-sourcing for solutions on social media, I was told there was probably no rhyme or reason for this collection of readings to go together, or that the connection might simply be 'God'. Someone else suggested it was 'squirrels', though I am not convinced they read the passages very carefully! The key may be that in Isaiah, God gives to the Emperor; and in the Gospel reading, we are to give to both God *and* the Emperor. In addition, both Cyrus (in Isaiah) and Caesar are pagan rulers to whom God's people owed some kind of obedience; and both Cyrus and the Thessalonians were called by God and had hope-inspiring work to do focused on a return. A certain artificial intelligence engine suggested that the uniting theme here is that God is the only one worthy of our worship and obedience.

In Isaiah 45, the Lord speaks to his anointed one, who startlingly turns out to be a pagan ruler, Cyrus. He has been anointed and called to subdue the nations and God will go before him to level the mountains and make this easier (echoes of the words of comfort to God's people in Isaiah 40:4). Although he does not know the Lord as his God, he will unwittingly do the work of the one true God, as an instrument in his hands for the good of his people and the execution of his plan. He will bring hope and a return from exile.

In the Gospel reading, the Pharisees and Herodians are not natural bedfellows. But when it comes to entrapment, they are skilled and deadly. While testifying to Christ's sincerity, truthfulness, and lack of partiality they give away their own sinful hypocrisy. Jesus shows that the real issue behind their enquiry about tax is something deeper: not just money, but loyalty and obedience to God. He will not be co-opted into their political agenda, however flattering they might be towards him and however much he *might* sympathise with their grievances about the burdens of Roman tax. He knows human hearts too well to trust himself and his name to their political campaigning! Instead, he calls on them, and all those made in God's image, to give their all to him.

The Thessalonians, to whom Paul writes perhaps his earliest epistle, are called and chosen by God (as Cyrus was, in Isaiah 45). They are keen to turn that call into obedient action with the work of faith, labour of love and steadfastness of hope for which Paul praises them (and thanks God for giving to them). Like Jesus, they face persecution but endure it with joy in the Holy Spirit. They render unto God what is God's by turning to him from idols.

The Thessalonians not only do the work of the living and true God, but worship and serve him knowingly and willingly. Their ongoing discipleship is characterised by both working and waiting: unlike many, they neither do God's work without knowing him nor claim to know him without putting their faith into action; and yet they are also patiently waiting for the arrival of their great King and true Emperor, Jesus – greater than Cyrus, greater than Caesar, even superior to their ancient local Macedonian hero, Alexander the Great. They look for the return, not of nationalistic days of glory, but of their truly divine Saviour. He rescues us not simply from ourselves and our sin, or even from our enemies, but from the coming wrath of God, says Paul, which is truly the greatest crisis facing any individual or society. The Thessalonians know that the one who came to bear that wrath in their place was coming to claim them as his own – a fact which inspired all their faith, hope, and love.

Proper 25

Sunday between 23 and 29 October inclusive

Leviticus 19:1–2, 15–18 · 1 Thessalonians 2:1–8 · Matthew 22:34–46 · Psalm 1

Love your neighbour as yourself.

Our readings this week focus on the golden rules of love for God and love for neighbour. Such familiar words – but are we putting them into practice?

The Pharisees are quick to pounce on Jesus once they hear that the Sadducees have failed to get the better of him. They enter the lists to test him, with a question of biblical scholarship. What is the greatest commandment? Jesus actually gives two answers, ranking love for God first and love for neighbour second. But on these two commandments hang all the Law and the Prophets. Everything in Scripture relates to one or both of these pivotal points. It is not as if we get to fill these basic categories of love with our own content; the rest of the Bible fleshes them out for us perfectly clearly. God himself defines what love is.

While he has them hanging on his every word, Jesus also throws back a challenge to the Pharisees to end this section of the Gospel where he has been questioned at length on various subjects of relevance to different groups at the time. He asks them about what the Bible says concerning the Messiah. He shows them that they have not understood it in its fullness. The Messiah may be the Son of David, but Psalm 110 was also clear that the Messiah would be *Adonai* ('Lord') too. Not merely subservient to David, but his master, relating in the heavenly counsel to the Lord (*YHWH*) himself, who decrees victory and supremacy over his enemies. No one can refute his handling of the Bible: not only does he have a perfect understanding of the big picture of the whole; but he knows and reverences every last detail and word, relying on its divine inspiration and utter truthfulness in everything.

Leviticus 19 shows us that 'love your neighbour as yourself' was not something invented by Jesus in the New Testament, but a text from within the Old Testament itself. The verses set for the reading relate relational love to divine imitation: we love others as part of the command to be holy as God is holy. This cashes out in specific circumstances: rendering just judgments which favour neither the poor nor the political elite in their evenhandedness; not gossiping or profiteering, or bearing a grudge. We cannot just leave someone to get on with their sin: we must reprove them or incur guilt ourselves. This is part of what it means to love our neighbour – it is far from loving to watch them go to hell for want of a loving rebuke, an attempt to arrest their slide into judgment. Above all, the Law says, love must start in the heart: too many rebukes and too much self-righteousness are infused with a lack of heartfelt love and compassion.

In the epistle, the apostle also interweaves the idea of loving and pleasing God with care for others. He had declared the good news about Jesus to the Thessalonians despite opposition, with courage and care. It is far from loving to withhold the gospel from people (or give them something more worldly and less wholesome as a substitute), but we must speak the truth clearly 'to please God who tests our hearts'. It is sadly possible to herald the message of love with hard, compassionless hearts, which may save our hearers (since the word itself has power) but condemns our deceitful and impure motivations. Flattery, greed, seeking power and praise – all are condemned, along with those who speak God's gospel without gentleness.

4th Sunday before Advent

Sunday between 30 October and 5 November inclusive

Micah 3:5–12 · 1 Thessalonians 2:9–13 · Matthew 24:1–14 · Psalm 43

When you received the word of God, which you heard from us, you accepted it not as a human word, but as it actually is, the word of God.

There is a huge difference between ministers who proclaim the pure, unvarnished word of God and those who preach only what is good for their own livelihood. Some lead people into darkness; the others will rejoice with faithful disciples in the kingdom of God and of glory. Can you discern the difference?

Micah preaches against prophets, priests and rulers whose gangrenous theology is nothing but self-serving, self-affirming slogans. They lead the people astray: not into deeper, costlier loyalty to the one true God but into a blind obsession with whatever keeps the deceptive, worldly peace. As they cover their ears against the clear word of God, they find their mouths are shut along with their minds and emptied of all good words. Their strategies and prayers produce no results; the sky above them is cold as iron. There is no answer from God. They abhor righteousness, as if it was sin, and pervert what is right and good in order to build their earthly kingdoms. Laws are changed to serve vested interests, for the promise of party funding and the alluring prize of media backing. Consciences and values are casually exchanged for votes. Because the priests and prophets collude in this magisterial deviance for the sake of their own gain, they are assured of the destruction of their beloved holy hill and the tottering system which supports their cuckoo corruption.

Likewise, Jesus also speaks of the destruction of the Jerusalem Temple. Not one beautiful stone will be left on top of another, he says, prompting intense and furious questioning from his disciples. 'Beware that no-one leads you astray,' he says (using the same verb as in the Septuagint of Micah 3:5). The danger is that, because of the ever-present threat of wars and various disasters, they will believe the messianic pretensions of false prophets and substandard saviours. Anarchy and the amoral reign of those opposed to God's kingdom and people will dampen the ardour of many tempted saints. But those who endure what the world, the press and the devil can throw at them will assuredly be delivered from this present evil age. Torture and betrayal, though sadly inevitable, cannot strangle or suppress an enduring global testimony to the good news of Christ.

Despite much persecution, the Thessalonians (for example) received the apostolic testimony. They embraced it, despite the cost, not as a merely human philosophy but as the unerring word of the living God. They could also testify to the blameless conduct of Paul, the authentic minister who, in contrast to others, worked hard to give instead of taking. By his authentic words and authentic life he, like all true ministers of the gospel, urged them to live a life worthy of God's kingdom and glory, rather than tailoring his message to the earthly ambitions or secret desires of his audience. They are urged to remember his fatherly exhortation and the word at work within them, while he rejoices in the fruit of his spiritual labour and gives thanks to the God of all grace.

So don't be led astray by inauthentic preachers who proclaim an inauthentic message. Compare those in Micah 3 and Matthew 24 with the apostle in Thessalonica, and you will know who to avoid, and whose word to follow.

3rd Sunday before Advent

Sunday between 6 and 12 November inclusive

Amos 5:18–24 · 1 Thessalonians 4:13–18 · Matthew 25:1–13 · Psalm 70

Woe to you who long for the day of the LORD!

Our readings today give a perfect opportunity to speak about some of the issues thrown up by memories of war. They teach that a final cataclysmic day of reckoning is coming, for which prepared Christians can hope while others ought to fear.

Amos 5 speaks to the warmongers who long for a big battle to sort the men from the boys, so to speak. Do not desire that decisive day, the day of the Lord, in such a mood. Might does not make right when uncoupled from righteousness. The religious zeal of Amos's audience is utterly misplaced; their hypocritical noise is offensive not pleasing and its solemnity sickening to the God who loves justice more than pomp and outward show. Those who rush headlong into the fray in such a context will quickly find the end is worse than the beginning, and their hopes of resolution will be dashed by evils greater than they foresaw. Mock religiosity is an inadequate preparation for the sudden onrush of God's judgment.

Jesus's parable of the ten 'bridesmaids' (or literally 'virgins'), reminds us that the day that is coming will be a day of separation, and of disappointment to many who are not truly prepared. The foolish ones look ready, with their lamps, but do not have the fuel required to light a flame. All become drowsy and sleep before the great and long-anticipated arrival of the groom. Yet when that moment suddenly comes, preparation in advance is all that counts. There is no second chance to grab some oil and not just *look* ready but *be* ready. The door will be irrevocably shut at that unexpected hour.

Paul writes to the Thessalonians who were eagerly waiting for the day, because he had told them of its splendour. Macedonians longed for a great king to restore the glory days of their great Alexander, but the parousia of Jesus, *his* royal visitation, would be more magnificent than anything that great homegrown general had laid on in his vast empire. Yet some of the Thessalonian Christians had died without seeing the day, causing confusion among the church. Paul writes to alleviate their concerns about their fallen Christian comrades.

They would grieve for their brothers and sisters in the faith because, as Queen Elizabeth II once said, 'Grief is the price we pay for love.' But Christians can grieve with hope in their hearts. All who trust in Jesus are united to him: just as he died and rose again, so shall they. When he comes again, they shall accompany the King. They shall not be disadvantaged by their death before the day, but take a privileged position of precedence ahead of those who remain alive until that time. A cry of command, an angelic call, and a divine trumpet blast will herald the descent of Christ from his seat at the Father's right hand to his place of honour in the new world. The dead in Christ will rise first, whenever and however they died. We who are left alive at that time shall only then be caught up to meet them.

We will be with the Lord for ever. Judgment Day for some is reunion day for Christians. No wonder Paul urges us to encourage one another with these words. They give strength and hope to suffering and grieving believers who can long for 'that day' with more than wishful thinking. Hope is guaranteed by the solid reality of Christ's own resurrection from the dead.

2nd Sunday before Advent

Sunday between 13 and 19 November inclusive

Zephaniah 1:7, 12–18 · 1 Thessalonians 5:1–11 · Matthew 25:14–30 · Psalm 90:1–12

Teach us to number our days, that we may gain a heart of wisdom.

Our readings this week challenge the attitude of complacency which many have as they anticipate the end of all things. The day of wrath for some is a day of salvation for many, but only such as do not rest on their laurels as they wait for the coming of the day.

Zephaniah 1 is almost unrelentingly dark. It speaks of a day of darkness and gloom, ruin and devastation, distress and anguish. It is aimed especially, verse 12 says, at those who rest complacently. These people doubt that God will act at all. He will neither do good nor harm, they claim. He will remain silent and distant, without getting involved in our worldly affairs. He will keep his hands clean, away from the mess of our broken world. It is a practical atheism, a philosophy of despair.

At the same time, these complacent deistic doubters think to rest on their earthly wealth or achievements as protection on that day if it ever arrives. But Zephaniah warns it will be a bitter day for any who trust in 'things' to rescue them. The images are alarming – they will be like dust or dung on that terrible day, he says, fit only to be cast aside. A blunt warning not to be found on the wrong side of God as history draws to its inexorable close.

1 Thessalonians 5 is more of a reassurance to believers, who anticipate the coming of the Lord with a thrilling joy in their hearts. We have not been appointed for wrath on that day, but for salvation says the apostle. As 1 Thessalonians 1 has already assured us, Jesus

has rescued us from the wrath to come, a reminder that it is still real and coming – not cancelled as some fool themselves into thinking. Paul is clear that the day will come suddenly, but should not be a surprise to Christians. His burden is to warn us to stay sober and alert as we wait, not missing the announcements along the way like drowsy travellers at an airport, oblivious to the clear and certain notices of the impending arrival and departure. Using the military images he develops further in Ephesians 6, he calls us to be good soldiers of Christ, ready to get up and stand firm at a moment's notice, not falling asleep on duty by neglecting faith, hope and love.

Jesus's parable in Matthew 25 gives the same message in his characteristically engaging narrative form. Servants who wait for their master to return, must prove faithful and hardworking with the resources left at their disposal. He may be gone a long time, he says (which rather scotches the idea that the early church were deluded and disappointed, thinking he was returning any second). But seeming delay should not lull us to sleep or distract us from long term plans to endeavour great things for the Lord. Rather, it should foster an entrepreneurial spirit which seeks to leverage everything we have for the best possible return. 'You wicked and lazy slave!' would be a shocking and terrifying greeting on the great and terrible day of the Lord. Far better to hear 'Well done, my good and faithful servant!' The question then, is which do we prefer? And are we motivated by the desire to please Christ in all that we do, say, and daydream about in this period of calm before the storm? One thing our readings this week hold as absolutely certain: the day is coming. Be prepared. Be very prepared.

Sunday next before Advent (Christ the King)

Sunday between 20 and 26 November inclusive

Ezekiel 34:11–16, 20–24 · Ephesians 1:15–23 · Matthew 25:31–46 · Psalm 95:1–7a

All the nations will be gathered before him, and he will separate the people one from another as a shepherd separates the sheep from the goats.

The common thread in our readings this week is the gathering of sheep under a glorious shepherd with all authority who will judge between them for the benefit of his loving people.

Ezekiel prophesies that the Lord God, or Sovereign Lord himself (the name he uses is *Adonai YHWH*) will seek out his lost sheep. They have been scattered 'on a day of clouds and thick darkness', that is, through judgment and catastrophe they have found themselves in exile. But the Lord will gather the people from the nations to which they have been scattered and bring them into their own land, a land of good grazing and rich pasture. He seeks not just the lost, but those who have strayed, those who are injured, those who are weak, that he might restore, heal, and strengthen them.

Yet God will destroy 'the fat and the strong'. He will judge between the fat sheep and the lean sheep, he says. The fault of 'the fat' is that they pushed around the weak and ravaged the flock for their own advantage. But they will not be allowed to get away with this lack of love for ever. God will set up a single shepherd over them; and though we have just heard that the shepherd will be God himself, he also describes the shepherd-prince as 'my servant David', a Davidic king. So the people will be ruled by a king both divine and human, and just as God separated the light from the dark in creation, he will separate people from people.

In Matthew 25, the Lord Jesus, Son of David, Son of Man, describes his own coming in glory. Accompanied by the angels he will sit on his glorious throne to judge the gathered nations. He will separate the sheep from the goats; sheep on his right (the favoured position, just as Jesus himself is 'at the right hand of the Father'), and goats on his left. The chosen sheep are those who have been blessed by the Father, and they shall inherit the kingdom which God has prepared for them alone since before the world was created. Yet though they were chosen for this unique benefit of God's eternal plan, their temporal activity revealed their elect status: they cared for the members of the King's family and stuck together with them in the midst of a troubled and needy world. Those who were not chosen for the eternally prepared kingdom also revealed their true colours in their earthly behaviour, by not feeding, welcoming, or associating with the suffering people of God. How one treats the people of God reveals one's attitude to God himself. What we do in this life is an echo of eternity.

In his prayer in Ephesians 1, Paul gives thanks for the faith of the Ephesians and for their 'love towards all the saints'. Where we hear of faith and love, we know hope is not far away; and so he prays (verse 18) that they would grasp the hope to which they have been called, the rich inheritance of the people of God. He also prays that they would know God's power at work within them, to enable them to love and to endure, the power which was exerted in the resurrection and ascension of the Lord Jesus Christ, who reigns over everything in heaven and earth. He is head over all things for the sake of the church, his body, which is connected to him in the most intimate of ways. He rules for them and they live for him.

So Jesus reveals himself as the Sovereign Lord spoken of in Ezekiel, and Paul says that he is head over all things in heaven and earth. Will you serve him today, or be separate from him on the coming day of judgment?

YEAR B
1st Sunday of Advent

29 November 2026
2 December 2029
28 November 2032
2 December 2035
28 November 2038

ADVENT

1st Sunday of Advent

Isaiah 64:1–9 · 1 Corinthians 1:3–9 · Mark 13:24–37 ·
Psalm 80:1–7, 17–19

Oh, that you would rend the heavens and come down,
that the mountains would tremble before you!

This week sees the start of a new Church year, Year B according to our lectionary. And the theme of our readings for this first Sunday in Advent is waiting for the coming of our Lord Jesus Christ. Yet as the world gears up for Christmas festivities, it is not the first coming of Christ in his lowliness and humility that we are anticipating, but his revelation in glory at the Last Day.

Isaiah 64 looks forward longingly to the arrival of God, the anointed conqueror. Isaiah calls for God to tear the heavens open and come down, as he came down in the past to do 'awesome deeds' and shake the mountains. There has never been a God like him, 'who works for those who wait for him', rewarding the patient faith of those who remember him and gladly do what is right. This reminds us of the stunning basis of our faith – it is God who works for us in salvation, not we who work to earn his favour. Our works themselves, apart from faith, are worse than nothing; they are unclean in his sight. So his judgment is always justified, even when he hides his fatherly face from us for a time. Yet even so, we can appeal to him on the basis of his covenant with us: we are his people, whom he cannot forget.

1 Corinthians begins with thanksgiving, despite the fact that Paul has many difficult and piercing things to say to this seemingly

successful but deeply worldly church. The centre of his thanksgiving for them is that they are 'not lacking in any spiritual gift as [they] wait for the revealing of our Lord Jesus Christ'. They are enriched and blessed in him and there remains a strong testimony to his grace among them, despite their waywardness. So Paul is prayerfully confident that God will strengthen them further, with grace to persevere in blameless discipleship until the day Christ returns. God called them into fellowship with his holy Son, and will faithfully keep them in that sanctifying relationship. Paul's words of warning and exhortation and correction are, of course, godly instruments to ensure their spiritual preservation 'to the end'.

Much has been written on our reading in Mark 13, and some have suggested that it refers not to the final coming of Christ in glory but to his impending crucifixion (when the sun was darkened in the middle of the day, and the powers of heaven were shaken). Verse 26 seems, however, to fix our eyes on a future day when he will come in manifest power and glory, not the hidden power of his cross. On that day, the elect will be gathered in from around the world by the angels. The day is near, says Jesus, but no one can know exactly when it is going to come. Only the Father has it marked decisively on his calendar.

Our task, in the meantime, is to be alert and awake. Jesus's image of a fig tree teaches us that the time will come and we should watch and wait. His image of the master going on a journey teaches us that our waiting should be active and always alert. When the master returns we must not be found asleep or in a selfish stupor (or have lives characterised thus), but be sober and ready to welcome the happy day.

2nd Sunday of Advent

Isaiah 40:1–11 · 2 Peter 3:8–15a · Mark 1:1–8 · Psalm 85:1–2, 8–13

Prepare the way for the Lord, make straight paths for him.

In this second Sunday of Advent, we are reminded by our Sunday readings of the preparation required as we wait for the glorious arrival of the Lord Jesus.

Isaiah speaks to a church and nation exhausted by warfare and an experience of exile which it fully deserved. His message is one of tenderness and comfort: the promised end is in sight. Jerusalem has received not double punishment for her sins (which would be unjust), but the matching punishment, the appropriate discipline, the fitting chastisement (the idea of the dual form of the Hebrew word for 'double' here is of a matching pair, like-for-like, as in the game of Snap). Now is the time, therefore, for restoration and gentleness.

Now is also the time for crying out 'Prepare the way of the Lord!' (Isaiah 40:3). Get ready for his coming. Creation levels out to facilitate his arrival and make it easy for all to see. A herald of good news goes up into a mountainous pulpit to proclaim the glad tidings to fragile humankind, to tell them they can trust the enduring promise and word of God. No power of hell and no subtle scheme of the mighty can pluck them from the hand of this protective and loving shepherd, who comes to claim his own.

The arrival of John the Baptist in Mark's Gospel is announced with a text from Isaiah 40 and a similar line from Malachi 3. Thus the New Testament story begins where the Old Testament left off. The Saviour is about to arrive, the Son of God himself. John's role is to prepare the way for his cousin, Jesus, by calling people to repent of their sins. He preaches forgiveness, as Isaiah did, to Judea and Jerusalem, pointing away from himself to the Word of the Lord.

The apostle Peter was an eyewitness of those things. And in his second letter he proclaims a similar message to those who wait for the second coming of the Messiah. The delay before his arrival is a mercy to us from the eternal Father, who calls us to prepare ourselves for the Last Day by living holy and godly lives. 'It is only the diligent Christian who will be the happy Christian in the day of the Lord', says the beloved eighteenth-century commentator Matthew Henry on these verses.[1] This is the way not just to wait for but even to hasten his return, says Peter. There is disagreement among theologians and commentators about the precise meaning of this hastening, and how we might 'speed his return' by our actions here and now. Perhaps it is related to the idea that the gospel must be preached to all nations before the end comes, and hence is an encouragement and spur to our diligence in evangelism, not least among unreached people groups? God does not want them to perish but to repent and therefore participate in eternal life.

Yet what we can be certain of is this: when he returns, we will see the final fulfilment of Isaiah's great prophecies, a new heaven and a new earth (2 Peter 3:13; Isaiah 65:17). Since this will be a home for righteousness, let us be righteous in preparation.

---

[1] Henry, *Matthew Henry's Commentary on the Whole Bible: Complete and Unabridged in One Volume* (Peabody: Hendrickson, 1994), p. 2441.

3rd Sunday of Advent

Isaiah 61:1–4, 8–11 · 1 Thessalonians 5:16–24 · John 1:6–8, 19–28 · Psalm 126

The LORD has done great things for us, and we are filled with joy.

The readings this week focus our attention again on the coming of Christ, prophesied in the Old Testament, announced by John the Baptist and anticipated by those who await his final return in glory. Each passage directs our thoughts to the Lord God himself, who alone can save and sanctify us.

John's Gospel gives us a fascinating insight into the ministry of John the Baptist, whose identity is carefully spelt out. As chapter 1 of the Gospel begins, we hear about the Word who was with God and was God. We might expect verse 5 therefore to begin, 'There was a man sent from God, whose name was *Jesus*', to focus our minds on the earthly ministry of the God-man. We will get there eventually! But first, we take a step back to the historic ministry of the forerunner, who prepared the way before the Lord. He is clearly distinguished from the light himself. His name was John, which might also throw some first-time readers of what we call the Gospel of John! One thing the Evangelist and the Baptiser do have in common, however, is that they both testify to the light, so that all may believe through him: this is the purpose of the Gospel narrative itself (John 20:30–31), and of the first merely human character we are introduced to in it. Later in the chapter, in the face of public questioning, John repeatedly distinguishes himself from the Messiah he came to announce – a coming Messiah who is far greater than any herald, because he is the Lord himself.

Isaiah prophesies not just the arrival of the messenger to prepare the way for the Lord, but also of the anointed conqueror himself. Isaiah 61 is the very passage from which the Lord Jesus taught about himself in the synagogue (see Luke 4). His Spirit-anointed ministry is an evangelical ministry of the proclaimed word: he declares the day of the Lord and the day of vengeance. And that word to the oppressed binds up the broken-hearted and cheers up those who mourn. He will implement his everlasting covenant to bless his people, to display his own glory, he asserts. The people will greatly rejoice says verse 10, their *whole being* exulting in what God has done to clothe us in robes of righteousness which we have neither earned or deserved. He alone can cause righteousness and praise to spring up from such unpromising soil.

In his closing remarks to the Thessalonians, Paul has some all-encompassing words of encouragement for this fledgling church. They are to rejoice *always*, pray *always*, give thanks *always*; they are to test *all* prophecies, and abstain from *all* evil. On the other hand, God himself will sanctify them *completely*, their *whole spirit*, both soul and body. When the Messiah comes again, the Lord Jesus Christ in all his glory, he will finish this work of new creation in us. As the great evangelist George Whitefield (1714–70) put it in his version of the hymn *Praising Christ*, we will

> Sing ‘till we feel our Hearts
> Ascending with our Tongues,
> Sing ’till the Love of Sin departs,
> And Grace inspires our Songs.[2]

On that great day of his coming, we will be found blameless, by grace alone.

---

[2] John Campbell (ed.), *The Comprehensive Hymn Book. One Thousand Hymns, for Congregational, Domestic, and Private Worship; Originally Compiled by George Whitefield* (4th edition; London, 1852), p. 16.

4th Sunday of Advent

2 Samuel 7:1–11, 16 · Romans 16:25–27 · Luke 1:26–38 · Psalm 89:1–4, 19–26

I will establish the throne of his kingdom for ever.

The theme of our readings this week is the gospel revelation that Jesus, Son of Mary, would also be Son of God and Son of David – the promised eternal ruler for God's people.

2 Samuel 7 is a key text for the unfolding of God's plan in the Old Testament. King David finally establishes a settled, peaceful kingdom after the opening tumultuous years of his reign. Seeing that he has been secured in his palace by the Lord, he naturally desires to show his gratitude to God in some way. The obvious idea of building a more lasting, permanent temple to house the ark of the covenant is suggested, and the prophet Nathan encourages David to pursue this seemingly godly plan. Yet God has something simultaneously negative and positive to say in response: negatively, he tells David it is not up to him to decide when it's time for God to settle down; positively, he assures him that the Lord will continue to be with the king, and establish his dynasty not just for the foreseeable future, but for all time. The throne of David and the house of David are to be established for ever.

There will always be a Davidic king, into the furthest reaches of eternity. God will be with the Davidic king and bless him. The earthly dynasty does well in the next few centuries, outliving the more unstable dynasties of the Northern Kingdom. But how, after the exile and destruction of David's Jerusalem, this prophetic word can be fulfilled, is not quite clear by the first century, as Israel languishes under Roman occupation. Until that is, the angel Gabriel appears to a young woman engaged to a man 'of the house of David'. She doesn't understand it and is perplexed by the announcement that God is with her and favours her. As Isaiah said, this virgin will be with child and give birth to a son (Isaiah 7:14). God will give him the throne of his ancestor, David, and he will reign *for ever*. The words Mary hears are almost identical to the prophecy in 2 Samuel 7, but this fulfilment is far greater and more glorious than she could have anticipated.

This divine King, this God-man, will truly reign for ever, and secure the place of David's dynasty for all eternity, in himself. Mary *is* the 'house' in which this King will be brought to birth. In the Magnificat (the name given to Mary's song in Luke 1, taken from the first word of it in Latin), she praises God for keeping his promise, not just to David, but further back to Abraham – the promise to undo the Fall and spread blessing to a world under the wrath of God. She has a most intimate and special place in the fulfilment of God's rescue plan for creation. There can never have been a more significant and joyful response to an unanticipated teenage pregnancy!

Paul began his letter to the Romans by bearing witness to the gospel of Jesus, the Son of God and the Son of David. At the end of his letter, like Mary, he gives glory to God and magnifies his name. God can strengthen his people by the gospel, the proclamation that Jesus is the Christ, the anointed King.

This doxology (an expression of praise to God) acknowledges that the gospel is a mystery, formerly kept secret for long ages past, but now revealed in the coming of Jesus. This new disclosure of what was planned from eternity brings an 'aha!' moment for all, but especially for the Gentiles, who see for the first time in the prophetic writings of the Old Testament their own place in the cosmic plan of God. What was always there (by the command of the most wise God), but somewhat concealed in patterns and prophecies, now snaps into focus with the coming of the King – a glorious king who commands the loving loyalty and obedient trust of all the nations under heaven. Rejoice with Paul and Mary in being the subject of such a magnificent king.

CHRISTMAS

1st Sunday of Christmas

Isaiah 61:10–62:3 · Galatians 4:4–7 · Luke 2:15–21 · Psalm 148

So you are no longer a slave, but God's child.

This week our readings focus on the baby Jesus, who has come to save his people from their sins in fulfilment of a grand cosmic design. This child came so that you can be a redeemed child of God.

Isaiah's vision of the anointed conqueror continues with a splendid picture of him 'clothed in the garments of salvation'. The Lord has come to save and rescue his people, covered in a robe of righteousness. And it is righteousness and praise which he causes to spring up 'before all the nations' – a clear sign that this new birth is an event of significance for the whole world. Salvation will suddenly shine out like a burning torch in the darkness, to be seen by the nations – but especially by 'the kings', it says, (which is one of the reasons the Magi are sometimes seen as royal visitors). A name is given by the Lord himself to the conqueror, who will be a crown of beauty to him.

In Luke 2 we find the shepherds rushing to Bethlehem to meet this very child, lying in a manger with Mary and Joseph standing nearby. They share their amazing story and the angelic proclamation about the new baby. Mary stores up these things in her heart, pondering them and meditating on the dramatic events and divine signs that have accompanied the birth of her little boy. No doubt she often thought about them as she heard the Scriptures read in the synagogue in years to come and reflected on their significance in God's rescue plan. After eight days, the baby is circumcised in accordance with the Law of Moses and the promise given to Abraham. He is called Jesus, because the angel who had announced his conception had said that was to be his name. He is, as Isaiah had prophesied, given a name from the mouth of the Lord himself. The name means 'the Lord is our salvation'.

The apostle Paul reflects on these same moments in our passage from Galatians 4. Christ came 'in the fullness of time' – not a moment too late, nor a moment too soon. He was sent by God to be born of woman – to take human flesh, willingly and obediently. As the religious poet George Herbert (1593–1633) puts it in his poem, *The Bag*:

> The God of power, as he did ride
> In his majestic robes of glory,
> Resolv'd to light; and so one day
> He did descend, undressing all the way.[3]

But why did he undress and remove his robes of glory? Because 'he had new clothes a making here below'. In the womb of the Virgin he took frail flesh, because without it he could not die for those given to him by the Father.

After his descent to the earthly realm, as travellers are wont to do, he rested for a while. And he became obedient to the law of the place where he was staying, but only in order to redeem those who were under that law – to make the slaves into sons. And so the Son of God redeems, so the Spirit can indwell, and each heart call out, 'Abba! Father!' in fulfilment of the Trinitarian plan to adopt us and make us heirs of salvation. Did Mary make all these astonishing connections as she turned these events over in her mind? Do we see the eternal grandeur of what is unfolding in the Christmas story, or do we miss the deeper truths hidden in our homely nativity scenes?

---

[3] Ann Pasternak Slater (ed.), *George Herbert: The Complete English Works* (New York: Alfred A. Knopf, 1995), p. 148.

EPIPHANY

1st Sunday of Epiphany

Genesis 1:1–5 · Acts 19:1–7 · Mark 1:4–11 · Psalm 29

He saw heaven being torn open and the Spirit descending on him like a dove.

Our readings this week rivet our attention on the baptism of the Holy Spirit, which brings new life and a new start, separating night from day. Have you confessed your sins and started this new life for yourself?

Genesis 1 brings light from darkness as the Spirit of God sweeps over the face of the waters in creation. What was formless and void becomes, over the course of the chapter, a full and beautifully ordered world. In creation, God separates: light from darkness, day from night. A new beginning, out of water, by the Spirit.

The beginning of the new order for God's fallen creation is about to dawn as John the Baptiser appears in Mark's Gospel. The world is now corrupted and degenerate, but God has not sent his last and greatest prophet to announce doom, but to call for repentance, promising forgiveness of sins. So many respond to this call that Mark says *everyone* from Jerusalem and the surrounding countryside went out to meet John, confess their sins, and be baptised.

Repentance is turning away and changing one's mind and direction. But the new direction is set by the one who comes after John. He is more powerful – and his way will be more permanent and more effective than the old way of the Law. Even his cousin, the forerunner foretold in the Old Testament Scriptures, is not worthy to untie his sandals. John's watery baptism is only a sign of the cleansing and new beginning that will come with the arrival of the Messiah, when the Spirit of God will hover over the waters once more, to bring new life.

Why did Jesus himself need to be baptised? John felt instinctively that it didn't seem right, given what he had said about Jesus's superiority, and what he may have known about his sinlessness. Mark does not dwell on this question as many of us may do. Matthew 3:15 tells us it was 'fitting to fulfil all righteousness'. Jesus did everything that a faithful Israelite was meant to do, and accepted the watery judgment of baptism which he himself did not deserve. What Mark tells us, which Matthew and Luke do not, is that as he came up out of the water, Jesus himself saw the heavens torn apart. The others narrate what happened, but not specifically that Jesus saw it; evidence perhaps of the eyewitness quality of this Gospel (as Peter tells Mark what Jesus told him about this occasion). John 1:33 implies John saw it too. What the Son of God saw next was the Spirit descending upon him, as he hovered over the waters of baptism to distinguish this baptisand from all others; what he heard was the voice of the Father in heaven, expressing his delight and pleasure in his perfect Son.

Acts 19 narrates the exciting progress of the gospel to the major port city of Ephesus in Asia Minor. The apostle Paul finds some disciples of John the Baptiser there, enough to have their own synagogue. Strangely, they do not know about the baptism of the Spirit which John himself had prophesied would come. When Paul explains John's position in the history of redemption, and that he pointed to the one who would come after him, they believe in Jesus. When Paul lays hands on them, the Holy Spirit comes upon them – just as when the other apostles had caught up with the progress of the gospel in Samaria and laid hands for the first time on Samaritan believers (Acts 8). The Spirit moves to bring new life. Has he moved into you?

2nd Sunday of Epiphany

1 Samuel 3:1–20 · Revelation 5:1–10 · John 1:43–51 ·
Psalm 139:1–6, 13–18

We have found the one Moses wrote about in the Law, and about whom the prophets also wrote – Jesus of Nazareth, the son of Joseph.

The theme of our readings this second week of Epiphany ('manifestation') is the proper response to the revelation of God's word and the mystery of salvation centred in Christ. Are you as excited to tell others about him as Philip is?

1 Samuel 3 recounts a time when the elderly priest Eli was going blind and the lamp of God in the tabernacle 'had not yet gone out' (though it clearly did some time later in the Old Testament period). Most seriously, 'the word of the Lord was rare', and so people did not know the Lord or hear his voice. This includes Samuel, who (verse 7 tells us) does not know the Lord, and has not had his word revealed to him. The charming story of how Samuel comes to recognise the word of God who stands before him and calls his name demonstrates very clearly the proper response to such a divine call: 'Speak, Lord, for your servant is listening.' Once Samuel adopts the posture of an attentive servant, ready to obey further instructions, his eyes and ears are opened to further revelation and he becomes a trustworthy prophet. He is acknowledged by the nation as a mouthpiece of God, which is no mere institutional position such as that occupied by Eli and his increasingly corrupt sons and heirs. To hear and speak God's word is not a professional office or status, but a privileged vocation.

The Gospel reading narrates how Philip began to follow Jesus when he was called, and dragged his friend along too. Excitedly, he finds Nathanael to tell him he's discovered the one prophesied in the Old Testament. He has finally arrived and been revealed, but Nathanael is sceptical that anything good can really come out of the North! Jesus demonstrates when he meets Nathanael that he can see beyond the superficial, even if Nathanael cannot. What happened beneath the fig tree that made Jesus's knowledge of it so astounding, we are not told, but it seems he had some revelation, some secret, that only the Son of God could know, which kindles faith in the heart of the sceptic. 'You will see greater things than these', Jesus assures him – he will see what the patriarch Jacob saw (Genesis 28:12), a revelation of the meeting point between heaven and earth, an angelic witness to the universal centrality of Jesus, the Son of Man.

That same centrality is glimpsed in Revelation 5. Only the Lion of the tribe of Judah is worthy to open the scroll of revelation which John saw sealed with seven seals. Without him, there would be only tears, frustrated hopes and disappointment because there would be no insight, no disclosure. That Lion is also seen to be a Spirit-anointed, slaughtered Lamb, who receives praise from the four living creatures and twenty-four elders of heaven as representatives of heaven and earth. He is worthy precisely because he has been slaughtered, since by his death he has ransomed his elect people from out of every tribe and language and people and nation on earth. They will serve as priests and kings for God, just as Samuel served as his prophet, and sing prayerful praise to their beautiful Saviour through all eternity. Join that song today!

3rd Sunday of Epiphany

Genesis 14:17–20 · John 2:1–11 · Revelation 19:6–10 · Psalm 128

Blessed are those who are invited to the wedding supper of the Lamb!

In our readings this week, the blessings of salvation come out of God's city to feed and sustain his people. How blessed we are to be invited to the heavenly banquet with Jesus!

In Genesis 14, Abram returns from defeating a group of kings, including the wonderfully named Chedorlaomer, who had captured his nephew Lot. He is met by the enigmatic figure of Melchizedek, introduced as King of Salem, commonly believed to be Jeru*salem*. His name means 'King of righteousness' or 'righteous king', and he is king of a place called Peace (*salem*). He provided Abram with suitable refreshment. Jesus used those same elements of bread and wine in the Last Supper, of course, because they are so obviously indicative of basic sustenance.

The connection is not as close as some would like it to be: Melchizedek is not a pre-incarnate appearance of the Son of God. When Hebrews 7 does draw a comparison between Jesus and Melchizedek, it is telling that it neither alludes to any 'sacrifice' he may have made nor even mentions the bread and wine. They are both priests of God Most High about whom Scripture says nothing of their beginning or end. The Son of God truly has always been, from all eternity, and he lives for ever – unlike the Old Testament priests who died and needed replacing every few years. We give him, our sustainer, not just a tenth of everything, but all our heart, soul, mind and strength.

Psalm 128 is also about blessing and eating. It is a song of blessing for all those who fear God and walk in his ways. They are sustained in every way by him, and thrive: eating the fruit of their labour, surrounded by a faithful spouse and many children, enjoying the prosperity of God's city in peace and harmony. It is only a small picture of the delights of heaven, and a pattern of that city to come. But the basic joys of family, food, and flourishing provide us with a satisfying snapshot of that final destination, to fuel our prayers and hopes.

Revelation 19 is the orchestrated version of the basic melody in Psalm 128. The voice of a great multitude thunders out in John's vision. God reigns and rules, so we can rejoice. We are invited to a feast, to celebrate the marriage of the Lamb: the Lord Jesus will be with the enormous multitude of his people for ever, enjoying fellowship and great food, in fine linen with their fellow-servants of Christ. As the eighteenth-century hymnwriter, Augustus Toplady once put it, 'The kingdom of glory will both be more largely and more variously peopled than bigots of all denominations are either able to think, or willing to allow.'[4] That kingdom of the New Jerusalem will also be more gloriously enjoyable and refreshing and fulfilling than we could ever even imagine. Are you looking forward to it?

---

[4] Augustus M. Toplady, *The Works of Augustus M. Toplady* (London: Edinburgh: William Baynes and Son; H. S. Baynes, 1825), 5.335.

4th Sunday of Epiphany

Deuteronomy 18:15–20 · Revelation 12:1–5a · Mark 1:21–28 · Psalm 111

What is this? A new teaching – and with authority!

This week's readings confront us directly with the word of God in all its authority against Satan, his tactics and his minions. That same word confronts us with the question: will you listen to Jesus?

In Deuteronomy, we are reminded that when God originally spoke from Sinai, the people did not want to hear him. Moses ended up speaking for him, as a prophet, but with the same word and authority. Moses foresees this kind of arrangement continuing, with further prophets raised up to speak God's words to his people. If anyone does not listen to the prophet, they are considered to be not listening to God himself. They will be held accountable if they do not heed his words. But as usual, where there is genuine currency there is also counterfeit and forgery: other prophets will speak in the name of other gods, or presume to speak in the name of the true God a word they have not been commanded to speak. For spreading this false teaching, those false prophets deserve to die, says the Lord. That is how seriously he takes his word; his holy opposition to false prophecy is fatal. You cannot lead God's people astray with impunity. God will see that there are consequences.

We see throughout the Gospels that Jesus taught God's word in the synagogues just as other preachers would. A passage was read from the Law, the Prophets or the Writings, and an exposition would follow. Yet, in another way, Jesus is quite unlike all preachers. He taught as one having authority, we are told in Mark 1, and the people were astounded by it. He was not an indirect mediator of the word, passing on another person's message after consulting others on its interpretation. He confidently proclaimed the God-breathed word in the power of God's Spirit. On this occasion, he opposes not just the scribes who sit in Moses's seat, but the evil, unclean spirits who torment his people. His direct commands carry all the authority of the Holy One of God, and the spirits know they have met their match – the one who has ultimately come to destroy them and their demonic works.

That battle is portrayed in lavish symbolic fashion by Revelation 12, which draws on many other passages in Revelation and throughout the Old Testament. The woman of the sun, moon and stars is the faithful community of God's people (as in Joseph's dream in Genesis 37). The way Revelation describes the woman and her tribulations here does not fit with just one individual; rather, it is symbolic of the difficulties and persecution of God's people in general. They are opposed by the great red dragon, with seven heads like Rome's seven hills, sweeping away the children of God with his sharp and terrible tail, the sting of suffering and death. From this church under pressure comes the Messiah, pictured in verse 5 with an allusion to Psalm 2 (as also in Revelation 2:27). The dragon tries to kill him but even that fails; instead he rises and ascends into heaven to sit on God's throne. We have here the ancient conflict of a serpent with a woman and her seed (see Genesis 3:14–15). Verse 6 shows that after Messiah's ascension, the church will be looked after by God during the war (as in verse 14), which will not last for ever. Ultimate victory and vindication in the battle is guaranteed by the authority of God's word of promise. So cling to Jesus and his word, and you will be on the winning side.

ORDINARY TIME

Proper 1

Sunday between 3 and 9 February inclusive
(if earlier than the Second Sunday before Lent)

Isaiah 40:21–31 · 1 Corinthians 9:16–23 · Mark 1:29–39 ·
Psalm 147:1–11, 20c

Woe to me if I do not preach the gospel!

The theme which unites our readings this week is the priority of preaching the gospel. When there are so many needs in our world, why is this one so important to Isaiah, Jesus and Paul?

In Isaiah, it seems that the people of Israel have lost confidence in God. They need reminding of certain things about who God is. 'Do you not know? Have you not heard?' is repeated (Isaiah 40:21, 28), and Isaiah tries to bring them good news, to remedy their ignorance and forgetfulness. They have forgotten his transcendent power for a start: 'God sits enthroned above the circle of the earth', the prophet reminds them, 'he brings princes to naught and reduces the rulers of this world to nothing'. He is not a mere local deity, or an ineffective and powerless friend. He is incomparable, the strong and mighty Creator, who has made a covenant with them and can never disregard their interests or needs. Isaiah urges the people to trust in him, to hope in him, for he can never let them down. Eric Liddell is heard reading this section of Isaiah in the film *Chariots of Fire*. Because even Olympic athletes get tired sometimes and run out of juice; but God doesn't and never will. He will always be there to renew us and empower us in his service, through the proclamation of the good news about who he is.

In the Gospel reading, we encounter Jesus in the exciting and dramatic early stages of his earthly ministry. No sooner has he left the synagogue where he has driven out an impure spirit, than he is at home with James and John at Simon and Andrew's house. Simon's mother-in-law is unwell with a fever. Imagine if Jesus came to visit you and you couldn't even get out of bed! How frustrating it would be to miss him and not be able to show him hospitality! But it is an easy thing for Jesus to drive out a fever as well. 'Do you not know? Have you not heard? The Lord is the everlasting God, the Creator of the ends of the earth.' This unnamed but noble woman then expresses her gratitude by serving Jesus and his friends with grateful hospitality. She is a picture of all those who are made whole by Jesus to serve him with reinvigorated energy.

But no sooner has dinner been tidied away than all the sick and demon-possessed people of the town turn up at the door! Along with everybody else in Capernaum. Jesus, undaunted, restores them to health too. The hospitals in Capernaum would soon be going out of business. The kingdom of God had really arrived. What great news to hear! Jesus is also up early the next day to pray to his heavenly Father. Did he pray for renewed strength, to soar on wings like an eagle as Isaiah 40 suggested? Whatever he asked for, he was soon disturbed by the clamour of people demanding his help again. But his prayer to the Father reminded him too of the priority of preaching the gospel. 'Let us go somewhere else,' he said to his disciples, 'so that I can preach there also. That is why I have come.' I have not come just to threaten the livelihood of the health profession for a while. I have come to *preach* good news, which will echo down the centuries.

The apostle Paul is also fixated on preaching the gospel in our reading from the epistles. In 1 Corinthians 9 he says he is *compelled* to preach, to those who did know, and to those who had not heard. 'Woe to me if I do not preach the gospel!' he exclaims. He would happily offer it free of charge, unlike the peripatetic philosophers of the day who touted their wares for money all over the place. The worker was worth his wages, as Jesus himself had said (Luke 10:7, which Paul quotes in 1 Timothy 5:18). But Paul would give up all his rights and comforts for the sake of the gospel. He would do what he needed to do, and be who he needed to be (within God's word), to win everyone to Christ and save them.

Are our priorities the same as Isaiah and Jesus and Paul, or are we too attached to our privileges and comforts in this life to be concerned about the benefits and rewards of eternity? Remember those who do not know, and have not heard, and pray for strength to serve them.

Proper 2

Sunday between 10 and 16 February inclusive
(if earlier than the Second Sunday before Lent)

2 Kings 5:1–14 · 1 Corinthians 9:24–27 · Mark 1:40–45 · Psalm 30

Do you not know that in a race all the runners run, but only one gets the prize? Run in such a way as to get the prize.

In the readings this week we hear about people making mistakes in the various ways they respond to God. Perhaps we can learn from them, and not repeat those false steps ourselves?

General Naaman is the commander of an army which has attacked God's people. That was wrong for a start! But God brought good out of this mistake, by making sure one of his captives was a young Israelite girl who knew about the power of God. Naaman is a valiant soldier, but he also has leprosy. This young girl tells Naaman's wife, her mistress, about the prophet Elisha back in Israel. 'If only my master would see the prophet,' she says, 'He would cure him of his leprosy.' But Naaman was a great man, so he did things the way great men do: approaching his king, who gives him a letter for the King of Israel, and then taking silver and gold and other gifts with him, he's off on his mission to get cured. The King of Israel is rightly horrified by the suggestion that *he* could cure Naaman, but needs a prompt before he sends him to Elisha who *could*. Elisha tells Naaman exactly what to do; but it isn't what he expected, and seems a bit beneath him, so off he goes in a rage. Only when he does what he is told does he finally receive the healing he seeks. There are more wrong responses to God's grace later in this chapter too, as rather than rejoicing in what God has done for Naaman, Elisha's servant Gehazi tries to make a fast buck out of it.

In our reading from the Gospel, we see another man take a false step in his response to the Lord's grace. He too has leprosy, like Naaman, but goes straight to the one who can heal him. Both Jews and Gentiles can be saved by Jesus and made ritually clean in him. Jesus is indignant or angry, moved in some way at this point: probably with the leprosy, and the plight of this man rather than his statement that Jesus could heal him if he wanted to. And he heals him immediately (because everything happens 'immediately' in Mark!). Then Jesus tells him very sternly exactly what to do: follow the current Mosaic rules, make the prescribed sacrifice and be signed off by the priest at the Temple. And be quiet about all this. And does he gladly obey the Saviour who healed him? Of course not! He goes straight out and starts blabbing to everyone – which hinders Jesus's ministry because he can't enter a town openly any more, and therefore other people can't be similarly blessed. But it also keeps the priests from seeing with their very own eyes what would have been an eight-day ceremonial testimony to Jesus's power (and his intention not to overturn the Temple and the Law), which would have been a much more useful and powerful thing at this stage in Jesus's ministry. Perhaps, after all, Jesus was angry at the start because he could see that this would happen.

In 1 Corinthians 9, Paul contrasts two ways of serving God, only one of which 'gets the prize' in the end. He takes his illustrations from the world of first-century athletics, from running and boxing competitions. We have to take part according to the rules, he says, and that requires strict training. Serving God takes discipline. Athletes in the ancient Olympics had to turn up ten months before the games for special training and preparation. And they had to swear on oath that they had finished the training according to the rules, otherwise they were disqualified.[5] Don't think you can just turn up and do it your own way. That was Naaman's mistake and the leper's mistake in the Gospel. They didn't want to do what they were told

[5] See William D. Mounce, *Pastoral Epistles* (Nashville: Thomas Nelson, 2000), p. 510.

and follow the rules set down for them because they thought they knew best.

As the early church preacher John Chrysostom put it, 'It is not enough merely to believe and then contend in any which way. Unless we have run our race in such a way as to be blameless and to come near to the prize, it will not benefit us.'[6] How we run (serve God) is important, though many Christians ignore this and think that once they profess Christ's name, that is sufficient, and they can go on to serve him and even contend for his cause in any which way they choose, even using worldly weapons and tactics. So will we learn from others' mistakes?

[6] Gerald Bray (ed.), *1–2 Corinthians*, Ancient Christian Commentary on Scripture (Downers Grove, IL: InterVarsity Press, 1999), p. 88.

Proper 3

Sunday between 17 and 23 February inclusive
(if earlier than the Second Sunday before Lent)

Isaiah 43:18–25 · 2 Corinthians 1:18–22 · Mark 2:1–12 · Psalm 41

Have mercy on me, Lord; heal me, for I have sinned against you.

These passages teach us that we can stand firm and be forgiven only because of the faithfulness of Christ. It's not because of our righteousness (because we don't have any of our own), but because of God's mercy and grace that he heals and restores us.

In 2 Corinthians, we hear that God is faithful. He stands by all his promises to his people. Each promise finds its 'Yes' in Christ, to the glory of God, who makes Paul, Silas, Timothy, the Corinthians *and us* stand firm in our faith. The particular promise of the coming of the Spirit has been fulfilled at Pentecost, and when we believe the gospel we are sealed into Christ by that same Spirit, who is present in our hearts as a foretaste and a guarantee of what is still to come (see also Ephesians 1:13–14). The early church preacher John Chrysostom sums it all up: 'Paul's preaching promised many things. He talked about being raised to life again and of being taken up into heaven. He talked about incorruption and those great rewards which awaited them. These promises abide unchanging … they are always true.'[7]

In Isaiah 43, God promises to forgive the people of Israel and to give them a new start. He speaks to the people of Judah who will be languishing in Babylon, to tell them to forget the past and focus on their future. He provides for all his creatures, even the wild ones in the desert, so he can certainly provide for his wayward people in exile, those whom he chose and formed for himself. Just as God says that

[7] Bray (ed.), *1–2 Corinthians*, p. 202.

he formed Israel 'that they may proclaim my praise', so he also says he will forgive their transgressions 'for my own sake'. He doesn't do it because they are holy or righteous in fulfilling his Law – because they aren't. The only thing they have contributed is their sin: 'You have burdened me with your sins and wearied me with your offences.'

Despite their sin, God will blot out their transgressions and remember their sins no more. This 'blotting out', says the eighteenth-century Baptist commentator John Gill, is an 'allusion to the blotting of a debt-book: sins are debts, and these are many, and which cannot be paid by the sinner; Christ has made full payment; as the surety of his people: upon this the debt-book is crossed; these debts are remitted for his sake.'[8] God hits the delete key on our sins, our debts to him, because Christ has paid up on our behalf.

In Mark's Gospel, Jesus heals a paralytic, showing that he is a God who is able to both heal and forgive. The paralytic is brought to Jesus by his friends, who lower him through the roof of the house where Jesus is teaching. The Lord sees the faith of his friends and he heals him. Jesus then tells the paralytic that his sins are forgiven. The scribes are shocked by this, but Jesus says that although it is easier to say 'your sins are forgiven' than to say 'get up and walk', he can actually do both, with authority and power. The paralytic then literally stands firm. The shock and amazement at this must have been palpable, but note that it says the people who saw it 'praised *God*'. It was indeed God who had healed and forgiven the man.

The Gospel reading ends with the assembled crowd saying, 'we have never seen anything like this!' But God has been in the forgiving business for a very long time. He is even now willing to forgive *us* for our sins and to give *us* a new start. We can trust in his mercy and stand firm in his love. For the glory of his name, he will do it; and, because we are his people, what is for his glory is for our great good.

---

[8] John Gill, *An Exposition of the Old Testament*, vol. 5 of *The Baptist Commentary Series* (London: Mathews and Leigh, 1810), p. 251.

2nd Sunday before Lent

Proverbs 8:1, 22–31 · Colossians 1:15–20 · John 1:1–14 · Psalm 104:24–35

In the beginning was the Word, and the Word was with God, and the Word was God.

The theme of our readings this week is Christ as the pre-existent, eternal Creator and head of both the old and the new creation. Everything in the universe is centred on him (although we often think that the world revolves around us).

John 1 begins the story of Jesus in the way that Genesis began the story of the world. In the beginning, even before God created the heavens and the earth, there was the Word. That Word was with God and was himself God. So we begin to see a complexity in monotheism, which stands behind the narrative of creation. That 'divine Word-with-God' is the agent of creation and the source of all life and light. He spoke and they came into existence. Yet as the opening to John's Gospel progresses, we find the world estranged from its Creator, needing a witness to testify to the light when he became flesh and dwelt among us, because our darkened eyes could not recognise him and our corrupted hearts could not accept him. But – thanks be to God! – in his grace he gives to some the power to become children of God. They are not just his offspring by creation, but by the regenerative will of God, to the praise of his glory and grace.

In Colossians 1, Paul sings the same song as the apostle John. Jesus Christ is the image of the invisible God, making him known. He is the firstborn of creation, not because he is creaturely but because he is pre-eminent. He bears responsibility for the first creation, and not just for those parts of it which we can see, but for things visible and invisible, angelic as well as earthly. Not only did he create them, but they were created *for him*, and he sustains them. But he is also the head of the new creation too, beginning with the Church itself. As firstborn from the dead, the pioneer of our salvation, he leads the way into the resurrection state. And where the head has gone, the body soon will follow. As the great Italian Reformer, Peter Martyr Vermigli (1499–1562) once put it, 'Our head is risen from the depths of death. Even though we may appear to be overwhelmed in the mortal stream, yet we are risen in him. We must either deny that he is our head or acknowledge that we are members of his body – in which case we are compelled to affirm that our resurrection has begun in his.'[9]

By faith, says Paul to the Colossians, we are united with Christ, in whom the fullness of God was pleased to dwell. That means we can participate in the reconciliation he has accomplished through his peace-making death on the cross. Again, we see both old and new creations, with Christ's incarnation, atonement and resurrection in the pivotal centre between them, made necessary by our rejection and alienation.

Proverbs 8 is a more poetic vision of the same truths. Much has been written about the verb in verse 22: did the Lord *create* the wisdom personified in this poem, or did he *possess* it, or give birth to it, or something else? A group known as the Arians (followers of the heretic Arius) in the early church, denied that Jesus was God, and thought here that wisdom/Christ was an ancient creature, brought into existence by God at a particular point in time. There was a time 'when Christ was not', they claimed, though he was very important still in their scheme of things. The orthodox preferred to understand Proverbs as in harmony with John and Paul, which it is. In the beginning, Christ the wisdom of God was with God, and was God. He was the beginning of creation, that is, appointed as its head, and the head of the new creation too. Certainly the rest of the passage focuses on wisdom as ever-present with God in that mighty work, rejoicing with him and delighting in his people. And, wonderfully, verse 30 reminds us that God delights in Christ himself. Let that be our application too, to delight in Christ who is far more wonderful than we could ever imagine.

---

9 See Apostles' Creed, in J. C. McLelland (ed.), *Early Writings: Creed, Scripture, Church*, Peter Martyr Library (Kirksville, MO: Sixteenth Century Journal Publishing/Truman State University Press, 1994), pp. 47–8.

Sunday next before Lent (Transfiguration Sunday)

2 Kings 2:1–12 · 2 Corinthians 4:3–6 · Mark 9:2–9 · Psalm 50:1–6

This is my Son, whom I love. Listen to him!

The application of our three readings this week is that we must listen to the word of the glorious Son of God from heaven and not cling on to the things of this world.

In 2 Kings 2 we see the overlap of two powerful prophetic ministries, as Elijah and Elisha prepare for the former to be taken up to heaven. They travel together through places redolent of Israel's history: Gilgal, where they celebrated Passover after crossing the Jordan for the first time; Jericho, where the conquest of the Promised Land began; and Bethel, where Jacob saw the gate of heaven. Elisha is reluctant to see his master go, but the time for him to take over, as Joshua took over from Moses, draws near. Elijah crosses to the eastern side of the Jordan, to end his ministry in the same area as did Moses, and under similarly extraordinary circumstances. As Elijah ascends into heavenly glory, Elisha receives from his 'father' the 'double-portion' inheritance of a firstborn son: his prophetic word will now direct and protect the people. Since Elijah did not die in the normal way, the Old Testament ends with an expectation that one day he would return to earth again (Malachi 4:5–6).

Elijah appears again with Moses himself on the Mount of Transfiguration in Mark 9. Jesus, the true Son of the Father, is revealed in all his glory. The gate of heaven is once again opened, it seems, for mere mortals to gaze in; and just as Jacob wanted to mark the spot at Bethel (Genesis 28:16-19), so Peter in awestruck wonder wants to do the same. Having confessed that Jesus is the Christ, he now receives a glimpse of what that means, though it will take him a while to grasp that there is a cross on the way to the crown. Jesus will repeat that point to him several times in the coming chapters, and the voice of the Father from heaven demands that Peter and the other disciples listen to the beloved Son.

In 2 Corinthians 4, Paul also dwells on the glory of Christ in a context where the church was tempted to forget about or downplay his sufferings. It was bad PR in a place like Corinth to focus on the gory at the expense of the glory, but the gospel is a message about a crucified Messiah. Many Corinthians could not see the relevance or use of such a thing, and yet it was that incarnate image of God, the Messiah Jesus who revealed to us the face of God. The unbelieving world around them, says Paul, could not grasp the gospel because their eyes were veiled and their minds blinded by 'the god of this world'. This could be a reference to the devil, who lays claim to the kingdoms of this fallen world. Or it could refer to the idea that some people worship 'the now' and have a 'this-worldly' contempt for the things of another world (they worship the 'god' which is this world).

Just as Jesus served us by dying in our place, so we serve others for his sake, proclaiming his word. It will not always be accepted or acceptable to the worldly who are perishing with darkened hearts and minds. Yet only through that creative, light-bringing word of the gospel can we truly enter the gates of heaven and see the glory of God.

LENT

1st Sunday of Lent

Genesis 9:8–17 · 1 Peter 3:18–22 · Mark 1:9–15 · Psalm 25:1–10

For Christ also suffered once for sins, the righteous for the unrighteous, to bring you to God.

At the start of Lent, our readings remind us that salvation comes through suffering. This means more than the 'suffering' of giving up chocolate or crisps for a few weeks, of course, which some people do during Lent!

Jesus begins his public ministry in the reading from the Gospel by coming from Galilee to be baptised in the Jordan. He willingly identified with sinners and fulfilled all righteousness under the Law. He came up out of the water (implying, of course, an immersive experience here, whatever we might conjecture about other baptisms in the New Testament), to see heaven and earth meet in one astonishing moment of clarity. The heavens are 'torn apart' and the Spirit descends like a dove upon him. The voice of the Father thunders from heaven that this is his beloved Son. The Trinity is united in joy and delight around the person of the incarnate Son. The fact that all three persons of the Trinity appear here together counters any suggestion of 'modalism', the idea that God first appeared as Father, then as Son, and then as Spirit, in three successive modes. God is and always was a Trinity: as it was in the beginning, is now, and ever shall be.

It pleased the Spirit then to immediately thrust the God-man into the wilderness, where he would in a sense recapitulate the history of God's people in their desert wanderings. For forty days he is tempted as the nation once was for forty years. Mark does not give us the same detail as the other Gospel accounts. He merely tells us that Jesus was tempted by Satan, was with the wild beasts and had angels waiting upon him. It is a scene of furious and very real spiritual warfare. Jesus emerges, after the arrest of John the Baptist, to begin his public preaching ministry, tested and tried but ready for royal action. The time has now come: repent and believe the good news of the coming kingdom!

That kingdom would only come through the death and resurrection of the King, as the apostle Peter finally discovers. In his letter to the embattled Christians of Asia Minor, he rejoices in the suffering of the righteous King for our sins, accomplished once and for all, definitively, in place of unrighteous sinners. This, he says, has brought us to God. At the end of the chapter he reminds us also of the resurrection, ascension and heavenly power of the Lord Jesus, 'with angels, authorities, and powers made subject to him'. The way to glory lay through ill-report, contempt, and loss: as it was for Jesus, so also will it be for us. That is the main thrust of the complex and difficult paragraph in 1 Peter 3.

Baptised into his death and resurrection, we are assured that our final destination is as secure as the King's. The mention of baptism gives Peter the opportunity to inform us that baptism was prefigured in the cleansing salvation through water of Noah and his family. Every living thing on earth died, except those who were graciously contained in the ark as God promised. They suffered, but emerged safe. Suffering is not a waste, but a necessary path to glory. It was thus for Jesus and will also be for us.

Genesis 9 is the primeval story of God's covenant with Noah as he came out of the ark. He re-establishes the covenant of creation, in language reminiscent of Genesis 1–2, and promises that he will never again open the floodgates of heaven to destroy this earth. I remember as a child learning the colours of the rainbow using the mnemonic 'Roy G. Biv', or (to do double-duty in both history and physics) 'Richard Of York Gave Battle In Vain'. But this beautiful phenomenon of refracted light is itself a memory aid. It is a physical sign to remind us of God's historical promise. Every time we see the giant archer's bow aimed upwards at God, we are assured that he keeps his covenant promises, on pain of death. He will be reminded constantly to do so. That is why it is a sign designed to bring us such delight. The pleasure our eyes feel at seeing the colourful arch of the covenant is like the solid joy of our souls delighting in his steadfastness. He rescues and saves not apart from but *through* judgment and suffering. So if we are suffering now, it is safe to trust him still.

2nd Sunday of Lent

Genesis 17:1–7, 15–16 · Romans 4:13–25 · Mark 8:31–38 · Psalm 22:23–31

Get behind me, Satan! ... You do not have in mind the concerns of God, but merely human concerns.

One of the key things in our readings this week is the idea of correcting those who go astray and err in matters of faith. This is a 'primary' – life and death – issue. The Church of England's Collect (set prayer) for today pleads with God to 'show to those who are in error the light of your truth, that they may return to the way of righteousness'.

Jesus had to have words with the apostle Peter himself on this score. Jesus taught publicly and openly that his path to glory was through suffering, rejection, death and resurrection. Yet Peter thought he should correct the Lord on this and rebuke him for such defeatism and negativity. 'Don't you know that the Messiah comes in power and glory, Jesus? Don't distance yourself from the movers-and-shakers of the religious establishment so quickly! There's a better way for us to win the day.' A puny creature puts the Creator straight.

Yet ever so kindly, out of his great love for Peter, the Lord Jesus censured his satanic strategy for a cross-less path to glory. The very earthy Rock was setting his mind on the things of this world rather than learning to accept God's ways and means. Peter's private impudence, motivated by fear and shame, would be subject to a humiliating public admonition. Only those who are willing to follow Jesus by turning their backs on what seems to be for their own advantage, to take up his way of ignominious weakness, will be saved. Only they shall be recognised and embraced on the Last Day, and not deservedly cast aside with an adulterous and sinful generation, says Jesus.

Paul is also in a corrective mood in Romans 4. It is a telltale sign whenever he starts to tell us how something did *not* happen, and traces through the implications of an alternative position, saying it is 'null and void'. The big idea is that law and works are the opposite of faith and promise, which Paul feels he must be clear on because presumably it is being denied by someone somewhere, either implicitly or explicitly. As the sixteenth-century theologian John Calvin says in his commentary, if salvation depended on the keeping of the Law then 'consciences would have no certainty, but would be harassed with perpetual inquietude, and at length sink into despair'.[10] No one wants 'perpetual inquietude' or despair! It is always good to remind ourselves that the personal, spiritual consequences of so-called 'abstract' theological error can be very serious indeed. We must continue to look for our 'justification' not from works of any kind, but by trusting in the one who was delivered over to the wrath of the Law for our sins, and was raised to life again for us.

Abram and Sarai have their names 'corrected' in the reading from Genesis 17. As Abram trusted in God's astonishing promise, his faith was reckoned as righteousness, so 'as good as dead' Abram became Abraham, the father of many. And this, not via the satanic, human method of circumventing God's path (Genesis 16:1–2), but just as God had said, through Sarah, the 'princess'. Both Sarah and Abraham laughed at the news and seemed to doubt; though Romans 4 assures us that Abraham was unwavering in his faith. However we reconcile Paul and Genesis, it's clear that Abraham believed what God said about life from the dead, because he followed the sharply painful path of immediate and unquestioning obedience, regardless of intimate personal discomfort.

So may we all pray, with the Church of England's Collect for today: 'Grant to all those who are admitted into the fellowship of Christ's religion, that they may reject those things that are contrary to their profession, and follow all such things as are agreeable to the same.'

---

[10] John Calvin, *Commentary on the Epistle of Paul the Apostle to the Romans* (Bellingham, WA: Logos Bible Software, 2010), p. 170.

3rd Sunday of Lent

Exodus 20:1–17 · 1 Corinthians 1:18–25 · John 2:13–22 · Psalm 19

The foolishness of God is wiser than human wisdom, and the weakness of God is stronger than human strength.

Our readings this week remind us that God's ways are not our ways, nor his thoughts our thoughts. We have to change our thoughts and our attitudes to be more like his. But how difficult that is!

What would Jesus do? WWJD? People often ask this question, thinking it might provide guidance in a particular situation. As one born under the Law, a perfectly obedient Son, he would of course always do what pleased his Father. His life was therefore in harmony at all times with the Ten Commandments, brought to us for the first time in Scripture in Exodus 20. Few can recite these Commandments any more (in any order), but they reveal to us the basic answer to WWJD.

It is customary to divide the Commandments into two: those which speak of how to love and honour God and those which flesh out how to love our neighbours as ourselves. These are prefaced by a covenant declaration: the Commandments come from the God who has saved us and called us his own. That is why we serve him and not another; why we worship him as he thinks best and not as idolatrous humans might naturally prefer; why we hallow his sacred name; why we remember the Sabbath he set aside. He saved us from slavery to sin that we might be a people who reflect his own glory, which is why we honour the institutions he designed for our flourishing in a rightly ordered family life and a contented, truthful engagement in community relationships. Lives lived thus are appropriate for a kingdom of priests, a royal nation. And also for the King himself. But the Law does not describe the natural inclination of the fallen human heart, which everywhere inverts it. We, like the

Wicked Bible (a sixteenth-century typographic curiosity), by nature prefer to omit the word 'not' from the Commandments.

Our Gospel reading shows us how easily we turn the goodness of God into an opportunity for personal gain. The institution of the Temple was God's gracious way of indicating his presence among his people, enabling them to approach and worship him, enjoying the revelation of his character and purposes. Instead, the church of Jesus's day had turned it into a straightforward money-spinner. They traded on the pious longings of God's people and were gripped by the consumerist impulse to take advantage of market forces. WWJD? Well, a whip of cords and overturned tables was the answer. Not because he submitted to an impatient iconoclastic urge (as we are sometimes tempted to when things don't go our way), but because he was consumed by zeal for God's holy Temple, as the Scriptures prophesied (Psalms 69:9, 119:139). Purity must always surround the place where God dwells – the Temple, the Messiah, his people.

The Temple traders certainly weren't expecting that. They thought they would be approved by God as 'purveyors of Temple merchandise by appointment of the King'. Yet the King was not pleased, because he doesn't think as we do. Their great expectations were for something altogether earthly and visceral. His kingdom is not of this world. Power and glory would be his, but through emptiness and ignominy and agony.

This was foolishness in the extreme to the Corinthian mindset, that may have been thrilled by Jesus's powerful oratory and carried away by his impressive zeal but would baulk at the cruciform path that he laid out for himself and his disciples. Jews demand signs and Greeks demand wisdom, says Paul. WWJD? He died, decidedly and deliberately. This was not the Corinthian strategy for advancement, as 1 Corinthians makes clear. They considered it dubious and perverse, but God tips us upside down and shakes our proud imaginations. His thoughts and ways are not like ours. The only hope for a crooked and depraved generation, like ours, is to re-orientate our thoughts to be more like his.

4th Sunday of Lent

Numbers 21:4–9 · Ephesians 2:1–10 · John 3:14–21 ·
Psalm 107:1–3, 17–22

For it is by grace you have been saved, through faith – and this is not from yourselves, it is the gift of God.

Our readings this week remind us that salvation is a gracious gift from God, which we do not deserve and cannot earn. It does not leave us to continue walking in the ways of the world.

The clear link between the Old Testament and Gospel readings is provided in John 3:14. It is not immediately apparent if Jesus's explanation to Nicodemus breaks into editorial comment somewhere around here or not, but certainly a link is created between the work of Christ and a brief incident in the desert wanderings of the Exodus generation. The bronze serpent was lifted up in the wilderness so that any Israelite bitten by a poisonous serpent could look at it and live. There is no direct therapeutic connection, that we know of, by which looking at bronze can cure a snake bite! Yet if God wills it to be a means of grace for his impatient people, it is so. Their grumbling against God and against Moses, as if the redemption achieved for them was pointless and paltry in its provision, receives a due retribution. This is part of God's bigger plan to deny entry to the Promised Land for the generation who have rebelled against him; yet his grace to the people continues even in the midst of judgment, in response to the prayers of their covenant mediator. Despite discipline, however, murmuring distrust will continue.

In the same way, despite it being unworthy and sinful and blind to the goodness of God (like Nicodemus was), God so loved the God-hating world that he gave his only Son to be lifted up outside a city wall. Whoever looks to the Son, believing in him, will not perish but have eternal life. Those who believe are not condemned, but those who don't … not only will they perish, but they are condemned already, even in advance of the sentence on Judgment Day. The serpent's poison is left to do its work on those who will not look to the light but prefer the darkness of secretly angry ingratitude. Their deeds are evil, the passage says; but on the other hand, any good deeds of those who look to Jesus 'have been done in God' – God's work in them is evident.

The same emphasis on a gracious salvation from darkness is clear in Ephesians 2:1–10, a much-loved passage. Despite the fact that we were dead in sin and therefore spiritually impotent; despite the fact that we were voluntary slaves to the world, the flesh and the devil; despite the fact that like everyone else we were by nature fully deserving of God's wrath and indignation against us, God's merciful love stepped in. As the eighteenth-century hymnwriter Charles Wesley wrote, in one of the unsung verses of his hymn, 'And can it be?', 'Still the atoning blood is near, that quenched the wrath of hostile heaven.'

What God did for Jesus the head in Ephesians chapter 1 – raising him from death and seating him at the right hand of the Father – God does for the body, those who are united to him by faith. We are made alive in him, raised up and seated with him – to the praise of his glorious grace and to demonstrate to the universe the immeasurable kindness of God. Yet, as always, the grace that saves us also leads us, into a new life of obedience for which we were created. As Wesley again so eloquently sings, 'No condemnation now I dread! Jesus and all in him is mine. Alive in him, my living head, and clothed in righteousness divine.'

5th Sunday of Lent

Jeremiah 31:31–34 · Hebrews 5:5–10 · John 12:20–33 · Psalm 51:1–12

Jesus became the source of eternal salvation for all who obey him.

Our focus this week is on the depth of eternal salvation which Christ our great high priest gloriously achieved on the cross for us. Yet he achieved this joy for us through his own grief and suffering.

Jeremiah prophesied a new covenant between God and his people. The Sinai covenant was smashed to pieces by the disobedience of the people, their spiritual adultery even, against God their 'husband'. The Babylonian exile which the prophet speaks about throughout the book is a clear sign that the covenant curses have fallen upon Israel. Even within the Mosaic Law, however, there are signs that God knew this would happen and had planned a way for Israel to be restored and saved.

The other prophets also spoke of a new and eternal covenant by which God would transform and redeem his people, and Jeremiah outlines some of the benefits of that fresh compact: he would write the Law on their hearts, not just on tablets of stone; he would expand the knowledge of God so that even the very least in the new kingdom would truly know the Lord; and most importantly, he would forgive and forget their sin, wiping it out.

Yet this was no easy task. According to our reading from Hebrews, it involved the appointment of a new high priest, in the order not of Aaron (like the Old Testament priests) but of Melchizedek. And for the new arrangement to stick, the new high priest would need to stick around. If sins are to be forgotten for ever, then the priest must also similarly endure in glory. To prepare and equip such a great high priest, there would be suffering, tears, and death as he stood in the place of his condemned and sinful people. 'And having been made perfect,' says Hebrews, 'he became the source of eternal salvation for all who obey him.' Now, looking to Jesus and following him, we have eternal and complete salvation in our eternal and complete high priest – whose own blood sealed the new covenant for his people. As Hebrews makes clear elsewhere (e.g. 7:24), in the words of St Athanasius (296–373), Christ 'has a priesthood that does not go by succession to others'.[11] We have and need only one such Melchizedekian priest, because he lives for ever, incorruptible and unchanging – utterly sufficient for all our needs.

We glimpse some of his suffering on this earth in the Gospel reading from John 12. Jesus knew that once the Greeks started to ask for him, his hour was almost upon him; the time for him to die, in order to be glorified and draw all people to himself. The depth of his sorrow becomes more and more evident, yet he says here, with a troubled soul, 'What should I say? Save me? No.' He knows what he had to undergo, for the glory of the Father. He will be lifted up for us and for our salvation, to usher in a new world. As the seventeenth-century pastor and poet, George Herbert has Jesus say in 'The Sacrifice':

> Lo, here I hang, charged with a world of sin,
> The greater world o' the two; for that came in
> By words, but this by sorrow I must win:
> *Was ever grief like mine?*
>
> Such sorrow, as if sinful man could feel,
> Or feel his part, he would not cease to kneel,
> Till all were melted, though he were all steel.
> *Was ever grief like mine?*[12]

By his suffering, by his blood of the new covenant, what Jeremiah prophesied changes from promise to eternally secure reality.

---

[11] Athanasius, *Discourses against the Arians*, 2:9. NPNF^2 4:353.

[12] Slater (ed.), *George Herbert*, p. 30.

Palm Sunday

Isaiah 50:4–9a · Philippians 2:5–11 · Mark 14:1–15:47 · Psalm 31:9–16

Being found in appearance as a man, he humbled himself by becoming obedient to death – even death on a cross!

The readings this week focus on the passion of Christ, who gave himself up to an ignominious death for us and for our salvation, but was honoured and vindicated by his Father.

Isaiah 50 is a song of the Messiah, meditating on the things which God has given him. He has been given the tongue of a teacher, to delight those who are weary with falsehood, lies and law. He has given him an open ear, to hear God's word. In return, the Messiah gives his back to those who struck him, and gives himself up to shame, suffering, and spitting. Because of this faithful obedience to his will, the Lord God vindicates his servant. He cannot be disgraced for ever, or be finally defeated by his adversaries. No one can call 'guilty' the one that God has cleared.

Philippians 2 tells the same story. The innocent Christ is obedient to death, even death on a cross – 'the utterly vile death of the cross' as they called it, which couldn't be mentioned in polite conversation without a twinge of disgust. God himself gives up his high position and humbles himself. Not only does he take human form and flesh, with its limitations and liabilities, he follows the path of emptiness for the sake of others (which is what Paul is encouraging the Philippians to do as well). Because of his faithful obedience to his will, God highly exalts Jesus. The work of the covenant of redemption being completed, the Father rewards the Son with the position he deserves. In Isaiah 45:23, the Lord swore that every knee would bow to *him* and every tongue swear allegiance; in Philippians 2, Paul places Jesus in that place of divine honour and prestige, so that at *his* name everything in heaven and on earth will bow, and every tongue confess that he is Lord.

The long Gospel reading is the narrative on which the poetic reflections of Isaiah and Paul are founded. Mark 14 begins with a plot to kill Jesus and his proleptic anointing for burial. Judas agrees to betray the Master and give him up to the authorities. He is given his reward. Meanwhile, Jesus teaches his disciples about what he is going to do as the Lamb of God who takes away the sin of the world (John 1:29), as he gives them bread and wine. He suffers the shame and pain of Gethsemane, Sanhedrin, denial, mocking and cruel crucifixion. Mark 15 ends with the seemingly decisive stone rolled over the grave where he is laid.

Palm Sunday would not be complete without remembering the bitter irony of Samuel Crossman's poignant seventeenth-century hymn, 'My song is love unknown', which is often sung this week. Though the crowd which sang Jesus's praises was composed of different people to the one which bayed for his blood, the contrast of fickle human responses to the self-giving of the King is startling and sobering:

> Sometimes they strew His way,
> And His sweet praises sing;
> Resounding all the day
> Hosannas to their King:
> Then 'Crucify!'
> is all their breath,
> And for His death
> they thirst and cry.

Yet he gave himself up for us. As Crossman (an appropriate name!) concluded, 'What may I say? Heav'n was his home; But mine the tomb, Wherein he lay.' He took my place to give me his.

EASTER

Easter Day

Isaiah 25:6–9 · 1 Corinthians 15:1–11 · Mark 16:1–8 ·
Psalm 118:1–2, 14–24

The Lord's right hand has done mighty things!

The readings this Easter week naturally focus on the good news of the glorious resurrection of the Lord Jesus Christ. If this is not true, then our faith is futile.

Mark's Gospel ends, too abruptly for some, with the empty tomb of Jesus and an angelic proclamation. The three women approach the tomb in order to anoint the dead body of their beloved Master after the sun has risen. They find the Son has risen too (it's a different verb to the one in verse 6, but who could resist the wordplay and the parallel, especially given Malachi 4:2 which is often applied to Christ, 'risen with healing in his wings'). The weakness of the women is highlighted: even three of them are not strong enough to roll the stone away, and they end the scene running away in terror, not sharing the news they have been explicitly told by a young man (an angel?) to share with Jesus's disciples. They have not yet seen Jesus, but they will. The astonishing truth of what has happened begins to creep slowly into their consciousness; and as it does, their confidence will grow.

By the time Paul wrote 1 Corinthians 15, the message of the bodily, physical resurrection of Jesus was a matter of 'first importance' for the early Christian community. It was at the heart of the gospel which they received, passed on and firmly believed – the good news which saves. Christ has died, but he has also risen, and both 'in accordance with the scriptures'. This was the culmination of biblical prophecies and patterns; it was not a last-minute thought, but something God had planned and prepared and left hints of in Scripture for thousands of years – from the anticipated resurrection of the slaughtered firstborn (Genesis 22:5/Hebrews 11:19) to the songs of the Davidic king not abandoned for ever to the corruption of the grave (Psalm 16) and the Suffering Servant crushed to death by the Lord but confident of prolonging his days in satisfying light (Isaiah 53:10–11).

Paul reminds the Corinthians that they can depend on the apostolic testimony of Peter and the other apostles, and even him – 'the least of the apostles' – for the veracity of this claim. He mentions five hundred brothers, many still alive, who also saw the Lord, so there was an abundant witness to the fact of the resurrection if anyone needed further convincing. It happened. It was true. They could count on it.

Isaiah's 'little apocalypse' helps to explain the significance of the resurrection. It was not simply the resuscitation of a single, albeit important, individual. It was the beginning of the end for death itself. The Lord had planned a party, the most lavish and spectacular event 'for all peoples', an extravaganza of delights. But first, the veil that rested on all nations, the noxious suffocating shroud that had covered the earth since the Fall, would be removed and he would swallow up death for ever. It would never be allowed to return, and tears would be wiped away along with the sinful disgrace of his people. Christ died for our sins according to this scripture, and rose again in accordance with it. So we can sing Isaiah 25:9, 'This is our God … let us be glad and rejoice in his salvation.' Sometimes poetry says it best. So as the poet-pastor George Herbert (1593–1633) puts it:

> Awake, sad heart, whom sorrow ever drowns;
> Take up thine eyes, which feed on earth;
> Unfold thy forehead gather'd into frowns:
> Thy Saviour comes, and with him mirth.[13]

---

[13] Slater (ed.), *George Herbert*, p. 108.

2nd Sunday of Easter

Acts 4:32–35 · 1 John 1:2–2:2 · John 20:19–31 · Psalm 133

With great power the apostles continued to testify to the resurrection of the Lord Jesus.

The big message of our readings this week after Easter is that the apostolic testimony about the resurrection of the Lord Jesus Christ creates a grace-filled, joyous fellowship of forgiven sinners who have peace with God.

John's account of Jesus's post-Easter appearances to his disciples bears all the hallmarks of eyewitness testimony. Their fear is turned to joy as Jesus comes among them, demonstrating the truth of his physical resurrection. Several times the Lord declares 'peace be with you', and sends them out to declare that same peace to others. Thomas does not believe at first, but soon pronounces Jesus to be both Lord and God. Those who believe in the Messiah through Thomas's testimony and that of the other apostles, without even seeing the evidence for themselves, will be blessed with peace and life. That is the very purpose of John's Gospel itself (John 20:30–31).

In Acts we hear that the post-resurrection Christian community was of one heart and soul and shared everything they had. But it can be a problem working out what is normative and what is descriptive in Acts. It is notoriously tricky deriving ethics or tips for sanctification from narrative (genocide, rape, polygamy and various other things are *described* in the Bible without being *prescribed*!). This vignette of the early church seems entirely positive, of course, and the ideal setting for the apostolic testimony to the resurrection of the Lord Jesus. Great grace was upon them all and, in a foretaste of the kingdom to come, no one was in dire need.

We ought to be wary of claiming biblical sanction for Communism from this passage, however, or the abolition of the private ownership of goods. Falsely boasting that someone else's riches really belong to you (or the Church, or the State), seems to be a recipe for eventual tyranny and injustice, almost as evil as illiberal meanness.

One thing we certainly do have private ownership of is our sin. As our reading from 1 John reminds us, if we say we have no sin, we deceive ourselves. I always feel the urge to add the word 'only' to that sentence: we deceive *only* ourselves – nobody else is fooled! And yet the glorious truth is that as Christians we have an advocate with the Father who truly is righteous. He can cleanse us from our sins because he himself was the propitiation for them, turning away God's wrath and indignation against us and bringing us peace.

Because of that sacrifice in our place (both for our original guilt and our actual sins), we can now walk in the light, as he is in the light, having fellowship both with God and with one another. We participate in this fellowship through believing in the testimony of the apostles who saw and heard and touched the one who was the way, the truth and the life (John 14:6). Their message creates and nurtures faith and makes our joy complete. Has it had an impact on *your* life?

3rd Sunday of Easter

Acts 3:12–19 · 1 John 3:1–7 · Luke 24:36b–48 · Psalm 4

Repent, then, and turn to God, so that your sins may be wiped out, that times of refreshing may come from the Lord.

Our readings this week contain a curious mixture of boldness and doubt. In the Gospel reading, Jesus is confident in the fulfilment of Scripture, but the disciples are frightened and disbelieving; in Acts, the disciples are now courageous, but their hearers are gobsmacked and mistaken; and in the Epistle, God's children can be audaciously pure but the world looks on with incomprehension.

The Lord appears to his disciples in Luke 24, in the midst of a conversation they are having about him, to bring them peace. Still uncertain about the initial reports of his resurrection, they are startled and terrified, believing at first that he must be a ghostly apparition and not a solidly physical resurrection body. He seeks to calm their fears and doubts with evidence – 'touch me … watch me eat!' – which causes exhilarating joy to rise in their hearts, though not yet with unfettered exuberance. Only as the fog clears and their minds are opened to understand the Scriptures do they grasp the significance of what they are witnessing.

In Acts, those same disciples set about the task that Jesus laid out before them that day. They are to be his witnesses, and proclaim his name to all the nations, beginning in Jerusalem. That start in the capital is surprising and confusing to the people there. But Peter seeks to calm their astonishment and focus their minds. Rather than staring at him and John as if they have healed the lame beggar by the Beautiful Gate through their own power or piety, he directs their attention to the Author of Life. Their bewilderment turns to faith and assurance as Peter unfolds the plan of God that Jesus has unveiled. The God of the Scriptures, the God of the promise, foretold the recent events of that gloomy Passover – how the Messiah would suffer and be killed. They must respond in repentance and faith in the now living Christ, or face his judgment as Moses had foreseen. Acts 4:4 tells us many of them did just that, with the number of those whose sins were wiped out growing to five thousand men.

As Acts 4 also begins to show, many would not recognise what had happened or believe the testimony of the apostles to the resurrection. The Father's lavish love makes us children of God. Yet the world does not know us as such. It did not know God when he stood right in front of them. Even when he fulfilled the greatest prophecies of Scripture by dying for us before their very eyes, he was not acknowledged. When our eyes are opened, the truth is revealed. And one day, every eye will see him, and see *us* as we truly are to God.

The application of this glorious hope is plain and clear in John's letter. 'All who have this hope in him, purify themselves just as he is pure.' He was revealed to take away sin, and in him there was no sin. So how can we go on clinging to the very weights which relentlessly pressed his shoulders towards the depths of the grave? John, who saw the lame beggar walk, warns us that some will try to deceive us on this score. But the one who does what is right is righteous, not the one who claims to be a child of God but has not yet glimpsed the beauty of holiness. They will walk in the light, not wallow in sin and call it good. Let us be warned, and not doubt.

4th Sunday of Easter

Acts 4:5–12 · 1 John 3:16–24 · John 10:11–18 · Psalm 23

This is how we know what love is: Jesus Christ laid down his life for us.

Our readings this week rivet our attention on the voluntary self-giving of Christ for his people, which marks out a unique way for all of us to follow in building and pastoring the church.

In John 10, 'the great shepherd of the sheep' (Hebrews 13:20), defines his role as the Good Shepherd. He is not a mercenary, taking the pay (or the glory, or the stipend, or the vicarage and pension) without caring enough to give his life. He knows the sheep deeply and profoundly, and so lays down his life for each of them by name. Speaking to Jews, he tells them there are other sheep who belong to him in other folds, and that his plan is to build a united church. He will unite Gentiles to Jews in one fold, in him: one flock, one shepherd. This will happen as his voice is heard, because wherever they are, his sheep know his voice and will hearken to it as a sound they know and trust. That voice will ring out once he has both laid down his life and taken it up again, he says – emphasising his sovereign control over the whole process.

In Acts 4, we have one of the clearest statements of Christ's uniqueness in the New Testament. There is salvation in no one else, says Peter, filled with the Holy Spirit. There is no other name under heaven by which we can be saved, but Jesus. He is the only way, the one true Shepherd. And yet, this is said in a context where the very people being addressed had been responsible just a little while beforehand for the crucifixion of the God-man, the way, the truth, the life. He was indeed the cornerstone of God's plan of redemption, and yet they had rejected him as worthless, good for nothing. So Peter challenges them with these uncomfortable truths, and questions the way they wish to build the church. Christ did not lay down his life for them to lay down another cornerstone. He did not lay down his life needlessly, because there was no other way by which men and women could be saved.

In 1 John 3, the wicked rejection and power-grabbing cruelty of the crucifixion is presented not as an act of foolish men, but as a sovereign act of divine grace. Jesus laid down his life. He did not lose it in an unfortunate accident, or by chance, or by plot, but by divine design. He gave up his life willingly and voluntarily. And that selfless moment at the end of a selfless life provides the model for believers to follow. Jesus has left us a template to follow, a stencil, and it is cross-shaped.

But John does not leave that idea floating in the air like an abstract theological axiom. He applies it very directly. If the cross shows us what love is, and you claim God's love abides in you, then how can you refuse to help a brother or sister in need? For Christ did not ignore or neglect our need, or love in words and empty 'political' promises. He loved us in truth and action, as we must please God in the power of the Spirit by loving others in the flock and family of God too. If they obey his commandments, they abide in him; and if they abide in him, we cannot be deaf, dumb or blind but come to their aid in time of need.

5th Sunday of Easter

Acts 8:26–40 · 1 John 4:7–21 · John 15:1–8 · Psalm 22:25–31

Apart from me you can do nothing.

The readings this week reveal to us the infinite care that God has for his church, and they urge us to cheerful submission to his paternal love.

In the last of his great 'I am' sayings in John's Gospel, Jesus tells us that he is the true vine. The Father is the gardener, who lavishes his care upon the vine, that he may be glorified by its fruitfulness. For that to happen, unfruitful branches (such as Judas) must be removed, but others are pruned so they may bear more fruit. That pruning takes place by means of Jesus's cleansing and sustaining word, and the disciples are urged to pay attention to it that they may abide in Christ. There is also a warning that those who do not abide in prayerful, fruitful listening will, like a branch that has lost vital connection to the vine, be cut off, wither and die.

1 John 4 continues the theme of the Father's love for his people. Since he himself *is* love, they must also be characterised by love. His love, says John, was revealed among us by the sending of his Son to be the propitiation for our sins. Paradoxically, it seems, his love is most revealed as his wrath is averted: as Scottish theologian James Denney (1856–1917) once put it, 'So far from finding any kind of contrast between love and propitiation, the apostle can convey no idea of love to anyone except by pointing to the propitiation.'[14] The 'boldness on the day of judgment' that John speaks

---

[14] James Denney, *The Death of Christ* (London: Hodder and Stoughton, 1894), p. 152.

of (1 John 4:17) can only be ours if there is no punishment for us to fear on that day.

John also expounds the Father's love for the Church by telling us of the assuring presence of the Spirit. 'By this we know that we abide in him and he in us,' he declares, 'because he has given us of his Spirit' (1 John 4:13). John's scriptural testimony is designed to give us not only a spur to love one another as God has loved us, but also both assurance and joy.

'Whoever lives in love lives in God, and God in them' (verse 16) does not mean it doesn't matter who or what you love. This passage is talking about brotherly love in the church, for example, not romantic or erotic love. The rest of 1 John itself has much to say about what we love and desire. For example, 1 John 2:15–17 tells us not to love the world or things in it such as 'the lust of the flesh, the lust of the eyes, and the pride of life'. In 1 John, our loves are meant to conform to God's loves. If our loves, lusts and desires go against his will, we do not live in God and he in us, and we will not live for ever. 'The one who keeps God's commands lives in him, and he in them,' says 1 John 3:24. He loves us and so his commands are caring.

God's care for the Church is also illustrated in the reading from Acts. The revelation of God's love in the sacrificial death of the Suffering Servant is the grand theme of the book of Isaiah, from which an Ethiopian eunuch was reading one day. And through the compassion of God this barren foreigner is brought into contact with the revelation of his world-embracing purpose. Yet he doesn't understand it! So God graciously provides him with a means of grace, a teacher to expound the puzzling good news and to initiate him into the new covenant by baptism.

The Puritan divine John Owen (1616–83), put it beautifully when he reflected on both John 15 and 1 John 4. 'It was out of infinite love, mercy, and compassion, that God would at all reveal his mind and will unto sinners. He might for ever have locked up the treasures of his wisdom and prudence, wherein he abounds towards us in his word, in his own eternal breast,' he wrote. 'But it was from infinite love that he made this condescension, to reveal himself and his will unto us.' And what does Owen think our proper response to this divine condescension ought to be? 'This mixture of authority and love, which is the spring of the revelation of the will of God unto us, requires all readiness, willingness, and cheerfulness, in the receipt of it and submission unto it.'[15]

So let us, this week and always, cheerfully submit in the power of the Spirit, to the loving commands of God in Christ.

[15] W. H. Goold (ed.), *The Works of John Owen* (Edinburgh: Johnstone and Hunter, 1854), 20:37–38 (on Hebrews 1:1–2).

6th Sunday of Easter

Acts 10:44–48 · 1 John 5:1–6 · John 15:9–17 · Psalm 98

You are my friends if you do what I command.

Our readings this week emphasise the link between the spiritual realities we enjoy and the outward signs and evidences of them. They force us to ask whether we have just the outward appearance of being a Christian or whether we enjoy the spiritual truth of the faith in ourselves.

In Acts 10, the Spirit falls on all who hear the apostolic word of testimony to Jesus, even Gentiles. Peter's preaching was effectual and powerful. Since the Gentiles clearly now possess the spiritual reality of a new relationship with God, they cannot be denied the outward sign of initiation into the new covenant. They are baptised in the name of Jesus, just as the Ethiopian eunuch had been a few chapters earlier. The outward seal corresponds to the inward reality, and although we know the latter does not infallibly accompany the former, Peter makes the vital point that the sign cannot be denied to those with the reality.

A link between spiritual reality and visible sign is again established in 1 John 5. Those who believe that Jesus is the Christ have been born of God, spiritually born again. The fact that this happens can be observed in people's lives as they come to express their new relationship to God in obedience to him and his commandments. 'In fact, this is love for God: to keep his commands.' Faith gets busy in love, but it is busy in response to an accomplished victory on its behalf, not in an attempt to earn salvation by its effort. Good works are the fruit of faith, which does not lie dead in our hearts but is living and active.[16]

---

[16] See Gatiss (ed.), *The First Book of Homilies: The Official Sermons of the Church of England in Modern English* (London: Lost Coin, 2021), p. 69.

But many find their zeal for such obedience is dampened over time. John tries to rouse us from fatigue in this regard; as French pastor-theologian John Calvin (1509–64) says, 'For they who with a cheerful mind and great ardour have pursued a godly and holy life, afterwards grow weary, finding their strength inadequate.' Hence we are reminded that God's commandments are not 'burdensome' for his regenerate children, and despite ongoing struggles with sin we find that 'there is no real enjoyment except in following God'.[17] That we are already partakers of the victory Christ has won, spurs us on to fight more courageously and strenuously against the craftiness of Satan and the corruption in our own hearts that would otherwise leave us despondent.

In the Gospel reading we hear afresh that an abiding love for God is expressed in joyful obedience to his commandments. Not everyone will actively continue in this love and so experience ongoing joy. Yet, as beloved Bible commentator Matthew Henry (1662–1714) put it, 'The joy of the hypocrite is but for a moment, but the joy of those who abide in Christ's love is a continual feast.'[18] In particular, Jesus focuses on his commandment to the disciples that they should love one another as he had loved them. This is the greatest love, that he laid down his life for his chosen friends. His death was 'for them' in that it accomplished their salvation; but it was also 'for them' as an example to follow. Those who claim to be friends with Jesus should lay down their lives for others as he did; which seems here to involve a prayerfulness that bears fruit for others. The greatest fruit and evidence of our love for God, therefore, is a self-sacrificing spirit, that prays and works for the benefit of someone other than ourselves. Do we have that kind of love?

---

[17] John Calvin, *Commentaries on the Catholic Epistles* (Bellingham, WA: Logos Bible Software, 2010), pp. 252, 254.

[18] Henry, *Matthew Henry's Commentary*, p.2019.

7th Sunday of Easter (Sunday after Ascension Day)

Acts 1:15–17, 21–26 · 1 John 5:9–13 · John 17:6–19 · Psalm 1

Sanctify them by the truth; your word is truth.

This Sunday we are reminded in each of our readings of the kind and protective sovereignty of God over the Church, which testifies to his truth. Do we believe his truth, and trust his care for us?

As we prepare for Pentecost, we move back to chapter 1 in our readings from Acts. Here we see very clearly the sovereignty of God over the Church. The Scripture had to be fulfilled, Peter says – in imitation of his master, who treated God's word, the Bible, as unerring and unbreakable. God the Holy Spirit prophesied through King David that one allotted to share in the ministry of the apostles would deny the Saviour. He also prophesied that another must take his place (though curiously, verse 20 is officially omitted from the set reading). From those providentially prepared beforehand by their previous experience of Jesus's ministry, Peter asks that God would chose Judas's replacement. The lot is cast into the lap, but its every decision is from the Lord, as Proverbs 16:33 puts it.

Matthias therefore joins the apostles as a witness to testify to the resurrection of Jesus. John's first epistle takes up that same idea of testifying to the truth. God has testified to his Son, that eternal life is in him. If we believe in him, we have both him and all his benefits. As French theologian John Calvin (1509–64) put it in one of his sermons on Ephesians, 'we should be satisfied with the benefits of our Lord Jesus Christ, and that when we are grafted into his body and made one with him by belief of the gospel, then we may assure ourselves that he is the fountain which never dries up, nor can ever become exhausted, and that in him we have all variety of good things, and all perfection.'[19] There is also a warning that to *not* believe is to turn God into a liar. A dangerous way to treat the one who loves and cares for his people but is also perfect holy light.

In John 17, Jesus talks about how the disciples knew him and believed he was sent by the Father. He then prays for his own, because he is leaving them – in the world, but not of it. Because of the firm intra-trinitarian agreement between them, the Son can pray to the Father to keep his side of the bargain, as it were. 'Protect them in the world, as I have', he prays, although there was one that was always destined to be lost, in accordance with the Scriptures. The world will hate those who remain, as they carry his word. But they are sanctified by that same word and are safe in the hands of God.

The German Reformer Martin Luther (1483–1546) summed up the application of this passage well. He said,

> If you believe in the words of Christ, 'None of them is lost whom Thou hast given Me' (John 17:12), then, as a Christian, you must say: 'I acknowledge no saint here. I am a poor sinner deserving of death; but in defiance of sin and death I cling to Thee, and I will not let Thee go. I have taken hold of Thee, dear Lord Christ. Thou art my Life, and this is the Father's will, that all who adhere to Thee have eternal life and be raised from the dead. In the meantime let my fate be what it will. I may be beheaded or burned at the stake.' No other life – whether it be called the monastic life or the life of St Augustine or of John the Baptist – will arm a person for victory. Only faith in Christ can do so.[20]

[19] John Calvin, *Sermons on the Epistle to the Ephesians* (trans. A. Golding; Edinburgh: Banner of Truth, 1973), p. 355.

[20] Martin Luther, *Luther's Works, Vol. 23: Sermons on the Gospel of St. John: Chapters 6–8*, ed. Jaroslav Jan Pelikan, Hilton C. Oswald, and Helmut T. Lehmann (Saint Louis: Concordia Publishing House, 1999), pp. 75–6.

PENTECOST

Whit Sunday (Pentecost)

Acts 2:1–21 · Romans 8:22–27 · John 15:26–27; 16:4b–15 · Psalm 104:24–35b

The Spirit helps us in our weakness.

In today's readings, we see that the Holy Spirit comes at Pentecost to strengthen, revive and renew his people. Pentecost is a unique occasion in the history of redemption, but it also prompts us to ask for that same empowerment for ourselves today.

I have always found it strange that Acts 2 is referred to by some as 'the birthday of the Church'. It is true that some were born again at Pentecost, but it is not referred to in Scripture itself as the Church's birthday. Indeed, a few chapters later in Acts 7:38, Stephen refers to Moses and 'the church in the wilderness', which rather assumes there was a church 1,500 years or so before Pentecost! Jesus referred to 'the church' prior to Pentecost too (e.g. Matthew 18:17), and the Greek word for church, *ekklesia*, is not even mentioned in Acts 2 (though it is in the Greek of Psalm 22:22, which again rather implies there was a church before Pentecost). So I think we need a different way to describe the special events of Acts 2, one which is less misleading and doesn't make it sound as if gathering a church was a new idea for God.

Perhaps we might refer to it as the Church's Spirit-baptism, rather than its birth? The church was once baptised into Moses in the cloud and in the sea (1 Corinthians 10:1–2), but now it enjoys the promised baptism with the Holy Spirit. Not that the Spirit himself was not active in the church before then, of course. But something new had now arrived – 'power from on high' (Luke 24:49) which (as one modern commentator says) 'brings a new knowledge of the ascended Lord Jesus, and an experience of salvation among the fellowship of believers'.[21] The fact that this happened on Israel's 'harvest festival' (which is what Pentecost was, Leviticus 23), points to the purpose of it all – which was to equip the disciples for the harvest of world evangelisation (Acts 1:8).

As the much-used Reformation-era Heidelberg Catechism (1563) has it in Question 54: 'What do you believe concerning the "Holy Catholic Church"?'

> I believe that the Son of God, through his Spirit and Word, out of the entire human race, *from the beginning of the world to its end*, gathers, protects, and preserves for himself a community chosen for eternal life and united in true faith. And of this community I am and always will be a living member.

Pentecost is about equipping the Church afresh, not creating it from scratch. This is just as Jesus promised in our Gospel reading from John 15. When the Advocate comes, he said, he will testify on my behalf; and then in turn the apostles must testify too. This is precisely what happened at Pentecost and in the years that followed, as the message of the gospel rang out across the world. The apostles and those that come after them speak God's word to the world in the power of the Spirit.

Our reading from Romans 8 also speaks of those who have the first-fruits of the Spirit groaning inwardly, for our future hope to become a present reality. This is such an incomprehensible and joyful prospect that we cannot even get the words out properly to express our longing and desire for it. The Spirit encourages us to testify to others, but that hope (in a sense) leaves us deeply dumbstruck! Yet the Spirit helps us even in that weakness, interceding with sighs too profound for words, that our lips may be opened and every tongue may tell of his glory. May the Spirit give us a voice today.

---

[21] David G. Peterson, *The Acts of the Apostles*, The Pillar New Testament Commentary (Grand Rapids, MI; Nottingham, England: William B. Eerdmans Publishing Company, 2009), p. 61.

ORDINARY TIME

Trinity Sunday

Isaiah 6:1–8 · Romans 8:12–17 · John 3:1–17 · Psalm 29

The Spirit you received brought about your adoption to sonship. And by him we cry, 'Abba, Father.'

Our readings show us that the revelation of God the holy Trinity is something which makes us shout out loud in response. Do we cry 'Abba, Father', or 'Woe is me!' – that is the question.

In the year that a weak and ineffectual king died, Isaiah saw the powerful Lord of all. Uzziah had been disobedient by entering unauthorised into the Temple to burn incense, and was struck with leprosy. Isaiah enters the Temple in his vision, invited in for a glimpse of divine glory, and is struck by his own sinfulness. He sees, hears and feels the angelic worship of God. We read of this on Trinity Sunday because the so-called Trisagion, 'Holy, holy, holy', has often been seen as Trinitarian. In the early church, the theologian Origen (185–253) reported that he was taught by his Hebrew master to apply each 'holy' to a different person of the Trinity.[22] Others would downplay this, saying that the threefold repetition is not necessarily a sign of the Trinitarian nature of God, but of his superlative holiness. The sixteenth-century Reformer Martin

---

[22] Origen, *First Principles*, 1.3.4. *Fathers of the Third Century: Tertullian, Part Fourth; Minucius Felix; Commodian; Origen, Parts First and Second*, ed. Alexander Roberts, James Donaldson, and A. Cleveland Coxe, trans. Frederick Crombie, vol. 4 of The Ante-Nicene Fathers (Buffalo, NY: Christian Literature Company, 1885), p. 253.

Luther said it indicated 'that all holiness in the whole earth must be ascribed to God alone'.[23]

Either way, the apostle John says Isaiah saw Jesus (John 12:41), so it is certainly a reminder that the Old Testament God whom Isaiah saw is the same as our great God and Saviour Jesus Christ. John beheld his glory, just as Isaiah did – but in human form, emptied of that outward manifestation of glory for a season. And yet, just as Isaiah exclaims 'Woe is me!' when he comes face-to-face with the inescapable, majestic holiness of God, so also Peter, struck by the realisation of who confronted him, cried out, 'Away from me, Lord, for I am a sinful man' (Luke 5:8). As Bible commentator Matthew Henry (1662–1714) reminds us, 'A believing sight of God's glorious majesty should affect us all with reverence and godly fear ... Those are fittest to be employed for God who are low in their own eyes and are made deeply sensible of their own weakness and unworthiness.'[24]

Isaiah may have anticipated judgment for his sin from a holy God, and yet his sin was atoned for and his guilt taken away. In the same way, Nicodemus discovered from Jesus that God so loved the world that he gave his only Son, that whoever believes in him might not perish (in fully deserved judgment) but have eternal life. Yet he does not understand what is revealed to him about the essential nature of a new birth. Hearing of the work of the Spirit from the incarnate Son, his human wisdom runs out, and he cries, 'How can this be?' He did not grasp the enormity of the Trinitarian work that was necessary both for him and in him.

The apostle Paul did, and that's why he told the Roman Christians not to live according to the flesh, but by the Spirit, to put to death the misdeeds of the body. Those led by the Spirit in this holy war of sanctification are children of God himself, and the presence

---

[23] Martin Luther, *Luther's Works, Vol. 16: Lectures on Isaiah: Chapters 1–39*, ed. Jaroslav Jan Pelikan, Hilton C. Oswald, and Helmut T. Lehmann (Saint Louis: Concordia Publishing House, 1999), p. 70.

[24] Henry, *Matthew Henry's Commentary*, p. 1089.

of the Spirit within us makes us co-heirs with Christ, the Son of God *par excellence*. Yet, compelled by the Spirit within, we do not enter the fray crying out, 'Oh, Spirit!' but 'Abba! Father!' Rather, we suffer with Christ so that in union with him we might also be glorified, and finally rest in the Father's arms.

So let us revere the Trinity – Father, Son, and Holy Spirit – and be empowered by the Spirit to live for Christ today, to the glory of God the Father.

Proper 4

Sunday between 29 May and 4 June inclusive
(if after Trinity Sunday)

Deuteronomy 5:12–15 · 2 Corinthians 4:5–12 · Mark 2:23–3:6 ·
Psalm 81:1–10

For God who said, 'Let light shine out of darkness,' made his light shine in our hearts to give us the light of the knowledge of God's glory displayed in the face of Jesus Christ.

This week we will focus on one big question, mainly from only one of our readings, because it is the most important question of all. In our reading from Mark's Gospel, we see Jesus go head-to-head with the Pharisees over the issue of the Sabbath. Who does he think he is?

The Pharisees are cross because of what Jesus's disciples are doing. The Old Testament Law (our reading from Deuteronomy) said that no one should work on the Sabbath, so there was a regular spiritual, mental and physical break each week. Harvesting a field would have been work, though surely rubbing a few ears of corn together for a brief snack could only be counted in that same category if layers of man-made rules and regulations had been added to God's Law.

Jesus, however, doesn't point out that this can hardly be classed as 'work'; instead, he accepts the premise of the Pharisees' question. Not in order to suggest that the Law can be broken whenever we feel like it, or that God's word takes second place to our bodily desires, but to make them think about who he is. He compares himself to King David, God's anointed king in the Old Testament. In a time of need on urgent business for God, he and his followers had likewise eaten food that they would not ordinarily be permitted. Just as that was permitted then, so Jesus's disciples could eat now, since he is the Son of Man, the Lord of the Sabbath. As the psalm today says, 'I am the LORD your God, who brought you up out of Egypt. Open wide your mouth and I will fill it.'

Again they pursue Jesus to gnaw away at him with close questioning as he enters a synagogue in Capernaum (Mark 3:1–6). Their attitude towards him is hardening. When a man with a withered hand appears, they watch closely to see if he will heal him on the Sabbath, so they can again accuse him of breaking the Sabbath commandment, rather than waiting a day to make the man well again. Jesus goes beyond the minutiae of the Commandments to ask whether the Sabbath was for doing good and saving life or doing harm and killing, in order to provoke them to think through why on earth they are so opposed to something as positive and life-affirming as healing.

Jesus looks at them when they refuse to answer his simple question. What a look that must have been! He is angry. He is grieved at their hardness of heart. They seem to have no shame, no guilt, over their stubborn refusal to accept that the compassion of God has no boundaries or prescribed times. So when Jesus heals the man without even touching him, they are not gobsmacked with joy and wonderment, but lost in the wild entanglements of religious rage. Storming out, they begin to conspire with their political opponents in a joint operation of co-belligerence, to rid the world of this man who breaks their rules.

At the beginning of Mark's Gospel, then, we see various reactions to the arrival of God's King. The Pharisees hate him and ally themselves with the wily political Herodians who also see a danger here. The crowds flock to him, amazed at what he says and does but not really understanding his message or grasping his true identity. Then there are those few chosen disciples, who have begun, however falteringly, to follow him and listen.

Mark says Jesus is the Christ, the Son of God. But who do we think he is? And how are we responding to his work among us today?

Proper 5

Sunday between 5 and 11 June inclusive (if after Trinity Sunday)

Genesis 3:8–15 · 2 Corinthians 4:13–5:1 · Mark 3:20–35 · Psalm 130

And I will put enmity between you and the woman, and between your offspring and hers; he will crush your head, and you will strike his heel.

Our readings this week are related by the opposition we face as Christians from the world, the flesh and the devil. Where can we go for help in this cosmic battle?

Enmity begins, in a sense, in Genesis 3. That wily serpent, the great dragon Satan (Revelation 12:9), opened up a new front in his war with God by approaching Eve. After the Fall, God walks in the garden in the cool of day and calls to Adam, who is lost. Adam blames Eve; Eve blames the serpent; and the serpent, as they say, didn't have a leg to stand on. 'Upon your belly you shall go,' says God as he curses him, 'and dust you shall eat all the days of your life.' But it does seem, for the moment at least, that he has conquered the man of dust.

Until the promise, the *protoevangelion*, as it is called, of Genesis 3:15. There we discover that, although this enmity between the serpent and the offspring (collective singular) of the woman will continue into the rest of the Bible, God has a plan to overcome him. As it was prophesied in the Garden of Eden, the devil finally managed to bruise Christ's heel, with the nails that pierced him and pinned him to the wood. But this pyrrhic victory of evil over good, in Christ's cruel and callous death, was destined to be the very thing which enabled him to crush the serpent's head for ever.

Jesus alludes to this in the Gospel reading from Mark 3. Even his family thought he was out of his mind, or were worried about the possibility. The official ruling from the Regius Professors (the

Jerusalem scribes) was that he cast out demons by the power of Beelzebub, the ruler of demons. But Jesus refuted them, saying, 'How can Satan cast out Satan?' He can't, of course, because that would mean his end was nigh. And besides, they all knew, Satan would be cast out and defeated by the promised seed of Eve, who stood before them at that very moment, if only they had eyes to see! He would bind the strong man and plunder his house, 'striking the head' of the devil even as he himself bowed his head in death.

There is inevitable opposition to this proposition. Some will be guilty of the eternal and unforgivable sin – attributing to an unclean spirit what is truly the work of the Spirit of God. Others, even family, will try to restrain and silence and diminish and disbelieve. The world and the devil work together to prevent us doing the will of God.

Paul speaks in 2 Corinthians 4 of the 'slight and momentary affliction' that we face if we believe and speak the truth. We waste away, as the curse of death eats away at our flesh. But inwardly we are renewed day by day, in the hope of an eternal weight of glory beyond all measure, that will be ours when we are raised with Jesus for ever. This heavenly hope, Victory over Evil day, motivates us to endure whatever this life may throw at us. And so we pray in the words of the Anglican collect, 'O God, the strength of all those who put their trust in you, mercifully accept our prayers and, because through the weakness of our mortal nature we can do no good thing without you, grant us the help of your grace, that in the keeping of your commandments we may please you both in will and deed; through Jesus Christ your Son our Lord.'

Proper 6

Sunday between 12 and 18 June inclusive
(if after Trinity Sunday)

Ezekiel 17:22–24 · 2 Corinthians 5:6–17 · Mark 4:26–34 ·
Psalm 92:1–4, 12–15

For you make me glad by your deeds, LORD;
I sing for joy at what your hands have done.

The theme of our readings this week is the true long-term flourishing of those who seek to please God. We can trust that, although we may not be able to see it in our own day and age, God's plan will succeed and his people will thrive.

Mark 4:26–34 contains just two of 'many such parables' that Jesus used to speak to people about the growth of the kingdom of God. That growth is quiet and irrepressible and in some measure mysterious. The seed is scattered by someone, and then it sprouts and grows 'he does not know how', as if the earth 'produces of itself'. From a tiny seed comes a giant shrub so large that birds can make nests in its shade. In times and places where gospel growth seems painfully slow and slowly painful, or where Christians feel an embattled and insignificant minority, it is a great encouragement to know that one is part of something which will not end in an obscure whimper, and across time and space is truly flourishing.

Ezekiel's vision is of a sprig from a cedar, a tender shoot, being broken off and planted by God himself on a mountain. This is the source of the imagery Jesus used to describe the thriving of the global gospel, as 'under it every kind of bird will live; in the shade of its branches will nest winged creatures of every kind.' This will be a sign to everyone that 'I am the LORD'; that is, that God himself has sovereign care over his word and world. 'I will dry up the green tree and make the dry tree flourish,' he says, according to his will. He can make the seemingly unfruitful and the seemingly strong swap places. Just as in Jesus's parable, there is a hint of judgment to come, both in the outworking of God's providence and eschatologically (in terms of the end of the world).

But it is not for those with the upper hand to boast over others: throughout all the victories and losses of our earthly lives (military, political, ecclesiastical), the Lord is pursuing his own agenda for the success of *his* kingdom. As the puritan John Owen (1616–83) said when preaching on this passage to Parliament at the end of the English Civil War, as far as our human successes are concerned, 'should they not be brought into an immediate subserviency to the kingdom of the Lord Jesus, the Lord will quickly distinguish between them and his own peculiar design.'[25] We must not forget how the Lord delights to work his own purposes out in a way which appears foolish and weak to the eye of worldly observers. Any current triumph must prove itself subservient to the growth of Christ's kingdom, or it will be inexorably torn down.

Paul reminds us of these things too when he tells us in 2 Corinthians that 'we walk by faith, not by sight'. His confidence comes from knowing Jesus and so he always aims to please him. That is the only source of long-term prosperity, since one day there will be a reckoning for each of us before the judgment seat of Christ, who only rewards those who seek his favour. Loving him means putting ourselves out for others, as he did. His love urges us on to persuade others to follow the Way, which may look from a human point of view like a recipe for failure. We trust the one who died that we might live, and in trusting him we find we are born again into a new world. In that new creation we cease to look at things from a human point of view, and adopt instead the standpoint of eternity and the ultimate victory of God. How foolish it would be to adopt a worldly strategy and seek to flourish in the temporary climate of current political correctness, without reference to that final day.

[25] Owen, *The Works of John Owen*, 8:318.

Proper 7

Sunday between 19 and 25 June inclusive
(if after Trinity Sunday)

Job 38:1–11 · 2 Corinthians 6:1–13 · Mark 4:35–41 ·
Psalm 107:1–3, 23–32

Why are you so afraid? Do you still have no faith?

In the readings for this week, we are encouraged to trust in Jesus through all the storms and difficulties of life, because his authoritative word protects us; and we are rebuked if we do not!

After a long and thrilling day of teaching, the disciples set sail with Jesus for the other side of the lake. They are happy to serve their now famous master at first, no doubt, even when that means bailing water out of the boat as it fills up in the storm. But their terror gets the better of them and they (it is interesting that it is 'they' and not just one of them) chastise Jesus as if he did not care what they were doing and suffering for him. In turn, he wakes up and rebukes the storm and the sea, silencing them with a word. Then he rebukes his disciples for not trusting him through it all (as he would also rebuke Peter in particular, when he looked at the storm and not the Saviour on another occasion in Matthew 14:30–31). This, and the other miracles of nature coming soon in the Gospel, force them to ask the critical question: 'Who then is this?'

As Job listened to the Lord speaking out of the whirlwind, he heard that God 'shut in the sea with doors'. The Creator said to the ocean, 'Thus far you come, and no farther, and here shall your proud waves be stopped.' As in Psalm 104:9, God holds back the sea by his powerful word. Who then is Jesus?

As the Reformer Martin Luther (1483–1546) comments, 'If the water were not contained within a barrier by the power of the Word, it would overflow and lay everything waste. Thus our life is miraculously protected and preserved every single moment through the Word. Individual floods, by which at times entire cities or regions are covered with water, prove that we would experience such afflictions daily if it were not for God's providence.'[26] In the same way, the devil may rise up and hurl dire threats at the Church, stirring up violence or persecution to sift us like wheat and stretch us. But God has set a limit on such opposition, so that although we may be tested and traumatised for a while, trusting in him we will not be entirely submerged. The gates of death itself cannot prevail against even the smallest seed of faith in the strong name of Jesus.

Paul speaks about his own travails in 2 Corinthians 6. He speaks of his endurance through turbulence as a commendation of his ministry to them. He has suffered 'afflictions, hardships, calamities, beatings, imprisonments, riots, labours, sleepless nights, hunger', as well as ill-report, contempt and loss. And yet he rejoices through it all. He is a faithful servant of Christ, undaunted through the midst of all this commotion and dishonour, which would so irk and rile lesser men that they would abandon either their godliness or their perseverance. As French commentator John Calvin (1509–64) says, 'if one is drawn aside from duty by the ingratitude of men, that man shows that he had not his eye directed to God alone'.[27] The false apostles in Corinth were admired for their prosperity and worldly success; Paul desires the Corinthians to cherish and esteem him most for his more Christlike faithfulness in adversity, which they ought to value more highly.

So do we trust in God's word and ways to protect us? Or would we rather entrust ourselves to more worldly strategies?

---

[26] Martin Luther, *Luther's Works, Vol. 2: Lectures on Genesis: Chapters 6–14*, ed. Jaroslav Jan Pelikan, Hilton C. Oswald, and Helmut T. Lehmann (Saint Louis: Concordia Publishing House, 1999), p. 93.

[27] John Calvin, *Commentaries on the Epistles of Paul the Apostle to the Corinthians* (Bellingham, WA: Logos Bible Software, 2010), pp. 252–3.

Proper 8

Sunday between 26 June and 2 July inclusive

2 Corinthians 8:7–15 · Mark 5:21–43 · Psalm 30 · Lamentations 3:22–33

You, LORD, brought me up from the realm of the dead;
you spared me from going down to the pit.

In the readings for this week, we rejoice in God's power over death, which he gives to those who trust in him. In the face of our greatest enemy, will you entrust your whole life to him?

In Mark's Gospel so far, we have seen Jesus's power over sickness, over the demonic world and over the forces of nature. In the reading from chapter 5, we now see his power over our last and greatest enemy, death. The same trust in Jesus which heals the woman who has suffered for twelve years restores to Jairus his dead daughter. Many people swarm around Jesus that day, as they still do today, but few have that living connection to him by faith. We may not be able to see who they are, but the Lord knows those who are his, and their loving trust in Jesus is sufficient to calm all fears. Jesus is aware in Mark 5:30 that 'power had gone forth from him' – it is costly to him to heal and restore others, and since many troubled him (verse 35) it is not cheap grace he dispenses.

The Corinthians are urged by Paul to imitate the generosity of the Saviour. Though he was rich, yet for our sake he left his Father's throne above ('so free, so infinite his love!' as the hymnwriter Charles Wesley exclaims in 'And can it be?'), and exchanged the sapphire-paved courts of heaven for a manger (and an overcrowded city full of needy people). In doing so, he makes us rich beyond the measure of our deserving. In the same way, says the apostle, let us show the earnestness of our love for others by similar acts of altruistic grace – not forgetting to finish what we start and put into practice our initial impulses or benevolent intentions. The Corinthians have an example of this sort of self-giving steadfastness in Titus and others, co-workers sent by Paul to assist them at no insubstantial cost to themselves in terms of travel and time. I wonder if we would be willing to make the same sacrifices for the gospel?

In Psalm 30, the Psalmist also praises God, who lifts us up from poverty to profit. 'I will exalt you, LORD, for you lifted me out of the depths,' he sings, 'and did not let my enemies gloat over me.' He is healed, and he is 'brought up from the realm of the dead' (verses 2–3), restored to life again after the despair of 'the pit'. It is said that suffering either makes you bitter or it makes you better: the Psalmist realises that a temporary experience of God's heavy hand upon him (moving him from prosperity to dismay) will eventually lift as 'rejoicing comes in the morning'. There is no profit of praise in allowing him to die – 'Will the dust praise you? Will it proclaim your faithfulness?' But the Lord, our helper (the same word as for Eve, in Genesis 2:18, 20) is gracious and merciful, turning mourning into dancing. His grace leads to gladness, for all who call out to him. And as we thank him for small victories in this life, we can also look ahead to a future of eternal song. If we trust him. Do you?

Proper 9

Sunday between 3 and 9 July inclusive

Ezekiel 2:1–5 · 2 Corinthians 12:2–10 · Mark 6:1–13 · Psalm 123

Have mercy on us, Lord, have mercy on us,
for we have endured no end of contempt.

The theme which brings our readings together this week is the rejection of God's true messengers and the difficulties that it brings for them. Are you prepared to keep serving Jesus if it means suffering ridicule and contempt?

In exile Ezekiel receives a startling and frightening vision of God's glory. The Spirit enters into him and he hears God speaking directly to him, bringing a tough commission. He is to be sent to a nation of rebels, with a long history of not listening to God's messengers and indeed fighting against them. They are impudent and stubborn, says God, laying it on thick before repeating 'I am sending you to *them*.' His commission is to speak and faithfully pass on God's words, whether they listen to what he says, or not. The expectation is that they won't, of course ('for they are a rebellious house'). But either way, they will know in the end that a prophet has been in their midst, and God did not leave them without some glimmer of his presence.

Being addressed throughout as 'mortal' (more literally, 'son of Adam' or 'son of man'), an expression which is used almost 100 times in the book, Ezekiel is reminded of his fragility and hence the dangerous nature of the task ahead. Yet he stands up, prepared for action. As the old Bible commentator Matthew Henry (1662–1714) comments, 'God will speak to us, when we stand ready to do what he commands us,'[28] and will give us his Spirit to work in his faithful people whatever he requires of us.

Jesus himself, *the* Son of Man *par excellence*, found his call to mission was no different in these respects. In the Gospel reading, he faces questions about the origin of his message and about his own humble origins. The people – a rebellious nation that would not listen – were offended by him. Despite their history of such stubbornness, even Jesus was amazed at the unbelief when they were confronted not just with God's word but with his incarnate Word. As he sends out his disciples afterwards, he is careful to warn them that they may face the same reaction, equipping them to know how to react when their teaching is not welcomed. Courageously they go, proclaiming that all should repent, for God's message always confronts the minds and lives of those with whom it comes into contact.

The apostle to the Gentiles found this to be true no less in his missionary endeavours than with those who had gone to the rebellious house of Israel. Some used his seeming lack of worldly success and charismatic credentials as a way of undermining and dismissing his ministry. Yet he, like Ezekiel and like Christ, had stood in the presence of God, been caught up into Paradise itself and received exceptional revelations. As always, these were attended with difficulties, and to keep him from being too elated by such raptures, he was given his famous thorn in the flesh. My suspicion is that it was some kind of ocular affliction (after being blinded on the road to Damascus, and from the hints in Galatians 4:15 and 6:11). But whatever it was, it humbled him and taught him that God's power is made perfect in weakness. Hence, like the other truth bringers in our readings, he was content to suffer insults, hardships, persecutions and calamities, he says.

Are we similarly prepared and equipped in our mission, to face the ridicule and contempt that a rebellious church and misguided nation may direct towards us as we speak the truth in love?

---

[28] Henry, *Matthew Henry's Commentary*, p. 1341.

Proper 10

Sunday between 10 and 16 July inclusive

Amos 7:7–15 · Ephesians 1:3–14 · Mark 6:14–29 · Psalm 85:8–13

The land cannot bear all his words.

Our readings are united by church and government suppressing God's word of truth, which alone can save us. Is this a pattern that we can also observe today?

Amos confronts the corrupt government of his day with a message entrusted to him by God. The Lord holds up a discriminating plumb-line to the ruling elite and they are found wanting. Jeroboam had constructed human-made centres of human-made religion, 'the king's sanctuary' or 'the temple of the kingdom'. They went up in response to his word and worshipped as he commanded them. This was not an *established* church with the privilege of speaking 'the true profession of the gospel' to the nation (as the British monarch's Coronation Oath puts it), but a *state* church, which merely reflected the will and whims of the king. The land could not bear all the words of Amos, a true prophet.

As Martin Luther indicates in his sixteenth-century comment on the text, this is typical: 'Thus the ungodly with their own traditions always mock the preaching of the godly.'[29] Ironically, Amaziah seeks to banish Amos from the land, just as Amos has prophesied the exile of Israel. Yet Amos refuses to bow to pressure from the government and the state church which follows along obsequiously in its pocket. As many who follow the call of vocation have discovered, God's true

[29] Martin Luther, *Luther's Works, Vol. 18: Minor Prophets I: Hosea-Malachi*, ed. Jaroslav Jan Pelikan, Hilton C. Oswald, and Helmut T. Lehmann (Saint Louis: Concordia Publishing House, 1999), p. 175.

word is inescapable and must be preached, even if it means leaving the comfort zones and income levels of previous employment (Amos 7:14–15).

Bishop J. C. Ryle (1816–1900) spoke of a similar situation in his book, *Christian Leaders of the Seventeenth Century*. 'Wretched, indeed, is that country where low, sneaking informers are encouraged,' he writes, 'where the terrors of the law are directed more against holiness, and Scriptural religion, and freedom of thought, than against vice and immorality; and where the seat of justice is used for the advancement of political purposes, or the gratification of petty ecclesiastical spite!'[30] He was speaking of another century, but it is not so different from the days of Amos, or our generation.

It is not so different with King Herod either, in the Gospel reading, when he meets with God's true messengers. He imprisons John the Baptiser, who challenged his unnatural twisting of sexual and marital ethics. Inwardly he suspects he ought to listen, but his sinful nature kicks against the word and renders him indecisively perplexed. His lusts cause him to make a rash promise which forces him to make a definitive choice. And just as celebrity atheist Stephen Fry said about God, 'The moment you banish him, your life becomes simpler.'[31] When Herod subsequently rejects the Word incarnate, it brings a simpler harmony to his relationship with Pilate. But in eternity, there is no peace for those who respond to the word of God in this way.

This Sunday the lectionary begins a series of consecutive readings in Ephesians, which will continue for several weeks. The reading for today is a single majestic sentence encompassing eternal predestination, redemption in Christ and the consummation of all things in God's strategic plan for the universe. It urges us to praise God

---

[30] J. C. Ryle *Christian Leaders of the Seventeenth Century* (edited by Lee Gatiss; London: Lost Coin, 2015), pp. 47–8.

[31] https://www.irishtimes.com/news/social-affairs/religion-and-beliefs/stephen-fry-tells-gay-byrne-god-is-a-maniac-totally-selfish-1.2087438 from Sunday 1 February 2015 (accessed 12 April 2023).

that we have every spiritual blessing in Christ and are part of God's cosmic strategy through believing the word of truth. This is the message we are called to proclaim (to the state, the nation, and the world), and which God will bless as we do so.

This is in stark contrast to the earth-bound gospel of a worldly religion which listens only to those who bless the particular perversities of the age. As French theologian John Calvin (1509–64) once remarked, exposing our tendency to ask God to bless our personal agendas and disordered ambitions: 'How can any one have the effrontery to expect that God will aid him in accomplishing desires at variance with his word? What God with his own lips pronounces cursed, never can be prosecuted with his blessing.'[32]

[32] John Calvin, *Institutes of the Christian Religion* (1559), trans. Henry Beveridge (repr., Grand Rapids: Eerdmans, 1989), 3.7.9.

Proper 11

Sunday between 17 and 23 July inclusive

Jeremiah 23:1–6 · Ephesians 2:11–22 · Mark 6:30–34, 53–56 · Psalm 23

The Lord is my shepherd, I lack nothing.

This week's lectionary passages teach us about the pastoral ministry of Christ, the Good Shepherd, who cares for his sheep by teaching them truth and keeping them from error. Are you listening to his voice?

The Gospel reading opens with the apostles gathered around their shepherd, Jesus. He has been teaching them how they also might care for his people, and they report back on all they have done and taught (since shepherding is done by teaching). It had been an exhausting and intense time, and Jesus knows they need some time out. As they go ashore, a great crowd appears. Jesus, says Mark, has gut-wrenching compassion for them (the word 'compassion' here is related to the word for the intestines). They are sheep without a shepherd. What does Jesus think they need the most? Verse 34 continues, 'and he began to teach them many things'.

The Gospel reading then skips the feeding of the five thousand, though that would be appropriate since, as Reformation Archbishop Thomas Cranmer (1489–1556) once preached, Holy Scripture is 'the food of the soul'.[33] Jesus cares for the whole person and heals the sick as well as feeding them with bread. Yet people shall not live on bread alone, but on every word that comes from the mouth of God (Deuteronomy 8:3). We are to have the same compassion for people. The greatest lack of our shepherd-less generation is the teaching of God's eternal word which alone can bring eternal life.

---

[33] Gatiss (ed.), *The First Book of Homilies*, p. 34.

Ephesians 2 reminds us that those of us who are Gentiles have been brought into the sheepfold by the blood of Christ. We were outsiders to the covenants of the promise, and had no eternally secure hope. But now, the dividing wall of hostility between Jews and Gentiles, and between God and humanity, has been broken down in Christ's body. We all now gather around Jesus, on level ground, as his disciples. We are one in Christ now: united with God and members one of another. Jesus is the cornerstone of the church, which is built up by the Spirit himself on the foundation of the apostolic and prophetic teaching.

Refuting error, preaching the negatives, is just as important as proclaiming the positives of the faith if we are to flourish. It has always been so, not only in the Bible but in the creeds too; Christ himself is, we declare in the Nicene Creed, 'begotten, *not* made, of one Being with the Father' – the negative giving proper definition to the positive. And the Old Testament reading from Jeremiah also reinforces this vital fact. He pronounces God's curse on those who destroy and scatter God's flock by their neglect of true teaching and their ungodliness ('they commit adultery and walk in lies; they strengthen the hands of evildoers', verse 14). They have not gathered, but dispersed, 'speaking visions of their own minds' (verse 16), attending to themselves and their sinful desires instead of nurturing the flock. God promises to raise up other shepherds to find and comfort his people, and to lead them to the King who executes righteousness, and *is* our righteousness. But those who lead the flock astray will face everlasting shame.

Proper 12

Sunday between 24 and 30 July inclusive

2 Kings 4:42–44 · Ephesians 3:14–21 · John 6:1–21 · Psalm 145:10–18

The LORD is trustworthy in all he promises and faithful in all he does.

Our readings for this week teach us that God will do as he has promised, and provide for our needs in times of trouble. He works for his own glory, and for our greater good.

The brief story in 2 Kings 4 is set in a time of famine (2 Kings 4:38). Though as the old commentator (1662–1714) comments, in a neat reversal of Amos 8:11, 'A famine of bread there was, but not of hearing the word of God, for Elisha had the sons of the prophets sitting before him, to hear his wisdom, who were taught, that they might teach others.'[34] Indeed, this whole section of the narrative from 1 Kings 17 to 2 Kings 13 focuses on Elijah and Elisha bringing God's word to the people in dangerous times. Elisha enables the faithful 'sons of the prophets' to eat what would otherwise be poisonous food (4:38–41). Then he also makes a little food go a long way, feeding 100 men with the firstfruits donated by one faithful, obedient man (who, incidentally, refused to give his firstfruits to the *priests*, as would be normal, presumably because they had been contaminated by Baal-ised worship). Where the supply is dangerous or inadequate, the word of God can always be trusted. And as the Baptist missionary Hudson Taylor (1832–1905) found, 'God's work done

[34] Henry, *Matthew Henry's Commentary*, p. 528.

in God's way will never lack God's supply. He is too wise a God to frustrate His purposes for lack of funds.'[35]

In John's Gospel we see that someone greater than Elisha has come. The feeding of the five thousand is the only such miracle recorded in all four Gospels, and John adds his own unique details. Andrew approaches Jesus with a boy's packed lunch (fewer than the twenty barley loaves that fed 100 in 2 Kings 4) and asks the same sort of question as Elisha's servant: 'what are they for so many?' But Jesus's sufficiency is more than a match for our deficiency. He brings the word of hope, and is the Word of hope, in the midst of life-threatening crisis.

The people saw this miracle as a sign – it pointed to something else. Some realised that it pointed to Jesus as *the* prophet who was promised to the world. But others saw in him something more royal. Did they want to make him king because they saw his messianic potential? Or because they wanted an ongoing supply of free bread? Or even, perhaps, because they thought that providing the latter was an adequate job description for the former?

The apostle Paul sees the Christ as more than adequate for all our needs (the things we *really* need, not merely food). God is able to do far more abundantly than all we can ask or even imagine. His power is not just at work for us, but *within us* (that is, the faithful Church founded on the words of the apostles and prophets), that we in turn might bring glory to God. Hence in Ephesians 3, Paul prays that in accordance with the plan of God set out in the previous chapters of the letter, God would strengthen us through his Spirit (who is building up the people of God); that Christ may dwell in our hearts through faith (not physically since he is at the right hand of the Father, far above all); and that we would grasp his limitless love. This is summed up in one phrase: that we may be filled with all the fullness of God – satisfied in every way with him, our identity rooted in Christ alone.

---

[35] See Christopher Wright, *The Shortfall: Owning the Challenge of Ministry Funding* (Carlisle: Langham Global Library, 2021), p. 10.

As the French pastor John Calvin (1509–64) nicely expresses it, only when people are swelled with pride and empty trifles do they imagine that they have entire completeness in themselves; but those who have Christ have everything necessary for being made perfect in God.[36] Do you have Christ? Do you trust all his promises?

[36] John Calvin, *Commentaries on the Epistles of Paul to the Galatians and Ephesians* (Bellingham, WA: Logos Bible Software, 2010), p. 265.

Proper 13

Sunday between 31 July and 6 August inclusive

Exodus 16:2–4, 9–15 · Ephesians 4:1–16 · John 6:24–35 · Psalm 78:23–29

I am the bread of life. Whoever comes to me will never go hungry.

The readings for this Sunday bring us blessings from heaven to save us and feed us along the way to our promised rest. What is it that sustains you in your daily walk with God?

In Exodus, the Lord rains bread from heaven to feed the people on their way to the Promised Land. They are flailing about in the desert, desperate and despairing because they do not have the food they were used to. But God promises to provide for them on their way to their new home, where there will be milk and honey in abundance. How gracious that he did so, despite their doubting and complaining!

In the Gospel reading, the people are seeking Jesus because he graciously filled their stomachs with bread too. He challenges them to go further and seek the food which will give them eternal life. That bread from heaven satisfies in a way that no other bread can – it is Jesus himself. Only by being united to him, the inexhaustible fountain that never dries up, can they be truly filled.

In Ephesians 4, the risen and ascended Lord Jesus gives gifts to his people from heaven which enable them to live a life worthy of their calling on earth. These gifts are 'wordy': the foundational teaching of the apostles and prophets of the New Testament (see Ephesians 2:20 and 3:5); evangelists to declare and announce the good news; and pastors and teachers to unfold the life-bringing, light-giving Scriptures. Through their teaching, these all equip the saints (the people of God) to do the work of ministry – note well that it is not the pastors who do the ministry, but they who equip the congregations to do so! As the word is unleashed it brings a proper unity, stability and maturity to the people, who as a result will not be blown off course by every wind of false teaching or crafty scheming that comes along.

Christ comes to us clothed in his word. The Scriptures are our sustenance, and as the puritan pastor John Owen (1616–83) once wrote, 'the preaching of the word is appointed of God as food for our souls; and we shall never receive it aright unless we desire it and long for it to this end and purpose'.[37] If we come to Jesus, clad in his promises, looking for mere entertainment or for affirmation or for an intellectual challenge, we will not receive him aright.

So as a former Rector of St Helen's, Bishopsgate (Dr Thomas Horton, died 1673) once said, 'Let us not come to a sermon as to a prize, or a mere trial of wits, to see who can do best – only to spend our verdict on the preacher, or out of mere fashion and custom – only because others come before us. But let us come to it with meekness, and humility, and fear and expectation, as that whereby we must be judged, and whereby we must be saved.'[38] And, we may add, it is that whereby we must be fed and nourished, for the good of our own souls and of those we are called to love and to serve.

---

[37] Owen, *The Works of John Owen*, 21:555.

[38] Thomas Horton, *One Hundred Select Sermons upon several texts: fifty upon the Old Testament, and fifty on the new* (London: Printed for Thomas Parkhurst, 1679), p. 262.

Proper 14

Sunday between 7 and 13 August inclusive

1 Kings 19:4–8 · Ephesians 4:25–5:2 · John 6:35, 41–51 · Psalm 34:1–8

Taste and see that the L*ORD* *is good;*
blessed is the one who takes refuge in him.

Our readings this week teach us to turn to Christ in our human frailty and be sustained by our unity with him. No human power or human reasoning will be good enough to keep us going.

Elijah, the great prophetic challenger who defeated and slaughtered the prophets of Baal on Mount Carmel, turns to jelly when threatened by an angry Jezebel. Afraid for his life, he flees into the desert. Tired of life, he prays for death. This is no superman of unflinching faith – he is no better than his ancestors. He was impelled by the Spirit of God himself to slay the false prophets, but has received no word to withdraw and hide; he relies solely on his trembling reason, which says 'Run!' He curls into a ball under a tree and hopes it will all go away. Yet God sends an angel to raise him from his sleepy attempt to leave the stage, and provides him with food for the journey he must now make. Twice he is refreshed and given what he needs to make it to Horeb, and come to 'the mount of God'.

Jesus, who knows our weaknesses and has carried our sorrows, also provides food to his people for their journey. And better still, he teaches us that he himself is the bread of life. Refreshed in him, we will be raised up on the Last Day and enjoy everlasting life with the Father. He is manna for the journey we must make, but unlike our ancestors who ate the original manna in the wilderness of Sinai, if we feed on Christ we will not die. For he is living bread and if we are drawn to him by the Father we are connected to a source of life which sustains the stars and planets, and pulsates into eternity.

Jesus is not merely human, 'the son of Joseph, whose father and mother we know'. We need not entertain doubts that he is incapable of supporting and preserving us to the end. The Jews in John 6 are said to grumble or mutter or murmur against him. The same word is used in the Greek Old Testament to describe the Israelites complaining about their apparent misfortunes and lack of provisions. It is truly God who teaches us in Christ, the source of all being and life. Even death could not defeat him. So we can rely on his word and ought not to trust those who can only offer us cucumbers and melons (with slavery) back in worldly Egypt.

At first sight there is no connection of these culinary themes with this week's section of our series in Ephesians. Nothing goes into our mouths in Ephesians 4:25–5:2, though much comes out (lies, evil talk, bitterness, wrangling, slander, malice, etc.). But the link is Christ and our unity with him. God's plan is to bring all things together under one head, Christ. Christ having died for the Church, the Spirit is now building us into a holy temple in him. So the imperatives of Ephesians are all founded on the fact that we are one with him: put away lying, because we are members of one another in Christ; do not let the devil stir up anger between us, because we are united in Christ; give up stealing and help each other instead, because we are one family in Christ; don't tear each other down, but build each other up, because we are sealed by the Spirit into him.

And the sum of all is this: since those who believe in him are children of God, live a life of love in imitation of the Son who gave up his flesh for the life of the world. As Reformation commentator John Calvin (1509–64) puts it, 'If we desire to be partakers of this benefit, we must cultivate similar affections toward our neighbours'.[39]

[39] Calvin, *Commentaries on the Epistles of Paul to the Galatians and Ephesians*, p.304.

Proper 15

Sunday between 14 and 20 August inclusive

Proverbs 9:1–6 · Ephesians 5:15–20 · John 6:51–58 · Psalm 34:9–14

Be very careful, then, how you live – not as unwise but wise, making the most of every opportunity, because the days are evil.

This Sunday's readings in our lectionary point us to Jesus as wisdom for life. He does not merely enlighten our minds, but moves our hearts and changes our direction. Is his wisdom your daily delight, or do other voices and opinions crowd his out?

In Proverbs 9, Wisdom plays the hostess and issues an invitation to all. She has prepared a feast of bread, wine and meat and calls anyone who wants wisdom to participate in this lavish dinner which brings insight to the immature and sense to the simple. Her invitation is mirrored by Folly from verse 13 onwards, who appears to offer something similar, but is not all that she seems. What she offers is an illicit alternative to the wholesome fare on Wisdom's table, which often seems more exciting and enticing, but ends in the depths of Sheol.

Wisdom vs Folly is also the theme of our reading from Ephesians 5. Many will try to deceive us with empty words, saying that what God calls immoral or impure is actually perfectly appropriate for those who are called 'saints'. They tell us that such behaviour will not end in judgment, but is a perfectly acceptable lifestyle for Christians (Ephesians 5:6). In that context, we are not simply to refuse to associate with such soul-destroying seduction (5:7), but be careful about how we ourselves live. To avoid Folly, we must understand what pleases the Lord, and what he has revealed to us about his will for our lives.

God's will is not simply his distant, vague, benevolent hope for us, but his command. There is a battle going on for mastery of our hearts. That is the context of the instruction not to get drunk (Ephesians 5:18). When alcohol takes control, it leads to reckless debauchery. To be drunk is to be senseless, like those 'without sense' being appealed to by the persuasive ladies of Proverbs 9. The alternative is to be controlled, guided, steered, driven, inspired by the Spirit of God. This leads to an alternative lifestyle: the participles of verses 19–21 all look back to the imperative 'be filled' and so describe a Spirit-filled life.

So, like the drunken, people who are filled and led by God will sing: but their singing will be of an entirely different character. It won't be coarse or crude, greedy or gross, but spiritual, scriptural and full of thanksgiving to God. Those who are filled with Jesus by the Spirit will submit to one another out of reverence for Christ: wives to husbands; children to parents, slaves to masters – and fulfil their reciprocal obligations of loving care (husbands to wives; parents to children; masters to slaves).

Jesus also offered food to his people in the Gospel reading, when he said 'I am the living bread – eat me!' Just as Wisdom and Folly in Proverbs were not offering literal food, so Jesus's thought here is far from the monstrously cannibalistic. As he says in verse 63, it is the Spirit who gives life, not any carnal sense of eating. What he offers is spiritual union with him, that Christ might dwell in our hearts through faith, as Ephesians 3 puts it. The bread he offers is the food of his word, which we ought to delight in like a sumptuous banquet bringing life and health to the weary and famished. As the puritan commentator John Owen (1616–83) put it, 'Wherefore, the word being prepared as spiritual food for the soul, faith receives it, and by a spiritual eating and digestion of it, turns it into an increase and strengthening of the vital principles of spiritual obedience. And then doth the word profit them that hear it.'[40] Why would we want the fast food of worldliness (knowing what and where it leads to), when such a feast is on offer for free?

---

[40] Owen, *The Works of John Owen*, 21:250.

Proper 16

Sunday between 21 and 27 August inclusive

Joshua 24:1–2a, 14–18 · Ephesians 6:10–20 · John 6:56–69 · Psalm 34:15–22

Be strong in the Lord and in his mighty power.

Our readings this Sunday urge us to stand firm in the words of eternal life against temptation and trials. No other weapon but God's word is good enough to defend us in the battles we face.

With all the promises of God fulfilled and the Promised Land now in their possession, Joshua gathers together all the tribes of Israel and their leaders in the presence of God. There at Shechem, the very place where Abraham had first heard the promise 'To your offspring I will give this land' (Genesis 12:7), they ratify and renew their covenant with the Lord. Joshua recounts their history: just as Adam and Eve had left Eden and gone East, so they had come once upon a time from the East, and from serving other gods, to this place of redemptive promise.

Joshua then urges them, at this moment of rebirth, to serve God sincerely and faithfully – not listening to the rival claims of their distant past or recent Egyptian deities or indeed the Amorite gods of the place they now lived. For the temptations to soften or abandon our allegiance to God once he has rescued us from slavery or suffering are many and varied. Popular local idolatries can be insidious, and giving them just a little bit of space can seem an attractive or sensible policy. But Joshua is clear what the right approach should be: 'as for me and my household, we will serve the LORD.' The people agree and unite with him; and the words of this covenant are written down and kept on record.

Another Joshua, Jesus (in Greek the name is the same), was teaching the gathered people in Capernaum how to get to an eternal Promised Land, sustained by union with him. Some were offended by his sermon and many turned back from following him as a result. As Reformation theologian John Calvin (1509–64) sagaciously comments: 'We ought, indeed, to regulate our doctrine in such a manner that none may be offended through our fault; as far as possible, we ought to retain all; and, in short, we ought to take care that we do not, by talking inconsiderately or at random, disturb ignorant or weak minds. But it will never be possible for us to exercise such caution that the doctrine of Christ shall not be the occasion of offence to many.' Some people, as he says, 'suck venom from the most wholesome food, and gall from honey'.[41]

What they needed was solid spiritual food – 'the words that I have spoken to you are spirit and life' – but they did not believe and trust the God who speaks. Indeed, no one *can* believe in him and enjoy that inexhaustible fountain of nourishing goodness and truth, unless the Father himself gives them faith: it is not something we can summon up ourselves, but a gift from God which he sweetly presses upon us. No wonder John 6:65 was one of St Augustine's favourite verses against the Pelagians, who thought they had it in them to follow and obey God without much help.[42] Those who do believe instinctively know, with Simon Peter, that there is nowhere else to go but Jesus. He alone has the words of eternal life. No other God, no other words, can suffice. So when the chips are down, we must stick close to him and keep listening.

Paul's rousing conclusion to his letter in Ephesians 6 exhorts us also to 'stand firm' with the strength and courage that God provides. Our struggle is not a temporal battle with human enemies

---

41 John Calvin, *Commentary on the Gospel according to John* (Bellingham, WA: Logos Bible Software, 2010), p. 277.

42 Philip Schaff (ed.), *Saint Augustine: Anti-Pelagian Writings*, vol. 5 of *A Select Library of the Nicene and Post-Nicene Fathers of the Christian Church, First Series* (New York: Christian Literature Company, 1887), pp. 222, 379, 422, 448, 480, 504, 506.

and worldly weapons. Only spiritual armour can withstand spiritual assaults. Taking up key words from earlier in the letter, we are summoned to take up truth and righteousness, a readiness to unite in gospel proclamation, faith to fight the lies of Satan and 'the sword of the Spirit, which is the word of God'. The word and prayer, with boldness, may land us in irons like Paul. But the word itself is not chained, and brings eternal untouchable salvation to those who cling to it. So are you clinging to it, and wielding it in the fight?

Proper 17

Sunday between 28 August and 3 September inclusive

Deuteronomy 4:1–2, 6–9 · James 1:17–27 · Mark 7:1–8, 14–15, 21–23 · Psalm 15

Get rid of all moral filth and the evil that is so prevalent, and humbly accept the word planted in you, which can save you.

The theme of our readings this week is the purity that comes from welcoming the word of God in our hearts. If you want to be pure, have you humbly accepted the word planted in you by God?

In Deuteronomy, Moses called the people of God to pay careful attention to God's words, neither adding to them nor taking away. Their diligence in following what God said would be a witness to the surrounding nations, and make them jealous to have such a good and loving God. They were to welcome the word wholeheartedly, not just on the outside, to remember how God had dealt with them and pass these things on to their children.

For some reason, the lectionary misses out a few verses from the middle of the Deuteronomy reading, presumably because they recall an incident where sexual immorality led to false worship and judgment from God (the Baal of Peor incident, Numbers 25:1–5). Moses, however, thought it useful to remind the people of this, as an illustration of the Lord's attitude towards the behaviour of those who ignore his very clear commands. It may even be quite an appropriate message for our days; as French pastor John Calvin (1509–64) remarks, 'we gather from this passage that we then are truly wise, when we depend on

God's word, and submit our feeling to his revelations'.[43] Better that way round than subordinating God's word to our desires.

Jesus attacked the Pharisees for hypocritically adding to the Law with their own traditions, and taking away from it the inner obedience which was meant to accompany outward observance. They embraced external rituals and cleansing, and kept the Word himself at arm's length. Rabbinic legalism missed the vital essence of the Law, particularly on the issue of purity. As the old commentator Matthew Henry (1662–1714) says, 'We become odious in the sight of God by that which *comes out* of us; our wicked thoughts and affections, words and actions, these defile us, and these only … As a corrupt fountain sends forth corrupt streams, so doth a corrupt heart send forth corrupt reasonings, corrupt appetites and passions, and all those wicked words and actions which are produced by them.'[44] Since Jesus declared all foods clean, those who want to get fit and follow 'a biblical diet' need now to try cutting out evil intentions: 'sexual immorality, theft, murder, adultery, greed, malice, deceit, lewdness, envy, slander, arrogance and folly'. These are far more calorific, spiritually, than anything we can put in our mouths.

James tells us that the unchanging God has implanted his word of truth in our hearts and expects to see some fruit from it. That word gave us new birth, and has the power to save our souls but it is choked by anger and unrighteousness. We must therefore, he says, get rid of 'all sordidness and rank growth of wickedness' (the King James Version has 'superfluity of naughtiness') and instead welcome the word of God with humility. That means not simply hearing it, but doing what it says. This is not a new slavery, but looking into the 'law of liberty', persevering in that which brings us true freedom rather than coating our sin with a veneer of religion.

---

[43] John Calvin, *Commentaries on the Four Last Books of Moses Arranged in the Form of a Harmony* (Bellingham, WA: Logos Bible Software, 2010), p. 348.

[44] Henry, *Matthew Henry's Commentary*, p. 1792.

James also reminds us that true religion which welcomes the word is not only about inner sanctity and consistency of heart. The kind of religion that God finds pleasingly pure and priceless also involves caring for others, particularly the most vulnerable (orphans and widows are just two possible candidates in that category: we might perhaps add others, such as asylum seekers). But our epistle ends with the clear injunction to 'keep oneself unstained by the world'. How many would rather be accepted by the world and plunge with it into judgment, than open the door to unsullied and unsullying Scripture, which the world calls 'repressive' or 'extreme'?

Proper 18

Sunday between 4 and 10 September inclusive

Isaiah 35:4–7a · James 2:1–17 · Mark 7:24–37 · Psalm 146

The LORD watches over the foreigner and sustains the fatherless and the widow, but he frustrates the ways of the wicked.

The passages set for us this week teach us not to show partiality in our applications of the transforming gospel but to embrace outsiders and tell them about the goodness of our God.

Isaiah's prophecy of the redeemed of the Lord returning to Zion with everlasting joy is a beautiful picture of the new exodus he anticipates. Soaring over his own day and age, the centrepiece of this magnificent vision is the coming of God himself: 'Behold your God!' What happens when he comes to save? The eyes of the blind are opened and the ears of the deaf unstopped; the lame leap like a deer and the tongue of the speechless sings for joy. He is also to come 'with vengeance and with terrible recompense' (which in Isaiah 34 turned the once fertile nations into a haunt for jackals), but our passage this week focuses mainly on the positive side of God's arrival. That royal visit will see transformation and the world turned upside down: water in the wilderness, burning sand becoming an oasis. Places that once absorbed all moisture now provide it in abundance. Reversal and restoration come to an inhospitable environment where the dogs lie down and roam free.

In the Gospel, God incarnate goes beyond the borders of Israel to find a Gentile's daughter suffering at the hands of a demon (the Greek word he uses here for 'dogs' is diminutive; it is not the same word used in Isaiah 35, because the Greek Old Testament has no mention of jackals here). Though Jesus's mission at this point in redemptive history was first and foremost to the people of Israel, the wider saving purposes of God are foreshadowed in what he does. The troubled Gentile girl will lie down and sleep in peace because of the faith of her nursing mother (Lamentations 4:3), who comes to Jesus with persistent humility (like the jackals in Isaiah 43:20 who honour the Lord).

Continuing on his foreign adventure, Jesus goes from Tyre to Sidon to the Decapolis. The 'Galilee of the nations' in the North enjoys his light (as Isaiah 9:1–2 had prophesied). Just as Isaiah said, the ears of the deaf man were then unstopped and though he was once speechless, he is enabled to speak again, with joy. Jesus commanded people at this point not to talk about what he'd done: a very effective evangelistic strategy! (Many today find, ironically, that they become speechless and mute the moment they read Jesus's positive command to take the gospel to all nations!) People are astounded beyond measure at the great reversal and healing that he brings, even outside Israel.

James challenges us – do we really believe in the same glorious Lord Jesus Christ, who did these astonishing, levelling things, if we show partiality in our churches? He bites at the prejudices of his day, and the preferences we have for the comfortable classes who dress well and speak with the proper accent (and went to the right school, college, or camp). This is not a picture of the Sunday welcoming team showing favouritism as they allocate seating, though obviously it could apply. The context is more of 'judges with evil thoughts' in a church court, deciding a dispute between two parties – a court that has forgotten that Jesus promised a great reversal of the ways of the world: the poor would inherit the kingdom of God (Luke 6:20). We are not to run church the way the ungodly run the world, judging by outward appearance. And in the same way, we are not to simply wish pious thoughts over people's needs, but with living faith care for the needs of others, both in body and soul, as Jesus did.

Proper 19

Sunday between 11 and 17 September inclusive

Isaiah 50:4–9a · James 3:1–12 · Mark 8:27–38 · Psalm 116:1–9

With the tongue we praise our Lord and Father, and with it we curse human beings, who have been made in God's likeness.

Our readings this week teach us that there is no shame for the one who speaks true words, though the tongue can put us in great peril. Are you careful with your words?

In the third of Isaiah's great 'servant songs', the Servant is a teacher who knows how to sustain the weary with a word of encouragement. His ability to impart truth comes from his lifelong attentiveness to the word of God, as 'morning by morning' he listens to it himself and humbly submits to what he hears. This places him in harm's way, however, though quite why is not yet revealed (though it is startlingly clear at the cross of the Lord Jesus Christ). Certainly, speaking the truth with persistence can lead to pushback, but for the Servant there are those who would strike him, pull out his beard, spit on him and disgrace him. However, he does not draw back because he knows that ultimately he will be vindicated. The Sovereign Lord (*Adonai YHWH*) helps him, so he will not be put to shame, whoever his adversaries might be.

Peter's words in the Gospel reading are both shockingly right and sinfully brazen. Others have faulty perceptions of who Jesus is, but Peter is spot on. He confesses with his tongue that Jesus is the Christ, the staggering but inevitable conclusion after all he has seen and heard in Mark 1–8. But when Jesus tells his disciples plainly about the suffering (and glory) that is to come, just as Isaiah and others had prophesied, the Rock wades in with his own alternative plan, rebuking the Lord for not really understanding what being the Messiah was supposed to be about. He is rebuked in return, for daring to correct God incarnate about God's will. He had his eyes on the glory of being associated with the Messiah, but was keen to bypass the cross.

Jesus turns to teach both the disciples and the crowd a more excellent way. To follow him means taking up a cross, losing your life for Jesus and the gospel. Gaining all the glory of this world is nothing in comparison to the priceless salvation of one's immortal soul. But the way to obtain that unsurpassed good is through the scorn and hatred of an adulterous and sinful generation. It requires resilience in the face of such painful opposition not to be ashamed of the words and ways of Jesus. But there is no shame on the day of judgment for the one who sticks to the glorious Son of Man and his unerring words.

James teaches us that teachers themselves will be judged more strictly when that day comes. It is a noble yet fearful task to be called as a teacher in God's church. An unruly tongue is a great evil, and the tongue of a teacher can do far more damage than most. Sexual and financial scandals often engulf pastors and churches; but an uncontrolled and ungodly tongue can bring untold ruin, and is surprisingly more difficult to tame. As the old commentator Matthew Henry (1662–1714) wisely observes, 'Other sins decay with age, this many times gets worse; we grow more froward and fretful, as natural strength decays, and the days come on in which we have no pleasure. When other sins are tamed and subdued by the infirmities of age, the spirit often grows more tart, nature being drawn down to the dregs, and the words used become more passionate.'[45] So let us guard our tongues from the fiery influence of hell, that we might not be ashamed when our words are played back to us on the Last Day.

---

[45] Matthew Henry and Thomas Scott, *Matthew Henry's Concise Commentary* (Oak Harbor, WA: Logos Research Systems, 1997), Jas 3:1.

Proper 20

Sunday between 18 and 24 September inclusive

Jeremiah 11:18–20 · James 3:13–4:3, 7–8a · Mark 9:30–37 · Psalm 54

The wisdom that comes from heaven is first of all pure; then peace-loving, considerate, submissive, full of mercy and good fruit, impartial and sincere.

Our readings this week teach us that when there are plots and arguments within the people of God, true wisdom is found in imitating Jesus and trusting in God to judge. Do you love a good fight, or do you have that wisdom which comes from above?

In the short reading from a section of the 'confessions' of Jeremiah (Jeremiah 11:18–12:6), we hear the prophet lamenting the suffering he must endure for being a spokesman of God. There are iniquitous schemes against his life, from people *in his own home town*, who want to silence him for good (destroying both the tree – the prophet, and its fruit – his words). He feels he has been led like a lamb to the slaughter, but he commits his cause to the Lord who sees the whole conspiracy. Like Jesus, he trusts that his vindication will come from God 'who judges justly' (1 Peter 2:23).

The Lord Jesus continues in Mark's Gospel to teach his disciples about the conspiracy against him – how he will be betrayed and killed, but rise again. As every preacher (and every parent) knows, no matter how many times you repeat some things, they can take a while to sink in, and the disciples have not yet grasped what Jesus is saying about the intrigues against him and how they fit within God's wider purpose. The disciples have certainly not heard what Jesus has said about the cross. They continue to seek glory and positions of honour for themselves, realising that they are destined for something significant being associated with the Messiah, but not yet perceiving the primacy of humility. They argue and fight and try to be first, so Jesus teaches them that to be first they must be last and learn how to serve. Not only how to serve, but how to welcome others too – he takes a child in his arms on this occasion not to give them an illustration of meekness, but to teach them to embrace those who are lowly and without status. For in honouring those who are seemingly weak and unimportant they would demonstrate that they had understood what Jesus says about his own approaching degradation. They long to be in the inner circle of the glorious King of Kings; they must accept that the one sent by the Father will suffer an ignominious death on their behalf.

James shows in his epistle that he did later absorb the truth of what the Master taught. He speaks of how bitter envy and selfish ambition are the precise opposite of good works 'done with gentleness born of wisdom'. The way of Jesus is not the earthly, unspiritual, devilish road which brings disorder and wickedness along with sanctimonious pride. These are the stratagems of Satan, and do not lead to heavenly wisdom which is 'pure; then peace-loving, considerate, submissive, full of mercy and good fruit, impartial and sincere'. Our conflicts and disputes come from our covetous cravings, which suggest a whole host of evil machinations to our ungodly minds. James simply says 'You do not have because you do not ask.' And when we do turn to prayer, it is often for our own comfort and joy, not that of others.

The conclusion is that we must draw near to God, and submit to his counterintuitive way of blessing, as patterned for us in the wisdom of the cross and resurrection. As we resist the devil, his plots and his impulses of impatience, we are purified for Christ's service, and sow a harvest which in due time we will reap. Can we trust God to arbitrate all our disputes, and so be meek and merciful to those who stand against us?

Proper 21

Sunday between 25 September and 1 October inclusive

Numbers 11:4–6, 10–16, 24–29 · James 5:13–20 · Mark 9:38–50 · Psalm 19:7–14

Truly I tell you, anyone who gives you a cup of water in my name because you belong to the Messiah will certainly not lose their reward.

In the Bible passages set for this week, we learn that our complaints about what is appropriate or possible must be set in the context of God's far wider, eternal plan to deal with our sin. Why complain when God has it all in hand?

As usual, the people of Israel in the wilderness are groaning and dissatisfied. It was ever thus with the people of God. They quickly lose interest in salvation and grow impatient with waiting for the promises to be fulfilled. They begin meditating instead on all the lovely things they have left behind. Who cares that they were in slavery – there were cucumbers and melons! Who cares that they were brutalised and dehumanised? – there were leeks, onions and garlic!

Moses, the servant of God, joins in with some grievances of his own – why have you treated me so badly, God? 'These are not *my* people, but yours, so why do I have to find decent food for them and listen to all this moaning? I'd rather die than bear it any more.' Understandable, perhaps, but inappropriate and untrusting when you consider what this God can do. He inspires seventy elders to help bear the burdens, even surprising Joshua, who sees blessings in unexpected places that he thinks he might have to quash. Would that all the Lord's people were prophets.

In the Gospel, the disciples also get nervous when they see demons cast out in Jesus's name by someone who is not from their group. Jesus tells them not to suppress such deeds, for whoever is not against us is for us. Would that more were not against us. We might think no sacrifice is too small to achieve our dreams or secure our comforts. But Jesus says there is a reward for anyone who makes sacrifices motivated by his name. Hands, feet, eyes and health are nothing, if they are kept at the expense of offending God. It is worth any sacrifice to avoid the unquenchable fire and undying worm of conscience in hell. In the light of eternity, no merely temporal sacrifice is ever improper or malapropos. The radical problem of sin requires drastic surgery – not the literal lopping off of limbs and organs, but the vigorously comprehensive solution of a new birth – hands, feet and eyes re-animated by a sin-abhorring Spirit.

When we do suffer physically (and we are all terminally ill with mortality and decay), the temptation is always to protest, as if it were unusual or unfitting. The most appropriate response, says the letter of James, is to pray and seek spiritual support, not only scans and medication. Speaking to some who had failed to spot the lengthy shadow cast upon this world by the coming day of judgment, who were too interested in the here and now, he reminds us all that our greatest need is not to rise from our sickbeds and be well again, but to be raised on the Last Day and saved for eternity.

The problem is our sins, which we must confess to one another and bring to God for forgiveness. Healing from this most devastating and deadly of diseases is open to all. The prayers of those who are right with God are powerful and effective, says James, and like Elijah's can bring welcome refreshment and conversion. They can even save wanderers who are drifting away from the fountain of all goodness. Bringing them back to God saves their souls from eternal death – the kind of spiritual therapy which we ought to value far more highly than we do, in an age too devoted to the cult of present happiness and wholeness.

Proper 22

Sunday between 2 and 8 October inclusive

Genesis 2:18–24 · Hebrews 1:1–4, 2:5–12 · Mark 10:2–16 · Psalm 8

Let the little children come to me, and do not hinder them, for the kingdom of God belongs to such as these.

The theme of our readings this week is the image of God and the redemption of the family. God makes Adam and Eve in his own image, for intimate relationship, but he also includes children in his heavenly kingdom.

In the passage from Genesis 2, we read of the creation of woman and the first marriage. Eve is not only the solution to Adam's 'aloneliness', but the one who enables God's image in humanity to be fully manifest: 'in the image of God he created man ... male and female he created *them*' (Genesis 1:27).

Eve was formed from Adam's side 'so that it should be shown that she was created for the partnership of love', as the medieval theologian Peter Lombard (1100–1160) put it in his famous *Sentences*. 'She was made neither to dominate, nor to serve the man, but as his partner.'[46] The old commentator Matthew Henry (1662–1714) glosses Lombard's thought beautifully by commenting that she was 'not made out of his head to rule over him, nor out of his feet to be trampled upon by him, but out of his side to be equal with him, under his arm to be protected, and near his heart to be beloved'.[47] She was both suitable helper (a title

[46] Peter Lombard, *Libri Quatuor Sententiarum*, Book 2, Distinction 18, Chapter 2; Giulio Silano (ed.), *The Sentences: Book 2 On Creation* (Toronto: Pontifical Institute of Mediaeval Studies, 2008), p. 77.

[47] Henry, *Matthew Henry's Commentary*, p. 10.

often given to God himself, the help of Israel) and a match made in heaven – bone of Adam's bone and flesh of his flesh, in holy intimacy.

In Jesus's day, this was radical teaching. What God had joined together in the marriage of male and female was not to be rent asunder. But serial adultery had resulted when merely human legislation interposed. Christ taught his disciples to go back to the account of creation to learn the Creator's intention. Hard hearts and stiff necks meant divorce and separation marred God's perfect design. But it was not so at first.

Jesus also subverted another sinful relational perspective: the way people thought about children. They too were made in the image of God, and made to be part of his kingdom. Jesus says 'of such' is that kingdom. He is saying more than that we must be like children to inherit the kingdom (a point he makes elsewhere). Bearing in mind how the pronoun 'of such' is used in the Gospels, it cannot mean simply 'those *like* this' while excluding actual children. Jesus is saying that their low social status was no bar to their redemption and inclusion in the covenant family. This is not just a strong indirect argument for infant baptism, but (as the nineteenth-century Presbyterian theologian Charles Hodge put it) indicates that heaven is 'in great measure, composed of the souls of redeemed infants'.[48]

Sundays in October this year bring us a short series in the letter to the Hebrews. In the week's readings we learn that the one who created the worlds and sustains them by his powerful word was for a little while made lower than the angels. Now he reigns at the right hand of the Father, having tasted death for us. Christ took our flesh and blood so that, through his death, we might become bone of his bone and flesh of his flesh. He unites himself to humanity physically in order to save his children, his brethren, his people spiritually, giving himself up for his bride.

---

[48] Charles Hodge, *Systematic Theology* (Oak Harbor, WA: Logos Research Systems, Inc., 1997), p. 27 (2.3.A).

As French Reformer John Calvin (1509–64) preached, Jesus 'has taken a nature that is common to us, by which he has made himself intimate with us,'[49] an intimacy which is accomplished by his Spirit as we are united to him through faith. Christ is gathering together not just many individuals, but a new family for his kingdom.

[49] Calvin, *Sermons on the Epistle to the Ephesians*, pp. 600–601.

Proper 23

Sunday between 9 and 15 October inclusive

Amos 5:6–7, 10–15 · Hebrews 4:12–16 · Mark 10:17–31 · Psalm 90:12–17

Everything is uncovered and laid bare before the eyes of him to whom we must give account.

Our readings this week show us that if we are to be saved, Jesus must be merciful to us because he knows our hearts and can detect our lack of dedication to him, especially regarding our use of wealth. Did you realise that nothing is hidden from him?

Amos 5 urges us to 'seek the Lord and live' – or face the consequences. Amos addresses a people who had disregarded 'righteousness' in the public square, especially by misusing the power that comes with wealth, and by trampling over the poor. Yet God knows what they are up to. Whatever is done in secret, is still wide open to him. 'For I know how many are your transgressions, and how great are your sins,' he says. Even then, if they 'seek good and not evil' they may live, if the Lord of Hosts chooses to be gracious to the remnant of the people.

This Old Testament teaching puts the Gospel narrative into proper focus. A man (we know from elsewhere that he is a rich ruler: Luke 18), comes to Jesus and calls him 'Good Teacher'. One would expect this auspicious start to meet with approval, but Jesus provokes him straight away by asking, 'Why do you call me good? There is only one who is good.' In other words, not you, young man! (Which should prevent people saying, as they sometimes do these days, 'I'm good', when asked how they are.) Are you calling Jesus good because you recognise that he has been sent from the source of all goodness *himself*...? Or is he 'good' but not 'the greatest'?

This man seems to have kept all the commandments, though, ominously, Jesus (who loves him, despite his shortcomings) omits to ask him how he has done with regards to *coveting*. This gives him the chance to claim he has kept them all. So again Jesus provokes him and challenges him to demonstrate his obedience to the tenth commandment. He is shocked. He is sad. Because it is a big ask, and his identity is wrapped up in something other than in loving Jesus.

The disciples are shocked too when told that just because God has blessed someone with wealth this does not mean he will bless them with eternal life as well. Riches are a test, and a temptation, not testimony to our spirituality. We need mercy, and only God can help, because we so often fail such tests. Though all those who truly give up everything to follow Jesus – our greatest treasure – and serve his gospel will never be at a loss for friends, family, fields and persecutions. And in the age to come, eternal life. God is no man's debtor.

Hebrews 4:12 continues the same theme. The Word of God is alive and not inactive. This could be, as many take it, a reference to Scripture. The Bible cuts into our hearts and exposes our thoughts and intentions. But it is possible that Hebrews refers here to the Word of God incarnate himself (as in John 1:1, Luke 1:2, and Revelation 19:13). The next verse, Hebrews 4:13, continues the same Greek sentence and it seems to require a personal reference, so many have taken it this way and think the Word here is Jesus. But either way, we are unprotected and laid bare, and open to God's judgment.

Yet at the same time, we have a great high priest to whom we can run. He sympathises with our weaknesses. We can run to him for help and find both mercy and grace in time of need. Every time we open our wallets or complete our tax returns, it is just such a time! He knows every penny we spend, and our bank statements are theological documents, revealing what we truly believe about God and his promises.

Proper 24

Sunday between 16 and 22 October inclusive

Isaiah 53:4–12 · Hebrews 5:1–10 · Mark 10:35–45 · Psalm 91:9–16

Surely he took up our pain and bore our suffering, yet we considered him punished by God, stricken by him, and afflicted.

Our readings this week show us that the service of the weak is more effective than the power of the strong. Jesus exercised his power to save us, through enduring the weakness of the cross, and shows us the way to true greatness.

The poem of the Suffering Servant in Isaiah 52–53 is a carefully crafted passages of five stanzas, but only the final three are set for our reading. Verses 4–6 are the centre of the cross-shaped structure, in which we learn that the highly exalted and wise servant of Isaiah 52:13 is also subject to the punishment of weakness and death. As our substitute he bears *our* infirmities and carries *our* diseases. He is oppressed and afflicted, condemned by a perversion of justice and looked upon by human eyes as defeated.

But there is a purpose in his suffering: he takes away the sin of the world – wounded, crushed, punished in our place with our iniquity on his back. The hand of God lies behind this seeming miscarriage of justice: it was his will, his plan to lay sin on a substitutionary sacrifice. The result is a turnaround of cosmic proportions: God's will shall prosper, the Servant will see everlasting fruit from his labour, and out of the anguish of his soul he shall see light and find satisfaction. Though cut off for a time, poured out and spent, he ends up with a portion among the great, dividing the spoil with the strong. He not only died to bear the sin of many but because he now lives he intercedes for transgressors.

Hebrews 5 reminds us that this experience of weakness was part of Jesus's qualification for ministry as our great high priest. He can deal gently with us, the ignorant and wayward, because he understands our weakness, though he himself drank temptation to the dregs and still resisted every drop of its power. He was appointed by God as our priest in the order of Melchizedek – we now need no other priest in that or any other order, because Jesus is still very much alive and active on our behalf.

He learned obedience, qualified for the role of eternal high priest, and became the source of salvation for all his faithful people. As the early church preacher, John Chrysostom (died 407) says in application of this point, 'If he, though the Son, gains obedience from his sufferings, how much more shall we?'[50] All our afflictions have ultimate purpose.

In Mark 8 the disciples realise who Jesus is. In chapters 8–10 he repeatedly tells them that he must suffer in weakness before rising from the dead. Yet James and John, those sons of thunder, hear only the lines about the glory to come and long for personal greatness. So the Lord patiently teaches them again that the way which leads to glory lies through service of others, not through lording it over them, even when that results in pain and discomfort.

The early church writer, Ephrem the Syrian (died 373) once starkly said that 'the one who abased himself to such humility and suffering for his murderers is the Son of God'.[51] And if even the glorious Son of God and Son of Man did not come to be served and pampered but to serve those who were his enemies, how can we imagine that our path to eternity could be any less abasing or self-renouncing? He gives his life as a ransom for many; as we, in imitation, pour out our own strength for the sake of others too – even those we do not like. This is the way to true greatness.

---

[50] John Chrysostom, Homilies of St. John Chrysostom, Archbishop of Constantinople, on the Epistle to the Hebrews', in *Saint Chrysostom: Homilies on the Gospel of St. John and Epistle to the Hebrews*, ed. Philip Schaff, trans. T. Keble and Frederic Gardiner, vol. 14 of *A Select Library of the Nicene and Post-Nicene Fathers of the Christian Church, First Series* (New York: Christian Literature Company, 1889), p. 404.

[51] Erik M. Heen and Philip D. W. Krey (eds.), *Hebrews*, Ancient Christian Commentary on Scripture (Downers Grove, IL: InterVarsity Press, 2005), p. 72.

Proper 25

Sunday between 23 and 29 October inclusive

Jeremiah 31:7–9 · Hebrews 7:23–28 · Mark 10:46–52 · Psalm 126

He is able to save completely those who come to God through him, because he always lives to intercede for them.

The readings for this week rejoice in the everlasting salvation which Christ has brought to his people, opening their eyes to see his glory as they approach him by faith. Will you approach him today for help?

Jeremiah's prophecy of a return from exile for the remnant of Israel begins with loud shouts of gladness and praise to the one who saves his people. But it is more than a localised event – they come from the land of the North, but also from 'the farthest parts of the earth' to enjoy restoration and refreshment. And in this mass movement of people come not just the strong but the weak and vulnerable too: the blind, the lame, pregnant mothers. They come weeping, but will be consoled; thirsty, but will find brooks of water; as John Newton put it, 'through many dangers, toils, and snares,' led on a straight path back to God their Father.

In our Gospel reading, one particular blind beggar shouts out to the Lord and is saved. He can't be silenced by the stern rebukes of onlookers, but cries out even more to 'Jesus, Son of David' – the merciful King. Martin Luther, the German Reformer, once pictured those crowds trying to silence Bartimaeus as like the crowd of thoughts that seek to hinder us from praying, and upbraid us by saying, 'Why do you want to pray? Do you not know what you are and what God is?' Many voices tell us that it is pointless to pray and it accomplishes nothing, that Jesus cannot or will not give us what we need and want. They are 'burdensome for the spirit,' said Luther, 'and hinder very many'. Yet we must push through the crowds, for Jesus stands and bids us come to him. As Luther says, 'a truly great struggle of the spirit is necessary'.[52]

The blind beggar comes not just asking for money or help for the moment, but for sight. His spiritual perception is acute, for he recognises Jesus for who he is, and on this basis Christ restores his vision as well. It is a gift with a purpose – that the man might now follow Jesus in faith on the way.

Hebrews 7 speaks of a solid salvation which is accomplished once and for all, and never needs to be repeated or reiterated or re-presented. The priesthood of Christ, it says, is permanent because he is alive for ever. Priests under the old covenant needed to be replaced from time to time because they had a limited lifespan and tended to die eventually. But Jesus lives for ever! 'Consequently, he is able to save completely those who come to God through him.' He did not leave us for the glories of a distant heaven, passing on his priesthood to another (whether Peter, or anyone else). He continues to exercise it himself, personally and directly, making intercession for all those who come to him.

What's more, Jesus's sacrifice is far superior to the sacrifices made by any earthly priest. Unlike them he is holy, blameless, undefiled and utterly exalted. Yet he gave up his own life for weak and seedy sinners like us, as a perfect and definitive, once-and-for-all-time offering which needs no repetition. As the old hymn 'Before the throne of God above' by Charitie Lees Smith puts it, 'Because the sinless saviour died, my sinful soul is counted free. For God the just is satisfied, to look on him and pardon me.' The perfect priest offers the perfect sacrifice, and he 'ever lives and pleads for me' – he is alive for ever, continuing to apply the benefits of his saving work to his faithful people, so that 'no tongue can bid me thence depart'. So let us press through the crowds that would keep us from him.

[52] Martin Luther, *Luther's Works, Vol. 12: Selected Psalms I*, ed. Jaroslav Jan Pelikan, Hilton C. Oswald, and Helmut T. Lehmann (Saint Louis: Concordia Publishing House, 1999), pp. 317–18.

4th Sunday before Advent

Sunday between 30 October and 5 November inclusive

Deuteronomy 6:1–9 · Hebrews 9:11–14 · Mark 12:28–34 · Psalm 119:1–8

How much more, then, will the blood of Christ, who through the eternal Spirit offered himself unblemished to God, cleanse our consciences from acts that lead to death, so that we may serve the living God!

Our theme this week is the great theme of covenant love, which is shown most powerfully in the sacrifice of Christ on our behalf. Come to him with reverent awe and love, to experience his blessings.

Deuteronomy is Moses's farewell address to the people of Israel. In this long speech, he tells the Israelites all the commands, decrees and laws which God has told him that they must observe in the land he is giving them. Moses is about to die, but he wants those who are about to enter the land to enjoy a long life in the land, to flourish and increase. Central to this is the idea that they must fear the Lord, and that their children after them must fear the Lord. The word 'fear' conjures up to our modern minds certain ideas of terror, control, dread, anxiety and panic. But to the ancient Hebrews it means so much more than that. In this context, it is more of an inspiring reverence, an awe or devotion that they are to have for their God, who had brought them out of Egypt to be his treasured possession (Exodus 19:5).

The primary way in which people can fear the Lord is to love him with everything they are. So Moses says, 'Listen up! Hear, O Israel! What I am about to tell you is supremely important.' First and foremost they should love the Lord their God. Not just the Lord who is God, but the one who is *their* God, 'your God' –

their covenant Lord who has bound himself to them uniquely and exclusively by a solemn oath. They are to reciprocate the love he has shown to them in a holy monogamy, as their only God. They are to love God with all their hearts (not divided hearts, as the Psalmist confessed he had in Psalm 86:11). They are to love him with all their souls. And they are to love him with all their strength (or literally their 'very muchness'). That love will require them not to keep the covenant to themselves, but to talk about it excitedly and continuously with their children and surround themselves with reminders of it (symbols on their hands, posters on their doorframes and on their gates).

Someone who was devoted to the covenant law hears the Lord Jesus debating it with others, in the Gospel. Like me at the beginning of all these expositions of the Lectionary, he is enthusiastic about the practice of summarising things neatly to help him get a handle on things. So he asks Jesus what the most important commandment is in the Old Testament. There are around six hundred commandments in the Law, and he wants to know which was first, which summed them all up. In answer, Jesus recites the *Shema* ('Hear!' in Hebrew) from Deuteronomy 6, although we should note that in Mark's Gospel at least, Jesus adds 'with all your mind' to his translation of the original, to bring out the intellectual aspect of loving God with your 'soul and strength'. He also added a second great commandment: that we should love our neighbours as ourselves (see Leviticus 19:18). The teacher of the Law is impressed with this response, adding that love for God and for neighbour is surely more important than all the burnt offerings and sacrifices which the Law also laid down. Jesus says this answer was wise, and that he is on the right path to the kingdom of God.

Our reading from Hebrews 9 does not mention the word love at all. But it is very much concerned with the covenant and expounds a contrast between the old covenant and the new, particularly regarding those sacrifices and offerings laid down in the Mosaic Law. Hebrews says that what Christ came to do as high priest of the new covenant was not offer the blood of bulls and goats on the Temple altar, and sprinkle the ashes of a heifer on the ceremonially unclean. That was just a picture, a shadow of the reality. In a marvellously Trinitarian way, Christ offered his own blood, by the eternal Spirit, to God the Father. This cleanses us, not ritually, but really, in our consciences. And because of this once-and-for-all-time definitive act of atonement, we can now serve the living God. This act by which Christ showed his love for God and for us enables and inspires us in return to love him, and live for him each day with a clean conscience.

3rd Sunday before Advent

Sunday between 6 and 12 November inclusive

Jonah 3:1–5, 10 · Hebrews 9:24–28 · Mark 1:14–20 · Psalm 62:5–12

The time has come. The kingdom of God has come near.
Repent and believe the good news!

The passages set for this Sunday remind us of the one thing we must always keep before us in remembrance – the necessity of repentance and faith.

We begin with the bald assertion in Hebrews 9 that 'it is appointed for mortals to die once, and after that the judgment'. For the writer to the Hebrews, there is death, then judgment; after that there is heaven or hell, but as St Augustine (354–430) is reputed to have said, 'of a third place, we are utterly ignorant, neither is it found in the sacred Scriptures'.[53] Opinions have differed about that among Christians over the centuries, but the main point in Hebrews is to remind us how definitive the work of Jesus is and how soon we may face judgment.

Hebrews 9 gives us the hope that, just as we die once and then face judgment, Christ was offered once and for all to bear the sins of many, and will return again to save those who are waiting for him. The decisiveness of our death is mirrored by the definitiveness of his redemptive, substitutionary offering.

In the light of this, the remembrance of death calls us to repent and turn to Christ. After a faltering start, Jonah obeys the Lord and proclaims this message to his enemies in Nineveh. He warns them of serious judgment to come, and they believe God's word to them through the prophet. Great and small, they repent in sackcloth and fast in hope of forgiveness. Seeing them turn from their evil ways, it seems that God

---

[53] Pseudo-Augustine in *Hypomnesticon Vulgo Libri Hypognosticon*, Book 5 chapter 5. Migne, *Patrologia Latina*, 45:1654.

turned from his threat of calamity; though as we know 'there is no shadow of turning' with him' (James 1:17). He purposed to save them from his judgment all along; it just took his servant Jonah a while to come to terms with such outrageous grace, which flows to us in repentance.

The announcement of God's sovereign rule, when he would put all things right, is the great indicative of Jesus's own preaching. Once his cousin John, the greatest prophet of the Old Testament era, was arrested, the time for the new era had finally arrived. The inevitable corollary was a call to repentance – a change of mind and heart and life – and the embrace of a different way. He did not come merely to announce good news or show the way. Announcing a kingdom, he commanded as King that all must bow the knee. The decisive, imperative 'Stop that – follow me instead!' was clearly heard by Simon and Andrew, as well as James and John.

In the same way, we often stop what we are doing on Remembrance Day or Memorial Day or Veterans Day. Not just for two minutes of silent reflection on the horrors of war and our own mortality. We must hear again the call to follow Jesus and to leave behind our old life of self-serving labours. With apologies to the pagan poet Horace and the First World War poet Wilfred Owen, it is sweet and honourable to die to sin and live instead for righteousness.[54] Death relentlessly pursues the one who will not, and all who fight shy of repentance in this life will not be spared in the next. The pagan Horace concluded that 'virtue opens a way to heaven for those who deserve not to die'.[55] But in reality it is repentance and faith in Jesus Christ which opens the door for the undeserving, that we might know eternal life and peace.

---

[54] The ancient poet Horace said *dulce et decorum set pro patria mori*, 'it is sweet and right to die for one's country'. Horace, *Odes*, III.2.13. This was famously echoed in Wilfrid Owen's first world war poem, *Dulce et Decorum Est*, in which he called it 'the old lie'.

[55] Horace, *Odes*, III.2.24 translated by David West in *The Complete Odes and Epodes* (Oxford: Oxford University Press, 2008).

2nd Sunday before Advent

Sunday between 13 and 19 November inclusive

Daniel 12:1–3 · Hebrews 10:11–25 · Mark 13:1–8 · Psalm 16

You will not abandon me to the realm of the dead.

This Sunday we will mainly focus on the reading from Psalm 16, which is an expression of confidence in God's redemption and reward. It is a prophecy about Jesus and his victory over death, and those who rely on him will not rot.

Psalm 16 is a *miktam*, which is a Hebrew musical term related to the Hebrew word for fine gold. So it is no surprise that this is sometimes called the Golden Psalm of David. There are a few other miktams in the Bible (e.g. Psalms 56–60), and they are all calls for God to help and rescue King David in times of difficulty, when he's struggling with the Philistines or with Saul or someone else. We're not given any historical setting as such; there are no Philistines or evil dictators in the background chasing David as far as we know. The one great enemy in this psalm is mentioned in verse 10. David begins by praying for God to preserve him in verse 1, and in verse 10 he is confident of that divine help: 'For you will not abandon my me to the realm of the dead [or 'sheol'], nor will you let your holy one see decay.' David is praying to God, and is assured that God will answer. He is convinced that God will save him from death.

We may not face foreign foes or giants. But we do all face death. If David thinks God can save him from death, then perhaps there is some hope for us too? Perhaps here is the secret of eternal life, a real 'holy grail' that would be well worth inscribing in gold letters anywhere? Verse 11, for example, is well worth savouring: 'You make known to me the path of life; in your presence there is fullness of joy; at your right hand are pleasures for evermore.' This a stirring vision of a future beyond death, a secure future for my whole being, including my flesh. It's a physical future, more exciting and real than anything on this earth.

'I believe that when I die, I shall rot' the atheistic philosopher Bertrand Russell (1872–1970) once said. He did not 'shiver with terror at the thought of annihilation', he claimed.[1] Whatever he liked to believe, Russell was wrong about reality. Because the Psalmist says there is life beyond death, with no corruption or decay. The Bible says that when we die we are judged by God, and then live for ever. Annihilation is not an option. We live on – in either pleasure or agony, heaven or hell. As our reading from Daniel 12 says: 'Multitudes who sleep in the dust of the earth will awake: some to everlasting life, others to shame and everlasting contempt.'

The Psalmist says that he has been shown the path of life, the way to fullness of joy the secret of everlasting happiness. He's been shown the way to a place where God is neither distant or absent but right there to be known, to be enjoyed.

And yet, inside his tomb, David's flesh did not dwell secure. It went mouldy and decomposed. Bertrand Russell was right, in one way. But David spoke better than he knew. He was not just a king but a prophet. According to the New Testament (Acts 2, Acts 13), Psalm 16 is not only a psalm of David, but a psalm of his greater son, King Jesus. This is what Jesus is singing on the day between Good Friday and Easter morning. 'O Lord, you will not abandon me to the grave for ever…' He is devoted to God and delighted in him alone, so he is confident of God's continual care, even beyond death. He knows that there are pleasures beyond death for those who are wholeheartedly devoted to God. In other words, here is the main point: God's promise of a better life and a better world on the other side of that great river is for those who can sing 'O God, my refuge,

---

1 Bertrand Russell, *What I Believe* (1925), chapter 1 on 'Nature and Man'.

keep me safe: on you my good depends; O Lord, you are my Lord alone, your saints my choicest friends … My heart and soul rejoice in you and in your power to save: you will not leave your Holy One to perish in the grave.'[2]

So, as our Hebrews reading says, let us not give up meeting together, as some are in the habit of doing, but encourage one another with the thoughts of Psalm 16, 'and all the more as you see the Day approaching' (Hebrews 10:25).

---

2 *O God, my refuge, keep me safe* by David G. Preston, © Author / Jubilate Hymns. See https://www.praise.org.uk/.

Sunday next before Advent (Christ the King)

Sunday between 20 and 26 November inclusive

Daniel 7:9–10, 13–14 · Revelation 1:4b–8 · John 18:33–37 · Psalm 93

Your throne was established long ago; you are from all eternity.

This week's Sunday readings encourage patient faith by showing us that the kingdom of Christ and of God is a kingdom that is not of this world, but one which endures for ever.

The message of the book of Daniel is that God always remains the true God, so stay faithful to him despite pressure to compromise. The potential compromises presented to God's people in the first half of the book are seen in a more apocalyptic perspective in chapters 7–12. After the visions in the first part of chapter 7, coded references to earthly kingdoms, we are introduced to the One who reigns for ever.

Who is this? In the biblical worldview, this Ancient of Days can only be God. He is ancient and sits on the fiery throne, with the hosts of heaven serving him as he sits in judgment on the whole world. But there are two thrones set in place in verse 9, not just one. Who is the other one for?

This figure comes on the clouds of heaven. The way the Bible uses that phrase, only one person travels like that. It's God. As Psalm 104 puts it, the Lord 'makes the clouds his chariot; he rides on the wings of the wind'. He rides on a swift cloud (Isaiah 19). He rides on a fiery chariot with wheels, on an immense cloud (Ezekiel 1). And he is worshipped as a god. Two figures, two persons we might say, acknowledged as God. And one is like a son of Adam too. It is hard for us not to see here a picture of the glorified God-man, our Lord Jesus.

Here is *the* son of man. The one destined to rule over the world for eternity. A godly son of Adam who defeats the beastly kingdoms. Though when the representative of one of those beastly powers confronted him with a sword at his throat (as it were), in John 18, he made the good confession that his kingdom was not of this world. So his followers are not to physically fight, to crusade, to establish his dominion. His authority is established through what looks to the human eye like weakness, not strength. Yet his power is made perfect in weakness, and his weakness is stronger than any earthly power. Those who belong to the truth listen to his voice – through which he created, sustains, and will rule the universe.

Revelation 1 shows the climactic denouement of this biblical theme. The one who loves us and freed us from our sins by shedding his own blood is now the firstborn from the dead and ruler of the kings of the earth. His death achieved that victory and supremacy, a glory and dominion which endures for ever, unlike the transient kingdoms of this world. And when he returns in transparent glory, every eye will have an unmistakeable view of his true nature; most terrifyingly, perhaps, 'even those who pierced him' will see the unexpected result of their nefarious work.

Since this is our God, the risen and ascended Lord Jesus, how can we grow weary or lose heart in all our present battles? With our eyes fixed on him and the joy that is set before us in his kingdom, we can endure with patient faith whatever slings and arrows may be propelled in our direction by outrageous fortune. We have no need to take up arms against them, other than the weapons of spiritual warfare, the word of God and prayer. May we, like Jesus, be faithful witnesses even unto death.

YEAR C
1st Sunday of Advent

28 November 2027
1 December 2030
27 November 2033
30 November 2036
27 November 2039

ADVENT

1st Sunday of Advent

Jeremiah 33:14–16 · 1 Thessalonians 3:9–13 · Luke 21:25–36 · Psalm 25:1–10

Heaven and earth will pass away, but my words will never pass away.

The beginning of Advent, the new liturgical year (Year C in the lectionary), is upon us. Advent is a period of waiting and eager expectation in the Christian calendar. Strangely for many, however, we look forward at this point in the year not to Christmas and the celebration of the incarnation, but to the second coming of Christ in glory to judge the living and the dead.

Jeremiah prophesied that the days were surely coming when God would judge the world as he had always promised to do. He would appoint a righteous 'Branch' to execute his will, someone in the line of King David (which looked finished, to human eyes, in the prophet's own time). This approaching Judgment Day, however, is not something which God's people ought to fear, since Jeremiah calls it (literally, in verse 14) a 'good thing' or a 'good word' – justice is promised and it will be equitable, exemplary and demonstrably fair.

The Lord's people are not perfect, and so their safety on that day is not down to their own goodness or blamelessness; salvation is assured, but only because this Branch, the Lord himself, is our righteousness, for we have none of our own that could be sufficient. Our part is to repent and trust that risen Branch (Acts 17:30–31), the one who has become for us righteousness, sanctification and redemption (1 Corinthians 1:30). As the old commentator Matthew Henry (1662–1714) says, '"The Lord our Righteousness" is a sweet name to a convinced sinner; to one that has felt the guilt of sin in his conscience; seen his need of that righteousness, and the worth of it.'[3]

All the same, 1 Thessalonians 3 contains an excellent prayer for strengthening in progressive holiness and love in the light of Christ's coming. Pastor Paul feels both joy and concern for his new Thessalonian converts. He longs to teach them more about what they possess in union with Christ but for the time being he himself is separated from them and can only pray. His consistent prayer throughout the letter (see also 1 Thessalonians 5:23–24) is that they may be sanctified completely and appear before the returning Christ as blameless. Yet he cannot trust to their own strength, and so he commits this cause to the Lord, who is faithful and will surely work within them.

In the Gospel reading from Luke, Jesus himself helps us prepare our hearts for his majestic return. There will be signs of tumult, with fear and foreboding. Everything will seem to be shaken. Then he will return in the way that he left, 'coming in a cloud', but this time with evident power and glory. Again, it is not a day of fear for God's people – our redemption is drawing near. That is a good word that we can rely on.

In the light of that impending climax, we must be on our guard against the weight of worldly worries and allurements. As an old bishop, Leo the Great (400–461) once preached, we must prepare ourselves for Advent, 'For by daily experience, beloved, it is proved that the mind's edge is blunted by over-indulgence of the flesh.' Yet how good it is, instead, for our souls to 'have leisure for Divine wisdom in the palace of the mind, where, away from all the noise of earthly cares, it may in silence enjoy holy meditations and eternal delights'.[4] To stand before the Son of Man we need his strength, to resist the temptation to look down and around, instead of up.

---

[3] Matthew Henry and Thomas Scott, *Matthew Henry's Concise Commentary* (Oak Harbor, WA: Logos Research Systems, 1997), Je 23:1.

[4] Leo the Great, 'Sermons', in *Leo the Great, Gregory the Great*, ed. Philip Schaff and Henry Wace, trans. Charles Lett Feltoe, vol. 12a of *A Select Library of the Nicene and Post-Nicene Fathers of the Christian Church, Second Series* (New York: Christian Literature Company, 1895), p. 127 (Sermon XIX).

2nd Sunday of Advent

Malachi 3:1–4 · Philippians 1:3–11 · Luke 3:1–6

But who can endure the day of his coming?
Who can stand when he appears?

Our readings this week focus on the purity of the coming day of Jesus Christ. We may all long for justice and truth to be revealed, but it's only by God's grace that we ourselves can survive or thrive on that day.

The prophet Malachi speaks to a half-hearted people who think that God has forgotten his covenant and given up on them. They long for him to come among them again in power because their religion seems risible and their re-built temple appears poxy compared to the glories of the past and of the surrounding superpowers. It is scruffy and dirty and ragged. They are asking, 'Where is the God of justice?' because people were getting away with all kinds of evil things, seemingly without punishment. Through Malachi, God assures them, 'I am coming!' He will send a messenger to prepare the way before his own arrival in the Temple to renew his covenant publicly. They had better get their act together.

That 'day of his coming' would not be such a good one for those who had neglected the covenant themselves. The paltry sacrifices, teachings and lifestyles of the Levites would need purification before they were anywhere near to pleasing the Lord. But the covenant would stand and, by grace alone, so would they. As the priests are purified, so the offerings of the people are also made acceptable because of the work of this refiner's fire.

Luke's Gospel alerts us to the coming of the preparatory herald. John the Baptist arrives, proclaiming a baptism of repentance for the forgiveness of sins. He is the forerunner prophesied by Malachi and Isaiah, making straight and level the way for God to come.

Repentance rolls out the red carpet. After Malachi's prophecy we do indeed expect God himself to come to his Temple, as the very next act in the drama (the Old Testament here providing a beautiful testimony to the divinity of our Lord Jesus Christ, crystal clear as it is fulfilled). After Christ made purification for sins (Hebrews 1:3), 'the number of disciples multiplied greatly in Jerusalem, and *a great many of the priests* became obedient to the faith' (Acts 6:7). Their lives became offerings acceptable to God through faith in Jesus Christ.

Yet that final day of purification, when Jesus comes again, remains a future promise. Paul is joyfully confident that on that day, God's good work in the Philippian church will have been brought to completion. They have made an excellent start and partnered with him in the work of the gospel, even when it has landed him in trouble with the authorities. Just as the Levites of Malachi 3 present offerings to the Lord in righteousness, so these Gentile converts will produce a *harvest* of righteousness. He longs for them to express their faith in loving service of others to God's glory. And as they are filled with knowledge and depth of insight, he prays they will live a life that is pleasing to God, and be pure and blameless on that day.

And so we pray that God would cleanse the thoughts of our hearts, and purify us in body and soul so that when Jesus Christ comes again as judge and Saviour, we may be ready to receive him, who is both our Lord and our God.

3rd Sunday of Advent

Zephaniah 3:14–20 · Philippians 4:4–7 · Luke 3:7–18 · Isaiah 12:2–6

I will praise you, LORD. Although you were angry with me,
your anger has turned away and you have comforted me.

Our readings this week speak to us of wrath, repentance and rejoicing, reminding us that the coming of the Lord is a day we must prepare for well.

John the Baptiser urges the people of Israel to flee the wrath of God to come and bear fruit worthy of repentance. They must not presume on their status or heritage but be warned by the threat of imminent judgment on all those who do not repent. His application is tailored to different elements in his congregation: all must share out of their abundance; officials should be diligent but not greedily corrupt; soldiers likewise should be content with their rightful pay and not use force to extract more from the vulnerable. What would he say to our congregations? To you?

John reminds us that 'the good news' (for this is what Luke calls it) includes not just the arrival of our Spirit-endowed Saviour, but also the approach of decisive, divisive judgment. And there is division in the background of Paul's exhortation to the Philippians too. Rejoice in the Lord, he tells them, and be well-known for your gentleness. Two women in the congregation, Euodia and Syntyche, disagree with each other in Philippians 4:2–3, but moderation and gentleness requires forgiving others for the sake of harmony, just as God has forgiven us. But an outbreak of 'the peace of God' also relies on remembering that 'the Lord is near'. Whether that means his coming is imminent or that his presence is immanent, Paul is certainly challenging all those who squabble, especially within churches. As the German

Reformer Martin Luther (1483–1546) paraphrases here, 'Don't worry. The Lord stands by you ... Put aside all your fear, anger, and bitterness. If you intend to do any fighting, fight with prayers.'[5]

The Old Testament reading brings us the good news too. Zephaniah urges rejoicing and song because 'the Lord has taken away the judgments against you'. We certainly deserve to be judged, and not to fare well in the process, yet 'the LORD is in your midst; you shall fear disaster no more'. We will not bear the deserved reproach for our sins, but with God himself as our warrior champion, we will be free.

It is not hard to see in Zephaniah's prophecy here an intimation of salvation through Christ, who bears the punishment for our sins upon the cross and crushes the head of our satanic enemy. He will come again soon: 'At that time I will bring you home, at the time when I gather you', says the prophet.

So, as the French Reformer John Calvin (1509–64) prayed at the end of his lecture on Zephaniah 3:

> Grant, Almighty God, that as we are at this day so scattered on account of our sins, and even they who seem to be collected in thy name and under thy authority, are yet so torn by mutual discords, that the safety of thy Church hangs as it were on a thread, while in the meantime thine enemies seem with savage cruelty to destroy all those who are thine, and to obliterate thy gospel, – O grant, that we may hope in thy promises, so that we may not doubt, but that thou in due time will become our deliverer: and may we so patiently bear to be afflicted and cast down by thee, that we may ever raise up our groans to

[5] Martin Luther, *Luther's Works, Vol. 20: Minor Prophets III: Zechariah*, ed. Jaroslav Jan Pelikan, Hilton C. Oswald, and Helmut T. Lehmann (Saint Louis: Concordia Publishing House, 1999), pp. 139–40.

heaven so as to be heard through the name of thy Son, until being at length freed from every contest, we shall enjoy that blessed rest which is laid up for us in heaven, and which thine only begotten Son has procured for us.[6]

Through Jesus Christ, our Lord, Amen.

[6] John Calvin, *Commentaries on the Twelve Minor Prophets* (Bellingham, WA: Logos Bible Software, 2010), p. 272.

4th Sunday of Advent

Micah 5:2–5a · Hebrews 10:5–10 · Luke 1:39–55 · Psalm 80:1–7

Restore us, God Almighty; make your face shine on us, that we may be saved.

The theme of our readings this week is the promised coming of a strong, obedient ruler who will bring lasting peace to his people through his death. How merciful he is to us.

The prophecy of Micah to the humble hamlet of Bethlehem speaks of an ancient promise being fulfilled in her. This is in stark contrast to the current state of the nation, which is besieged and benighted. 'But', says Micah, a new hope will arise from a small and unexpected place, to work 'for me' – that is, for God's greater glory and advantage (unlike many rulers who reign only for themselves).

Israel will be without a king until the time that this one is born. He will stand for ever, to care for his flock, not with human cunning or military prowess, but 'in the strength of the LORD and in the majesty of the name of the LORD his God.' His kingdom shall spread to the ends of the earth, even beyond the borders of Israel, and so establish a secure and peaceful home for all who look to him.

In an often-neglected Christmas text, Hebrews 10 speaks about the moment when 'Christ came into the world'. He did not, of course, literally speak on the day of his birth; the writer puts into the mouth of the incarnate Christ the words of Psalm 40:6–8 to explain the significance of his coming. In the psalm, King David speaks of the powerlessness of the Old Testament sacrifices in and of themselves to please God; they are rejected, not as part of his ceremonial Law, but because they are nullified by the sinful hypocrisy of those who abuse them and do not look beyond them.

This is contrasted with the eager obedience of the Messiah, who comes to implement the will of God, in response to the long-written prophecies written about him. God has prepared a body for him. As the Athanasian Creed puts it, 'it is necessary to everlasting salvation that we also believe faithfully the Incarnation of our Lord Jesus Christ ... not by conversion of the Godhead into flesh; but by assumption of the Manhood by God.' He put on our nature to be our Redeemer.

This certainly does please God, and the humble strength of Christ achieves what no mere animal sacrifice could ever hope to. The once-and-for-all offering of his body definitively sanctifies all those who believe. The Law is abolished to establish God's perfect will, but the offering of a sinless body is necessary to achieve this – to reconcile the Father to us he must be a sacrifice not just for original guilt but for all our actual sins as well.

The Blessed Virgin Mary may not have known all the detail of this divine plan when she meekly consented to be a part of it. Yet Christ takes our human nature in the womb of the blessed Virgin. Even the baby in the womb of Spirit-filled Elizabeth is aware that something world-changing is afoot, and he leaps for joy in the presence of the one who will fulfil all the promises of God.

Mary's response is rich in Old Testament allusions; her magnificent song extols the power of God who keeps his promises and lifts up the lowly. God looks with favour on the little town of Bethlehem and the lowliness of his servant Mary. Both are greatly blessed. May we also be blessed as we contemplate his mercy towards us, in sending his Son to be born as a man and die on the cross in our place.

CHRISTMAS

1st Sunday of Christmas

1 Samuel 2:18–20, 26 · Colossians 3:12–17 · Luke 2:41–52 · Psalm 148

Bear with each other and forgive one another if any of you has a grievance against someone.

Our readings this week remind us that the Lord Jesus was dedicated to serving his heavenly Father from the earliest days of his childhood, and that since we too are to live every day in communion with him, after a whirl of activity over Christmas we may need to pause to forgive one another and restore peace in the household of faith.

The prophet Samuel is dedicated to the service of God as a child by his mother, who prayed at the tabernacle for his birth. Little Samuel will minister before the Lord, wearing a linen ephod, and Hannah will bring him a new robe every year when she and Elkanah go up to offer their annual sacrifice. And every year, Eli prays down a blessing on them before they return home, while Samuel himself grows in stature and in favour with both God and the people.

This Old Testament vignette is clearly the pattern for Luke's unique story of Jesus's childhood visit to the Jerusalem Temple. Like Elkanah and Hannah, Joseph and Mary go up annually for the Passover in response to the command of God, taking their miraculous child with them. The boy is remarkably devoted to God above all, and at the end we are told that he grew in stature and in favour with both God and the people.

Yet the Gospel narrative has puzzled many. How could Joseph and Mary not know Jesus was still back in the city when they left? Why does Mary refer to Joseph as 'your father', if she had truly been a virgin when he was conceived? Why did Jesus treat his parents like this and cause them such anxiety? Why does he say they should have known where he would be, when they spent so long searching the place? How could he, if he was truly the incarnation of the omniscient God, somehow 'grow' in wisdom?

It is a challenging story. No doubt it was perfectly natural for parents to assume their children were somewhere in the large crowd heading home, and it does seem the holy couple may have had other children to worry about by now too (see Mark 6:3 and Matthew 13:55–56). Joseph was regarded as Jesus's father by others who were not party to the secret of his holy conception, but he took his human nature from Mary – which means he had a real human nature which physically grew with all his powers together.

The main challenge of the story, however, is that Jesus was utterly devoted to his relationship to God, his Father. Even though he respected his parents and was obedient to them, he knew that his life must revolve around God. And the same message is there for us in Colossians 3. The word of Christ must dwell in us richly. As the old commentator Matthew Henry (1662–1714) says on this passage, 'Those who are the elect of God, holy and beloved, ought to be lowly and compassionate towards all. While in this world, where there is so much corruption in our hearts, quarrels will sometimes arise. But it is our duty to forgive one another, imitating the forgiveness through which we are saved.'[7]

Christmas can be a fraught and stressful time. So let us use the Sunday after Christmas to re-focus our minds on serving God above all, and serving our friends, family, and fellow human beings in the year ahead.

---

[7] Henry and Scott, *Matthew Henry's Concise Commentary*, Col 3:12.

EPIPHANY

1st Sunday of Epiphany

Isaiah 43:1–7 · Acts 8:14–17 · Luke 3:15–17, 21–22 · Psalm 29

You are precious and honoured in my sight … I love you.

In our readings this week we celebrate the baptism of Christ. It is a unique moment, revealing something deep and profound about his love for us.

The great medieval theologian Thomas Aquinas (1225–74) devotes six articles in his *Summa Theologiae* to the subject of John's baptism, and eight more to a discussion of the two verses where Christ himself was baptised.[8] So this brief episode throws up a multitude of theological puzzles which might easily fascinate or sidetrack us. It is a spectacular picture of the divine Trinity in action. All three persons appear before us at once, which rather scotches the fantasy that Father becomes Son becomes Spirit, as three evolving, sequential manifestations of the one God. Rather, their outward operations being indivisible, the three are united together publicly in beginning the work of cosmic redemption which they had planned from eternity.

Christ was baptised by John not because he needed to repent as others did, but in order (as Luke puts it) to fulfil all righteousness. He was born under the Law to redeem those under the Law, and so did what all pious Jews were commanded to do, that he might ultimately be their perfect representative and substitute. St Augustine (354–430) says in a sermon on the Epiphany that Christ was

[8] Thomas Aquinas, *Summa Theologiae*, III.38.1–6 and 39:1–8.

baptised 'because he wished to do what he had commanded all to do'. And St Ambrose (339–97) agrees when he says, 'this is righteousness, to do first yourself that which you wish another to do, and so encourage others by your example'.[9] A good leader won't ask others to do what he himself is not willing to.

The descending dove has occasioned much wrangling and speculation. But, in this context, the Spirit is of course a visible symbol of the Father's pleasure in his Son, and of the empowering grace bestowed upon him for his ministry 'to proclaim good news' (Luke 4:18). Likewise, in Acts 8, when the Samaritans accept that gospel about Jesus the Messiah, they receive the Holy Spirit as a clear sign that they have been included in God's plan. Again, there has been some debate about why the reception of the Spirit here had to await the arrival of the apostles who laid hands on the Samaritan believers. But the answer is the same as in Luke 3 – to fulfil all righteousness.

Jesus declared that the apostles would be his witnesses in Judea and Samaria. So sending them out as his official ambassadors at this key moment in salvation history is fitting and appropriate – not because an apostolic laying on of hands is essential to our reception of the Spirit, or because there is a second blessing available to some after belief and baptism (it being tricky to derive a generally applicable doctrine from such unique, one-off events). The apostle John had once asked if he could call down the fire of judgment on these people; his presence at this moment is a crucial signpost that salvation (not judgment yet!) has come equally to all.

That too is the message of our reading from Isaiah, who prophesies this unfolding of God's global purpose. The Creator of Israel, who formed a nation out of such unprepossessing material over the course of the centuries, assures them of his ongoing care. The gates of death shall not prevail over them; neither flame nor flood can harm them if he is with them (as Shadrach, Meshach, and Abednego discovered in the fiery furnace, Daniel 3:24–25).

---

9 As quoted by Aquinas in *Summa Theologiae*, III.39 *sed contra*.

Isaiah 43:4 is the only place in the Bible where God says the words, 'I love you'. Yet that message is writ large upon each and every page of Scripture. And according to Isaiah, that love extends to the North and to the South, and he gathers his children ('created for my glory') from East and from West. There is nothing he would not give to ransom his precious people, wherever they may be in this sinful and rebellious world.

2nd Sunday of Epiphany

Isaiah 62:1–5 · 1 Corinthians 12:1–11 · John 2:1–11 · Psalm 36:5–10

How priceless is your unfailing love, O God!
People take refuge in the shadow of your wings.

In this week's readings we rejoice that in the coming of Christ all things have been made gloriously new. Let us rejoice in that newness of life, however this new calendar year is going.

John's Gospel contains a number of 'signs' revealing Jesus's glory and pointing to his work of transformation (the word for 'revealed' in John 2:11 is related to the Greek word *epiphany*, which explains the use of this reading at this stage in the year). Here at the beginning of his public ministry, when his time has just begun and his greatest 'hour' of glory has not yet arrived in the Passion, it is still apparent that he has come to bring something startlingly, lavishly fresh. Not for his followers the insipid waters of the old, but the rich abundance of better wine, a Messianic feast.

The *Book of Common Prayer* (1662) alludes to this occasion in the service for the solemnisation of matrimony. It speaks of the honourable estate of marriage, 'which holy estate Christ adorned and beautified with his presence, and first miracle that he wrought, in Cana of Galilee'. His presence signified his approval of the proceedings, as man and woman were joined together. His encouragement of the festivities and celebration pointed forward to the glory of the new creation and the wedding supper of the Lamb (Revelation 19:9), since marriage is a picture of Christ and the Church. Our presence in certain places, especially if we are public persons and not simply private individuals, can also signify approval and blessing. Though naturally we reach out to those in darkness, we must take care not to bless and adorn naively those things of this present world which led Christ to the agony of the cross.

Continuing the marriage theme, Isaiah 62 expounds God's irrepressible ambitions for his betrothed people. They may be forsaken and desolate now, but Zion shall one day be delightful and married. With unstoppable patience, he will ensure that rather than slumbering in her sins, she will be stunningly righteous, and publicly saved from current captivity and obscurity in the sight of nations and kings. She who once was by nature corrupted and filthy will be called by a new name, and be a crown of beauty to adorn the glory of God. As the French theologian John Calvin (1509–64) rightly concludes, 'Let us therefore be aroused by this goodness of God to the desire of leading a holy life, that his image may more and more be formed anew in us.'[10]

For the next three weeks we have a brief series of epistle readings, working consecutively through 1 Corinthians 12–13. Paul's discussion of spiritual gifts is prompted by the Corinthians themselves (the 'Now concerning…' in 12:1 picks up the same phrase in 7:1 and 8:1). They are, as he has already declared in his opening thanksgiving, a church 'not lacking in any spiritual gift'; but the worldly use of those gifts has occasioned a certain level of disorder and confusion because there is still too much Corinth in the Corinthians.

The apostle teaches them that the Spirit of God reorientates a person, focusing their attention not on themselves and their pleasures and comforts but on the Son of God and his people. There are varieties of gifts, from the same Spirit; varieties of service, but the same Lord Jesus; varieties of activity but the same God animating and activating each. As Anthony Thiselton says in his shorter commentary on 1 Corinthians, 'Paul's emphasis upon unity-in-diversity is grounded in the nature of the one

---

[10] John Calvin, *Commentary on the Book of the Prophet Isaiah* (Bellingham, WA: Logos Bible Software, 2010), 324.

God, who is holy Trinity.'[11] The Trinity is at work in us, but not for our own excitation or exaltation – each manifestation is given 'for the common good'. No one has every gift, and therefore all are needed, and all are in need of the Church. This challenges and changes rugged individualists and undermines any basis for celebrity church culture.

So whatever other resolutions you may have made this year, let's resolve to live a new life every day, using our God-given gifts to serve our brothers and sisters in the Church.

---

[11] Anthony C. Thiselton, *First Corinthians: A Shorter Exegetical and Pastoral Commentary* (Grand Rapids, MI; Cambridge, U.K.: William B. Eerdmans Publishing Company, 2006), p. 197.

3rd Sunday of Epiphany

Nehemiah 8:1–3, 5–6, 8–10 · 1 Corinthians 12:12–31a · Luke 4:14–21 · Psalm 19

The law of the LORD is perfect, refreshing the soul. The statutes of the LORD are trustworthy, making wise the simple.

Our theme for this week is the necessity of the proclamation of God's word to the community of God's people. Let's commit ourselves anew to hearing and delighting in God's word, week by week and day by day.

Nehemiah 8 recounts the wonderful occasion on which Ezra, in response to popular request, brought the Law of God to the Israelite assembly (the Old Testament church). They gather with a reverent anticipation on the day when that Law itself said they should observe a day of solemn rest, 'a holy convocation' (Leviticus 23:24). This is a 'day to blow the trumpets' (Numbers 29:1). Reading from the word is to blow the trumpet and call God's people together.

They stand to listen, and weep when they were convicted of their sin. Yet they go away with 'the joy of the LORD' as their strength, 'to eat the fat and drink sweet wine'. For as Thomas Cranmer (1489-1556) urges, 'we should forsake our own corrupt judgment on things and the opinions of those who care only for their physical bodies, and reverently hear and read holy Scripture, the food of our souls. This is the well of life, far superior to the smelly old puddles of human reason and traditions which people often turn to for wisdom and guidance.'[12]

[12] See Gatiss (ed.), *The First Book of Homilies, The Official Sermons of the Church of England in Modern English* (London: Lost Coin, 2021), p. 34.

The reading from Nehemiah looks at first to be rather strange, because it is not simply listed as Nehemiah 8:1–10. On closer inspection, it is easy to see why two verses have been omitted in the middle of the reading: they are mostly lists of ancient Hebrew names, which many modern readers may struggle to pronounce! However, they also include the notes that Ezra stood on a purpose-built wooden platform to read the word – a biblical reference to a pulpit or reading desk; and also the fact that the Levites in verse 7, 'helped the people to understand the Law'. Rather than omitting the verses altogether, it may be better simply to replace the names with 'various senior people' and 'the Levites' or some such circumlocution, if reading this in church.

It is noteworthy that Ezra involves those senior laypeople with him in this enterprise – the word of God is not the unique preserve of spiritual professionals, though it is their particular responsibility. Nehemiah wants us to see sound teaching as a demand and a need of the whole community.

Luke's account of Jesus preaching in the synagogue is somewhat agenda-setting for his whole Gospel. Filled with the Spirit, he preaches good news to those who need it, and proclaims spiritual liberty to those oppressed. All that was written in the Old Testament is fulfilled in him, though the people to whom he preached in Nazareth did not appreciate it. As the great evangelist George Whitefield (1714–70) once said of London in his *Directions How to Hear Sermons*, 'How aggravating, that light should come into the world, that the glad tidings of salvation should be so very frequently proclaimed in this populous city and that so many should loath this spiritual manna, this angels food, and call it light bread?'[13]

One wonders if the Corinthians were also less enamoured by the teaching ministry and sought more exotic or 'showy' gifts of power. Paul urges them in his epistle to respect each and every member

---

[13] Gatiss (ed.), *The Sermons of George Whitefield* (Wheaton: Crossway, 2012), 1.469–470.

of the body, and therefore to 'strive for the greater gifts' – that is, the gifts that build up the body rather than exalt the one who possess them. The word-proclaimers (apostles, prophets, and teachers) come first in his list of appointed gifts. Yet as with other gifts, not all possess them – 'Do all (in the body of Christ) speak in tongues?' for example, in verse 30, implies a firmly negative answer. His more excellent way (of which more next week) is a way where the word is released to equip the saints for the work of ministry, nurturing the body in loving unity. May the trustworthy word of the Lord refresh your soul today.

4th Sunday of Epiphany

Ezekiel 43:27–44:4 · 1 Corinthians 13:1–13 · Luke 2:22–40 · Psalm 48

God is in her citadels; he has shown himself to be her fortress.

The set readings for this week focus on the joyful impact of the living God's presence with his people. What a joy it is to know that he is with us and in us.

The prophet Ezekiel called upon Judah to align itself with the God of salvation through judgment after the profound trauma of the exile to Babylon. In the final part of his prophecy in chapters 40–48 he has a vision of a new temple, a new land, a new city and a new law to restore hope to those who saw the glory of the Lord depart from Jerusalem, leaving Solomon's beautiful Temple to be destroyed.

Ezekiel 43 begins with God returning to the Temple that he left in chapter 11, through the gate that faces east (43:4). Our reading then continues with God accepting the people as the priests offer sacrifices on a new altar in that restored Temple. The gate facing east remains shut as a reassurance that God will not be leaving again. The new name for the city will be 'The LORD is There' (48:35), and his glory will fill the new Temple, as it once filled the Tabernacle and the Temple of Solomon. The somewhat mysterious figure of 'the Prince' is the only one permitted to sit in that east gate, to eat with the Lord. But all benefit by his presence there.

Luke 2 narrates how the Lord incarnate comes to his rebuilt Temple centuries later. More than once, Luke tells us that what happened was in fulfilment of 'the Law of the Lord', as Jesus is presented in the Temple as God's holy firstborn Son and a sacrifice is offered. Filled with the Spirit, Simeon awaits him, looking for the consolation of Israel in response to a promise that he would see the Messiah before he died. Prompted by the Spirit to enter the Temple, when Jesus and his parents arrive he praises God in the words of the song known as the *Nunc Dimittis* ('Now dismiss…').

Simeon's song reveals that this child is salvation itself, for both Jews and Gentiles. And Simeon can depart this life in joy having seen and held him. As the old commentator Matthew Henry (1662–1714) puts it, 'What a poor thing doth this world look to one that hath Christ in his arms and salvation in his eye!'[14] He also has a prophecy for Mary, that Jesus will shake up Israel and be greatly opposed – and also cause her great maternal suffering. Also led by the Spirit, the prophetess Anna bears witness that Jesus will redeem Jerusalem, that holy city, as seen by Ezekiel. How little Simeon and Anna saw of the wisdom and power of Christ; yet they greatly rejoiced to see the Lord they sought suddenly come to his Temple (Malachi 3:1). Filled with the Spirit, Anna and Simeon praise Jesus and tell others about him.

By contrast, the Corinthians thought themselves very spiritual, but it seems from Paul's letters to them that in many ways theirs was a spirituality of self, chained to this world and bereft of love. In that context, the famous hymn of praise to 'love' in chapter 13 snaps into focus as a painful rebuke of their childish immaturity. Without love, their much vaunted 'knowledge' and prophetic gifts are worse than useless.

Love is patient – they are not. Love is kind – they are not. The Corinthians are envious, boastful, arrogant, and rude – which is not the way of love. Insert your own name into the poetic rhythms of Paul's praise for love, to see how much it might sting: do I insist on my own way? Am I irritable or resentful? Can anyone but Love himself recite it thus without blushing?

Whatever we think we know, we only know in part and have no reason to be puffed up. But one day, when we see him, we will rejoice for ever in his presence. May the things of this world become strangely dim as you contemplate that glorious future.

---

[14] Henry, *Matthew Henry's Commentary on the Whole Bible: Complete and Unabridged in One Volume* (Peabody: Hendrickson, 1994), p. 1830.

ORDINARY TIME

Proper 1

Sunday between 3 and 9 February inclusive
(if earlier than the Second Sunday before Lent)

Isaiah 6:1–13 · 1 Corinthians 15:1–11 · Luke 5:1–11 · Psalm 138

By this gospel you are saved, if you hold firmly to the word I preached to you. Otherwise, you have believed in vain.

Over the next three weeks, the Lectionary gives us the opportunity to focus on something which the apostle Paul says is 'of first importance' – the resurrection. Since that is evidently so vital for Christians to understand, we will spend a little time soaking in 1 Corinthians 15. This week's reading from that chapter shows us how important the physical resurrection of Christ is for the Christian faith.

1 Corinthians 15:1–11 tells us three things: First, it says only one gospel is good enough to save us. Then, that life after death is at the heart of the gospel. Finally, Paul declares that it doesn't matter who tells you about it, as long as you believe. Paul says in verses 1–2 that the gospel was preached to them, they received it, and they took their stand on it. It is by believing this message of good news that they are saved. Otherwise, everything about the Christian faith is all in vain. If we change the message, it becomes useless. If we let go of it, we lose out. But if we hold firmly to it, then we will be saved.

Paul reminds the Corinthians – who seem rather too fond of their own ideas and their own ways of doing things – of what that message was. He says life after death is at the heart of the gospel. He tells us what is 'of first importance' in the gospel which brings salvation. And that is, that Christ died for our sins, and that he was raised again to life: his substitutionary atonement – his death in our place for our sins – and his glorious, bodily resurrection. The real resurrection of Jesus and the idea of life after death is absolutely fundamental to the Christian message. This is why Christians all over the world and throughout history declare in the Creed, 'On the third day, he rose again.'

Jesus appeared in public to his disciples. That's why Paul lists some of the people he actually appeared to in 1 Corinthians 15:5–8. He appeared to Cephas (another name for Simon Peter, who was first called in our Gospel reading), to the twelve apostles, to Paul himself, and even to 500 people all at the same time. This couldn't possibly just be an hallucination or wishful thinking from bamboozled minds. It couldn't be some pious 'spiritual' delusion. Resurrection, to first-century Jews, meant something, as scholar N. T. Wright puts it, 'emphatically physical'.[15] Paul even says many of the witnesses to this event (and it was an event, not a mere academic conception) were still alive as he was writing. So they could be interrogated and asked about it, and their reliability as witnesses assessed.

The Truth is out there – and he had been seen and touched and heard by hundreds of people. If that was not true, the early Christian movement would have died out pretty quickly, like every other Messianic movement of that century. The logic of history suggests that the best explanation for why billions of people have since believed in the resurrection, is that it is – amazingly – true.

Jesus's resurrection from the dead was not a party trick. He really did die; and when he rose again from the dead, he was not a ghost. He ate and drank with his disciples (Luke 24:41–43), which would be a bit icky if he was a ghost! Doubting Thomas was invited to

---

[15] N. T. Wright, *The New Testament and the People of God*, Christian Origins and the Question of God (London: Society for Promoting Christian Knowledge, 1992), p. 323.

touch the wounds Jesus still had from his death on the cross (John 20:24–28), and so were the others: 'See my hands and my feet, that it is I myself,' said Jesus, 'Touch me, and see. For a spirit does not have flesh and bones as you see that I have' (Luke 24:39).

It doesn't matter who tells you about this, says Paul, finally. This is the gospel which saves us. The gospel of Jesus Christ our risen Lord. So accept no substitute gospels, however elevated the messenger might be. Believe in this trustworthy message, no matter how despised or intellectually inferior its advocates might appear. Because without this, your life, and everything about church, is simply self-righteous religious entertainment to indulge in before we rot and disappear for ever.

Proper 2

Sunday between 10 and 16 February inclusive (if earlier than the Second Sunday before Lent)

Jeremiah 17:5–10 · 1 Corinthians 15:12–20 · Luke 6:17–26 · Psalm 1

If Christ has not been raised, your faith is futile;
you are still in your sins.

We continue to soak ourselves in the message of 1 Corinthians 15, which Paul says contains matters 'of first importance'. This week's reading from 1 Corinthians 15:12–20 tells us that if Jesus was not physically raised from the dead, then everything is pointless.

Christ did truly rise again from the dead. That is the faith we have inherited. Yet there have always been some people who deny this core and central truth of the Christian message and say Christ did *not truly* rise again from death. Usually, they take the logical step from denying the resurrection to not bothering to be a Christian. On the other hand, there are some today, just as there were some in Corinth, who want to retain the name Christian and be part of the church, but who can't quite get their heads around the fact that Jesus really did rise bodily, and that we shall too.

So Paul addresses those people in today's epistle reading, just as he addressed others in 1 Corinthians 5 who thought they didn't have to repent of the sexual immorality of their surrounding culture in order to follow Christ. Underlying both of these serious Corinthian errors was a gnostic, dualistic idea that the body is not an ultimate thing; what really counts is soul, or spirit. So it doesn't matter what I do with my body, because it's just sex, a bodily function; and bodily resurrection is not what we're hoping for, because the ultimate prize is *disembodied* spiritual bliss.

The apostle pops this heretical bubble by pointing out how the basic facts of Jesus's story show their philosophy to be in error. 'Now if Christ is proclaimed as raised from the dead, how can some of you say that there is no resurrection of the dead?' Like the members of the Athenian council on Mars's Hill, some scoffed at the idea of people rising from the dead (Acts 17:32) and didn't really care for it. But as the Gospel reading today says, 'Blessed are you when people hate you, when they exclude you and insult you and reject your name as evil, because of the Son of Man' (Luke 6:22). Yet, asks Paul, plugging away at the faulty logic: if people don't rise from the dead, then why is 'Christ has risen' a basic part of the Christian message? Indeed, verse 13, 'if there is no resurrection of the dead, then not even Christ has been raised. And if Christ has not been raised, then our preaching is in vain and your faith is in vain.' That is the merciless logic here. If you throw this aspect of Christian doctrine away, you may as well throw out the lot.

Paul seems mortified by the idea that Christians would proclaim something that couldn't actually be true and that they didn't really believe in. If dead people don't rise – if that's a fundamental axiom of existence and the limit of your scientific imagination – then neither did Jesus. Which means we misrepresent God in our public confession of faith. To be straightforward: we are blasphemous liars, leading people astray. Plus, 'you are still in your sins' (verse 17). You can never be forgiven, and have nothing to offer the guilty consciences of those who know they are sinners before a holy God, because 'he was raised to life for our justification' (Romans 4:25). All those dead Christians who clung to the hope of forgiveness and eternal life, and lived their lives with godly boldness as a result, have simply perished into nothingness (verse 18).

Quite a lot seems to hang on this basic truth of the physical, bodily resurrection of Christ in real space and time. Someone might claim that we can still derive comfort and joy and goodness and inspiration from the Christian story, which can make a difference in this world. Paul says, 'If in Christ we have hope *in this life only*, we are of all people most to be pitied' (verse 19). Christianity minus bodily resurrection is a ludicrous, risible joke. And so are you, if you believe it.

But the glorious truth is that he really did rise, and so shall all who cling to him by faith. He is just the first, the trailblazer, the 'firstfruits' of those who have died. Our resurrection is guaranteed by the solid reality of his.

Our readings from both Jeremiah 17 and Psalm 1 encourage us to meditate deeply on these truths. Because if we do, far from having a futile faith, we will be like a tree planted by streams of water, never failing to bear fruit or withering in the heat.

Proper 3

Sunday between 17 and 23 February inclusive
(if earlier than the Second Sunday before Lent)

Genesis 45:3–11, 15 · 1 Corinthians 15:35–38, 42–50 · Luke 6:27–38 ·
Psalm 37:1–11, 39–40

Just as we have borne the image of the earthly man, so shall we bear the image of the heavenly man.

In these three weeks, just for a change we are focusing mainly on the reading from the epistle, because Paul says it is about a matter 'of first importance'. In our reading today from 1 Corinthians 15, we learn that the resurrection body that we are looking forward to is a glorious, imperishable, powerful spiritual body.

The idea of the resurrection of the body, though it features in the Nicene Creed and is a standard Christian doctrine, has always given rise to a huge number of questions. It was disbelieved in the Gospels, when the Sadducees questioned Jesus about it and tried to trick him into admitting its apparent absurdity. They were in error because they did not understand the Scriptures or the power of God (Matthew 22:23–33). The chin-scratching puzzle that Paul addresses here concerns the kind of bodies that we will have when we are raised from the dead. His main point is that, as modern commentator David Prior puts it, 'These physical bodies of ours simply are incapable of coping with the glory of God. If we are going to be resurrected in Christ, we need also to be transformed into his likeness.'[16]

It could well be that the Corinthians had a bit of a downer about bodies in general. That would have made the idea of being

[16] David Prior, *The Message of 1 Corinthians* (Leicester: IVP, 1985), pp. 271–2.

resurrected with a body, rather than as pure spirit or something like that, a little disgusting and unattractive to them. 'Why would we want to have bodies? Surely the point is to transcend this base matter! Why would I want my corpse to be reanimated? What hope is that?' Paul seeks to address this concern by telling them that the good news is better than they ever thought. For Paul, resurrection did not mean mere resuscitation, but glorious transformation.

To get to this answer, Paul employs a number of analogies taken from everyday experience, particularly the picture of seeds dying in the ground and rising again as wheat. Or as German Reformer Martin Luther (1483–1546) puts it,

> 'He fairly showers and drowns us with illustrations, so that we find examples and illustrations in abundance wherever we look. And every peasant, even though he is unable to read, has this article before his eyes everywhere and can feel it in his hands. In short, we have as many living proofs of the resurrection as we behold kernels and seeds sown or sprouting in the field or in the garden. And so we say: "Life is emerging from death everywhere."'[17]

The new bodies that we shall enjoy in the new creation will be far superior to those we have endured in this life. Sin and death and corruption shall be no more. Bad backs shall be no more. Blind eyes, deaf ears, weak hearts and creaky knees shall be no more. What was sown as perishable shall rise in glory as imperishable. What was weak shall be powerful. The naturally earthly body shall be raised as a spiritual body – which does not mean it won't be physical, but that it will not be subject to decay, or the infirmities and limitations of our current bodily existence. As the *Book of Common Prayer* (1662) expresses it, in a memorable and profound moment from the Burial Service, 'we therefore commit this body to the ground, earth

[17] Martin Luther, *Luther's Works, Vol. 28: 1 Corinthians 7, 1 Corinthians 15, Lectures on 1 Timothy*, ed. Jaroslav Jan Pelikan, Hilton C. Oswald, and Helmut T. Lehmann (Saint Louis: Concordia Publishing House, 1999), p. 179.

to earth, ashes to ashes, dust to dust; in sure and certain hope of the Resurrection to eternal life'.

Paul's greatest illustration of this is Jesus himself. Adam, the first man, was of the dust of the earth (Genesis 2:7). But Jesus, the second man, is of heaven. And we will have resurrection bodies like his resurrection body. He was raised, never to die again (Romans 6:9) with a new incorruptible and undying body that yet had certain continuities with the body which died on the cross (he is still a man, for example). That too is our hope. It still raises many questions about what it will be like. But the answer to all our questions can only be known in the eventual enjoyment of these bodies – if by faith we cling to Christ who will raise us to life.

2nd Sunday before Lent

Genesis 2:4b–9, 15–25 · Revelation 4 · Luke 8:22–25 · Psalm 65

You are worthy, our Lord and God, to receive glory and honour and power, for you created all things, and by your will they were created and have their being.

This week's readings teach us that the one whose word made and sustains the orderly creation for our benefit is worthy of all our praise. Give thanks today for God's creative and sustaining power at work within you.

The reading from Genesis 2 focuses in on the creation of man from the dust of the ground, which has already been mentioned in the sweeping account of Genesis 1. We are reminded of our place in God's grand scheme of creation, placed in the garden of Eden to work it and take care of it. God commanded Adam that he could eat of every tree in the garden except the tree of the knowledge of good and evil. His word would prevent Adam's death, and bring him inestimable blessing.

Here, for the first time in Genesis, something is pronounced to be 'not good', not quite right and perfectly functioning, and God quickly acts to remedy that situation. Woman is created as a helper-partner for man, more suitable in that role than any of the animals that the Lord God had made. She is quickly recognised as such, a blessing from God. This pattern of man and woman coming together in partnership is then noted as the origin of marriage. The words of Genesis 2:24 describe how because of this original design, men continue to leave their parents and become one flesh with their wives. They were perhaps written down by Moses; yet Jesus claims they are the words of the one who created us himself (Matthew 19:5), revealing his good purpose and order for human flourishing.

Revelation 4 describes a mighty otherworldly scene and reflects on the purpose of creation. Upon the beautiful throne of heaven sits one dressed in white, with a rainbow like an emerald for a halo or a crown. Around him are assembled twenty-four elders dressed in white with golden crowns on their heads. There is an awesome display of majesty and power, a sea of glass and the seven spirits of God. Living creatures are also assembled, crying out praises to the Lord God Almighty.

Meanwhile, as the living creatures give glory to the one on the throne, the elders fall down and worship him. The liturgy of heaven requires them to cast their crowns before him in orderly reverence and awe. They sing that he is worthy to receive all this glory and honour and power *precisely because* he is the Creator. His creation and preservation of everything that exists gives him the right to receive such worship. They exist because of this will and his word, and so praise is due to him.

The story in Luke 8 shows the majesty of the one seated on the heavenly throne interacting with a disordered rebellious world. Adam did not listen to the word of his Creator, but chose a different path, so creation became wild and death entered in. Now he faces danger from the elements, from the roaring wind and raging sea, such as the disciples are experiencing in their fragile little boat. They fear death is approaching, the death they would not know if man had listened to his Creator and believed his word.

Jesus wakes up – how had he been sleeping? Why had he been sleeping? He addresses the threat to his ordered creation, rebuking the wind and the waves, restoring the sea to a place of blessing for their travels rather than a threat. When the calm returns in obedience to him, he asks them the pointed question: where is your faith? Why did you not trust me?

And they are totally freaked out. Who on earth is this? Whose word can still the storm? The one whose word made and sustains the orderly creation, and who is worthy of all praise. Why do we not trust him?

Sunday next before Lent (Transfiguration Sunday)

Exodus 34:29–35 · 2 Corinthians 3:12–4:2 · Luke 9:28–36 · Psalm 99

We all, who with unveiled faces contemplate the Lord's glory,
are being transformed into his image with ever-increasing glory,
which comes from the Lord, who is the Spirit.

The theme of our readings this week is the glory of the Lord Jesus Christ, whose word we must hear and serve. Will you listen to him?

In Exodus 34, Moses returns to the people of Israel with the renewed edition of the Ten Commandments, after being with God on Mount Sinai for some time. His face, wrinkled by the burdens of leadership during the exodus and no doubt ashen by the years, now shines resplendent 'because he had been talking with God'. The early church writer Ephrem the Syrian (306–73) considered this poetically as 'a symbol of old age that in Eden again becomes young',[18] though the Israelites at the time saw it as a rather more frightening portent and were too terrified to even go near him. God's glory is but faintly reflected in Moses' face as he passes on God's word to the people, but they can only bear it unveiled for a few moments at a time.

Having taught them not to be ashamed of his words when he would come in all his glory, Jesus takes Peter, James, and John up another mountain to pray. As he is speaking with God, his face too begins to change and even his clothes are fluoresced with the glistening brightness of that glory in which Moses and Elijah also appeared. They speak together of his departure, literally in Greek his forthcoming 'exodus' – his death and resurrection which are about to be accomplished in Jerusalem.

---

[18] Joseph T. Lienhard and Ronnie J. Rombs, eds., *Exodus, Leviticus, Numbers, Deuteronomy*, Ancient Christian Commentary on Scripture (Downers Grove, IL: InterVarsity Press, 2001), p. 155.

The disciples, despite the drama of the occasion, are weighed down with sleepiness – just as they will be in Gethsemane as Jesus prepares to reveal his self-emptying glory on the cross. Our eyes cannot look directly into the sun without being overwhelmed and shutting down; in the same way, the incomprehensible magnificence of God's glory is too much for the bodily perceptions of our sinful flesh to endure. Even so, Peter does not want the experience to end, and as he sees Moses and Elijah leaving he longs for the sweetness of the moment to continue. But until the perfect comes, we see not face-to-face but ear-to-word or face-to-book: 'this is my Son,' the Father declares, 'listen to him'.

2 Corinthians 3 contrasts the transitory glory of Moses's Old Testament ministry to the ever-increasing glory of the ministry of the Spirit through the word. He was an unremittingly bold servant of Christ, despite much opposition and persecution, precisely because of the superior transfiguring glory of the new covenant. In the gospel, we may contemplate the Lord's glory with unveiled faces and be transformed into his own image. Paul's resilience was built not on his ability to engage in creative marketing or on a deceptive distortion of the truth, but on the open proclamation of the word. Would that all churches were built the same way, designed so that listening to Jesus's word is central to all we do.

Paul sees in the veil which covered Moses's face an analogy to the veil which lay over the hearts of many of his Jewish contemporaries (and the minds of all unbelievers). They could not grasp the true meaning and significance of the words they so often read and reverenced because they were stupefied by a lack of faith in Christ. Only turning to Jesus and reading from a position of loving trust and obedience pledged in advance removes the cloud of obscurity from our eyes. In God's mercy he has entrusted the key to those who proclaim not themselves but Jesus Christ as Lord, that we might see the naked truth and rejoice in his eternal glory.

LENT

1st Sunday of Lent

Deuteronomy 26:1–11 · Romans 10:8b–13 · Luke 4:1–13 ·
Psalm 91:1–2, 9–16

For it is with your heart that you believe and are justified and it is with your mouth that you profess your faith and are saved.

Our theme this week, as Lent begins, is the sufficiency of God's gracious provision for us, and the response for which it calls. Do you believe in your heart and profess the truth with your mouth?

In the reading from Deuteronomy, we hear about the giving of first fruits from the land to God. Having been saved by unmerited grace alone from slavery in Egypt, the people have a new relationship with the Lord. It is not quite true that grace means love given freely and without expectation of return. The idea of giving first fruits was a clear and powerful testimony that all they possessed belonged to God; they held the Promised Land as tenants, as it were, of a good and gracious landlord. He gave freely without regard to their goodness, but not without some expectation of a return, a change in relationship, or an acknowledgement of that personal bond. His grace is incongruous – it doesn't weigh the status or worth of a recipient, as we might do. But it comes with a prompt, a call to action. The liturgy and action of the giving of first fruits recount the power and goodness of the Lord, so that giving back to him is placed entirely in the context of celebration.

Romans 10 reminds us that with the coming of Christ, God's gracious call has gone out to the ends of the earth. Everyone who calls on the name of the Lord will be saved, whoever they are, whether

Jew or Greek. Whatever our background, be it Muslim or secularist, nominal or fundamentalist – and whatever we may have done or been – 'the same Lord is Lord of all and is richly generous to all who call on him'. The word is plain and clear, and near to us – but it needs to be acted upon; as French pastor John Calvin (1509–64) says here, 'For wherever the word of the Lord is, it ought to bring forth fruit; and the fruit is the confession of the mouth.'[19]

Christ himself is our example and our leader. As St Ambrose (339–97) puts it, 'Jesus, full of the Holy Spirit, is led into the desert for a purpose, in order to challenge the devil. If he had not fought, he would not have conquered him for me.'[20] As he goes to this confrontation in our Gospel reading, he does not rely on physical strength (bolstered by food) or on human weaponry; he relies entirely on the sword of the Spirit, the graciously revealed word of God. In his three quotations, all taken from Deuteronomy as our first reading is, he does not merely confess the truths of Scripture with his lips, but lives as one believing their truth and therefore able to parry the temptations set before him.

Jesus does not doubt God's provision in the wilderness. He refuses to take the devil's easy road to power and glory, circumventing the path laid out for him by the Father. Neither does he fall for Satan's gymnastics of Bible interpretation, when he pits one text of Scripture against another. Jesus does not consider one part of Scripture to be contradictory to another. We are not to push the boundaries, search for loopholes and put the Lord our God to the test, but trust in the piercing clarity and full sufficiency of his word in every situation. As the Proverb says, 'Every word of God is flawless; he is a shield to those who take refuge in him' (Proverbs 30:5).

---

[19] Calvin, *Commentary on the Epistle of Paul the Apostle to the Romans* (Bellingham, WA: Logos Bible Software, 2010), p. 392.

[20] Arthur A. Just (ed.), *Luke*, Ancient Christian Commentary on Scripture (Downers Grove, IL: InterVarsity Press, 2005), p. 73.

2nd Sunday of Lent

Genesis 15:1–12, 17–18 · Philippians 3:17–4:1 · Luke 13:31–35 ·
Psalm 27

Teach me your way, Lord; lead me in a straight path
because of my oppressors.

Our readings this week reassure us that we should stand firm because God's saving promises will never fail, however much we may doubt or be opposed.

In Genesis 15, Abram seems to be beginning to waver. After his success against Lot's captors, the word of the Lord comes to comfort him as fresh fear and dread rush in: 'Do not be afraid, Abram!' God promises to protect and provide for him, but he cannot quite bring himself to believe it entirely. We can be assailed by opposition from within and without, especially after a moment of spiritual victory.

But whatever doubts or concerns Abram had, God speaks his word of promise in response – 'you *shall* have an heir, and more descendants than you can imagine'. And if he should question the pledge of land as part of his reward, God cuts for him a covenant – a bond in blood, sovereignly administered, which solemnly ratifies the promises.[21] A heifer, a goat and a ram are torn in two; and then, like a pillar of fire and cloud, God himself symbolically walks between them. Through this sacrament joined to the word he speaks powerfully and prophetically: 'May it be so to me, if I should break my word' (see Jeremiah 34:18). If the covenant is broken, God will take the curse upon himself. Faith can rest in such fatherly goodness.

In Luke 13, the Pharisees try to scare Jesus into obscurity. 'Herod is trying to kill you,' they say; which may well be true, but they

[21] See O. Palmer Robertson, *The Christ of the Covenants* (Phillipsburg, NJ: Presbyterian and Reformed Publishing Co., 1980), p. 15.

magnify the threat by repeating it and urging Christ to flee. As Reformation commentator John Calvin (1509–64) says on this place, the Pharisees' design was 'to awaken in him such fears as would drive him to some place of concealment … that his whole doctrine would vanish away'. And in the same way as Satan endeavoured to terrify Jesus, 'so he constantly invents and hatches up new grounds of alarm, to strike the ministers of Christ with dismay, and to constrain them to turn aside'.[22] Cunning ploys to suppress God's word are beloved of Herodian foxes everywhere. Exhorting self-censorship and self-protection, their apparent mindfulness is only malice in masquerade. Yet Jesus knew the deadly path that he was on, and would continue his work undaunted, trusting in the 'deeper magic' of a brooding love which loses self in service. He longed not for his own comfort or glory, but to gather his people together in the city chosen for long ages past as the place of substitutionary sacrifice.

In Philippians 3, Paul speaks with tears of those who live as enemies of the way of the cross. Their minds are set on earthly things, and they boast of things they ought to be ashamed of – wearing their sins on their sleeves and their lapels. They have divinised their own physical pleasures, so that gratification of their bodily desires has become the god they serve and revere. Their end, declares the apostle, is destruction. The broad road is theirs.

We, on the other hand, must not fall for such worldly allurements because we are citizens of another kingdom, another city. Out of his great love, Paul urges the church to aspire to a different style of life, despite the mocking of the opposing lobby and the struggles of the flesh. Macedonians may have longed for another Alexander the Great to arise, but these in Philippi know that their true Saviour is coming from heaven. Paul assures them that when he comes, Christ will transform their bodies and their fortunes – if only they (and we) stand firm in joyful hope.

[22] John Calvin, *Commentary on a Harmony of the Evangelists Matthew, Mark, and Luke* (Bellingham, WA: Logos Bible Software, 2010), pp. 157–8.

3rd Sunday of Lent

Isaiah 55:1–9 · 1 Corinthians 10:1–13 · Luke 13:1–9 · Psalm 63:1–8

Because your love is better than life, my lips will glorify you.

This week's readings remind us of how ignorant we are when we think and act as if the gracious call of God was not always accompanied by a demand for a decisive break with sin. Unless we repent, we will all perish.

Isaiah 55 calls us to enjoy free, unmerited covenant blessings which alone can deeply satisfy. Because of the work of the Suffering Servant who has paid every necessary cost for his people, a lavish feast is spread before us – without money and without price. We could never afford it, and given the corruption of our desires would not (unaided and unbidden) choose something so good and truly delightful.

Yet free as it is at the point of need, this grace is not, says Isaiah, unconditional. To appropriate it we must seek the Lord at the opportune moment – he will not always be close at hand. To grasp his goodness we must forsake our wickedness and turn to him; his righteousness and ours cannot stand together or be held onto simultaneously. Yet with nothing in our hands but sin, we will find pardon lies with him. Because he doesn't work like we do, repaying like for like. His thoughts are higher and his ways more graciously exalted.

The apostle Paul also warns us not to forget the call to repentance which always rides along with grace. He does not want the Corinthians to be ignorant or unaware, he says, that those who enjoy the sacraments of grace may still be struck down by God's displeasure. As the Old Testament narrative amply illustrates, great spiritual privilege does not necessarily make one great spiritually. All those Paul alludes to fell in the desert because of their evil desires, despite experiencing some of the most earth-shattering moments in redemptive history.

The Corinthians too were not lacking in spiritual gifts; but our participation in the immense blessings of the covenant do not put us a cut above the rest in some spiritual premier league, though we may sometimes speak and act as though they did. None of us are invulnerable to the typical temptations faced by saints and sinners of old. The devil has no new tricks, because he doesn't need any new tricks; we're quite content, it seems, to keep falling into the same old traps of idolatry, ingratitude, and immorality.

There is nothing unusual about our temptations. But there is also no such thing as an irresistible urge, for those who are in Christ. This side of the Promised Land he does not promise to remove our temptations, or the fallen inclinations on which they prey. 1 Corinthians 10:13 doesn't even promise he will strengthen us to withstand them, though often that may be wonderfully true. What we are assured of here is something slightly different: he will temper the power of our adversary and guarantees to provide us an escape hatch. In temptation, make for the exit. Flee to the ark of safety he unerringly provides.

In the Gospel reading, Jesus intimates that there is a radical equality between us all. The Galileans who suffered at Pilate's hand and those upon whom the tower of Siloam fell, were no better or worse than the wilderness generation, the Corinthians or us. All alike must repent or perish, says Jesus. He is patient with us, persistently looking for the fruit of penitence and giving us every assistance. But his patience will not last for ever.

So let us not be content with external asceticism during Lent, but ask for the gift of repentance which, as the old Puritan John Owen (1616–83) defined it, is 'Godly sorrow for every known sin committed against God, with a firm purpose of heart to cleave unto him for the future, in the killing of sin, the quickening of all graces, to walk before him in newness of life'.[23]

---

[23] W. H. Goold (ed.), *The Works of John Owen* (Edinburgh: Johnstone and Hunter, 1854), 1:487–88.

4th Sunday of Lent

Joshua 5:9–12 · 2 Corinthians 5:16–21 · Luke 15:1–3, 11b–32 · Psalm 32

Blessed is the one whose transgressions are forgiven,
whose sins are covered.

This week's readings remind us that God is able to remove the stain and separation of sin and grant us a second start at the feast where we belong.

Having crossed the Jordan in preparation for the assault on the Promised Land, in Joshua 5 the men of Israel are told to stop and be circumcised (having failed to be so on their wilderness wanderings). Uncircumcision was considered a matter of ritual shame, reproach or 'disgrace' (see Genesis 34:14 where the same word is used). Former slaves wandering around the desert could be slandered as mere fugitive rebels, but God reminds the world by this sign that he had long ago taken this people under his special protection. As French commentator John Calvin (1509–64) says, 'they were again made the peculiar property of God when they were anew stamped with this mark'.[24] With no fear of the past catching up with them, they can move forward into the new world God has set apart for their enjoyment, celebrating their liberty through the Passover, and finally eating from the land of milk and honey – their new home.

In 2 Corinthians 5, the apostle Paul unwraps an even greater reality, declaring that 'if anyone is in Christ, there is a new creation: everything old has passed away; see everything has become new!' Just as he promised, God has swallowed up death for ever and wiped the tears from our faces – 'the reproach of his people he will take

---

[24] John Calvin, *Commentary on the Book of Joshua* (Bellingham, WA: Logos Bible Software, 2010), p. 81.

away from the earth' (Isaiah 25:8). It may not be apparent in an external sign, but there is a new song in the heart and on the lips.

Not counting our sins against us, Jesus has done everything necessary to reconcile the world to himself on the cross. Through his apostolic ambassadors sent into every nation, he entreats those who are still far off to be reconciled to God, not by ritual but by repentance and faith. There is no other solution for sin, but that alone: as the wonderful old hymn 'Before the throne of God above' rejoices, 'because the sinless saviour died; my sinful soul is counted free: for God the just is satisfied, to look on *him* and pardon me.'

The message of forgiveness, cleansing, a fresh start and a new home was magnetic to those who heard it from the lips of the welcoming Saviour himself. In Luke 15, 'sinners' and tax collectors flock to Jesus and eat with him at the start of their new lives. There is joy in heaven as they return to God, but no rejoicing in the hearts of those who felt they themselves deserved even more.

The parable of the wasteful son, disgraced by a very un-kosher downfall into the pigsty but cherished by a lavishly, prodigiously forgiving Father, resonates with all who wish to leave their sin behind and come home. The parable of the irritated elder son, who had everything but contentment and the compassion shown by his father, convicts those who understand little of what it means to serve a gracious God. Both belong at home, feasting joyfully on the fattened calf; but only one has used the pain of separation as a goad to spur him back to his father's embrace.

So as the psalm for today reminds us, there is great joy in turning back to God in repentance: 'I said, "I will confess my transgressions to the LORD". And you forgave the guilt of my sin.' Do you know that liberating freedom? Why not pray and confess to him now, in the sure and certain hope of his forgiveness and warm embrace?

5th Sunday of Lent

Isaiah 43:16–21 · Philippians 3:4b–14 · John 12:1–8 · Psalm 126

The LORD has done great things for us, and we are filled with joy.

Our theme for this week is that when we are truly saved from the barrenness of death, it leads to honour and praise for God above all. Let today be a day of rejoicing for all the great things the Lord has done for you.

Isaiah's prophecy speaks of a greater exodus to come, which will make the rescue at the Red Sea seem insignificant. God's promise to permanently extinguish our enemies and bring new life to the desert is rooted in a firm covenant relationship with his elect people. He has chosen and formed us for himself, that we might declare his praise, just as the wild animals of the desert will also honour him when he opens the floodgates of life-giving water in the wilderness. 'I am about to do a new thing – do you not perceive it?'

Many did not perceive it when the Son of God came to accomplish and fulfil these things. He demonstrates his power over the grave in John's Gospel by raising Lazarus of Bethany (the 'house of the poor/afflicted'). And the week before his own death, he eats with Lazarus and his sisters, who serve and honour the one who will die in their place as the Passover lamb of God. The Gospel gives primacy to this 'first love' relationship; it takes precedence over all over identities or offices or actions we might own. However much we do for the poor and vulnerable, for example, it is not pleasant or acceptable to God, but rather sinful, if we do not first honour his Son by faith.

The early church scholar Origen (185–253) once said that just as Lazarus's house was filled with the fragrance of this pure nard, so also the world is to be filled with the fragrance of the Christian's good deeds.[25]

[25] Joel C. Elowsky (ed.), *John 11–21*, Ancient Christian Commentary on Scripture (Downers Grove, IL: InterVarsity Press, 2007), p. 40.

But this must be kept in right perspective. St Augustine (354–430), in an oft-repeated illustration, used to compare those who do good works without trusting in Christ to a racehorse which expends huge amounts of energy running *outside* the course, to no ultimate avail.[26] We must seek him first, honour him while he is near, and there will always be time to do our duty to others. As the ancient theologian Cyril of Alexandria (376–444) put it, 'love for the poor is very praiseworthy, only let it be put after veneration of God'.[27]

In the Gospel, Judas doesn't really care, anyway, about either the poor or the Lord. He places a higher value on Mary's perfume (300 denarii, about a year's wages) than he later does on Jesus's life when he betrayed him (thirty pieces of silver, about four months' wages). But how might *we* show our proper love and esteem for Jesus? Jesus himself tells us plainly here that he will not be with us physically after his ascension (which also took place at Bethany – see Luke 24:50). So we need not look now to adore him that way. His hair and feet are now seated at the right hand of the Father until he comes again in glory to judge the living and the dead.

In Philippians Paul directs us, rather, to regard our earthly gains as loss. No family advantage, no ecclesiastical preferment, no spiritual achievement can rival the righteousness we are gifted by God through faith alone. Knowing Christ and his resurrection power is all. With that in hand we strain forwards to reach the goal he has set before us. We are not perfect, but we make progress towards the prize with our eyes fixed firmly on him. As we share in his sufferings, we share in his power; that is the pattern of discipleship. As the psalm today puts it, 'Those who sow with tears will reap with songs of joy'. You can trust that promise today.

---

[26] See Augustine's second exposition of Psalm 32:1 in E. B. Pusey (ed.), *Expositions on the Book of Psalms by S. Augustine* (Oxford, 1839), 1:281. This illustration is also used in the *The Glossa Ordinaria on Romans* (trans. Michael Scott Woodward; Kalamazoo, Michigan: Medieval Institute Publications, 2011), p. 211 (on Romans 14:23) and in Peter Lombard's *Sentences*, 2.40.1.2 in Guilio Silano (ed.), *The Sentences: Book 2 On Creation* (Toronto: Pontifical Institute of Medieval Studies, 2008), 198. Cf. Gatiss (ed.), *The First Book of Homilies*, p. 82.

[27] Elowsky (ed.), *John 11–21*, p. 47.

Palm Sunday

Isaiah 50:4–9a · Philippians 2:5–11 · Luke 23:1–49 · Psalm 31:9–16

In your relationships with one another,
have the same mindset as Christ Jesus.

The readings this week reflect on the plots against Jesus, the man of sorrows. He would have identified with the psalm for today when it says, 'Because of all my enemies, I am the utter contempt of my neighbours and an object of dread to my closest friends – those who see me on the street flee from me.' And yet ultimately, he was safe in the shelter of God's love.

The psalm reading is part of a prayer for mercy from someone in deep trouble and distress. His strength is failing, and he has become a byword to those around him, feeling forgotten and forsaken. Despised by opponents and deserted by his friends, he looks to God in the midst of the whispering conspiracy against him. He trusts in God and clings to the one who has covenanted to be *his* God (remembering that 'I will be *your* God' as the highest privilege of the covenants of grace and redemption). He prays for the covenant blessing, that God's face would shine upon him (cf. Numbers 6:25), and that he would be delivered from this situation – not because he deserves it *per se*, but because of God's mercy towards his servant.

The Lectionary officially says verses 17 and 18 of the psalm are optional. It is perhaps as strange to miss out these two verses as it is to omit the first eight and the last six. It is difficult to understand why some people are squeamish about asking God to put the wicked to shame and silence lying lips. Naturally we long for all to know the truth and repent; but let us not be more holy than God's word itself – though we are discouraged from taking matters into our own hands, the Bible has no qualms about praying for God's just vengeance against evil.

It is not difficult to see here a prophecy of Christ, in the midst of the Passion narrative in our Gospel reading. But it also presents an example of a believer under pressure who looks to God for deliverance in the midst of oppression and trouble, when everyone else has faded away. So as St Athanasius (296–373), no stranger to suffering and persecution himself, once said, 'When you see yourself hated and persecuted by all your relatives and friends because of the truth, do not be downcast either for them or for yourself; and when all your acquaintances turn away from you, do not be frightened, but ... keep your eyes fixed on the future, singing Psalm 31.'[28]

The longer Gospel reading is designed to help us catch some sense of the bitterness and seeming injustice of the Passion. It begins with the assembly of elders handing Jesus over to the Gentile court of Pontius Pilate, with trumped-up charges which are clearly false to anyone who has followed Jesus's teaching on paying taxes to Caesar and his reticence to be seen as an earthly kind of king. The only ones stirring up the crowds were the chief priests, not Jesus, and they continue to do so after Pilate pronounces him innocent and he is taken to Herod instead. Herod's soldiers badly mistreat him, and though he had no pretensions to such frippery (cf. Luke 7:25), they deck him out in splendid clothing and kick him back to the Governor, like a political football.

Despite repeatedly trying to declare him innocent and release him, Pilate fails to hold his nerve and do what is right. His final verdict is that his own verdict should be overturned by the howling of democracy. Jesus was crucified in the place of one who deserved to die and yet was set free; Barabbas could thank God for someone else taking the punishment he deserved that day. King Jesus could have saved himself all along. But how then would the Scripture be fulfilled (not least Isaiah 50:4–9), the penitent thief saved, and the centurion shown the truth at the end? And because he fulfilled the covenant by dying in our place, his God exalted him to the highest place (Philippians 2:9). In humility we too ought to value others above ourselves (Philippians 2:3).

[28] Craig A. Blaising and Carmen S. Hardin (eds.), *Psalms 1–50*, Ancient Christian Commentary on Scripture (Downers Grove, IL: InterVarsity Press, 2008), p. 226.

EASTER

Easter Sunday

Isaiah 65:17–25 · Acts 10:34–43 · Luke 24:1–12 · Psalm 118:1–2, 14–24

The wolf and the lamb will feed together, and the lion will eat straw like the ox, and dust will be the serpent's food.

This week we rejoice in the resurrection of our Lord Jesus Christ and the glorious harmony of the new creation which he has inaugurated. This is the wonderful future that we have to look forward to.

Isaiah 65 presents us with a beautiful picture of a renewed, re-created world, which is so beautiful that it causes all thoughts of the former world to vanish and be replaced by everlasting joy. Jerusalem, the city of God, is an essential part of this vision of a new creation, for in it are God's people, minus the weeping and distress of former years. The harlot city of Isaiah chapter 1 has been transformed. None of the things that spoil this world (such as untimely death or frustrating work) will be there. Neither will creation be set against itself with wolves and sheep, lions and oxen, the serpent and the people threatening each other like unsentimental predators. This recalls Tennyson's powerful words about God and nature at strife, with nature lending such evil dreams to the scene; the tension is expressed in famous lines, speaking of humanity,

> Who trusted God was love indeed
> And love Creation's final law

> Tho' Nature, red in tooth and claw
> With ravine, shriek'd against his creed.[29]

Isaiah 65 shows us that love does indeed have the final word. But there are also some potentially confusing details in Isaiah 65. I don't think verse 20 is meant as a literal picture of old age followed by death in the new creation, since we know from Isaiah 25:8 and from the New Testament (e.g. 1 Corinthians 15:54), that death itself will one day be swallowed up for ever.

In the Gospel, Jesus's first disciples experienced the anxious gloom of uncertainty and dereliction after his death. Perhaps they felt as Tennyson did in that poem (originally called 'The Way of the Soul'):

> If e'er when faith had fallen asleep,
> I hear a voice 'believe no more'
> And heard an ever-breaking shore
> That tumbled in the Godless deep;

Yet the women still came to anoint his body. They were startled, however, by two figures who rebuked them for seeking among the dead the one who had prophesied resurrection. Suddenly remembering these very words, they ran with alacrity to instruct the apostles. Indeed, as Reformation commentator John Calvin (1509–64) puts it, Christ gave them 'no ordinary reward' and 'bestowed on them distinguished honour, by taking away from men the apostolic office, and committing it to them for a short time'.[30] They were not immediately believed, but Peter ran to check, just to make sure. The new age, the new world, had arrived. Jesus was indeed, the firstborn from the dead (Revelation 1:5).

In the reading from Acts we see how Peter's doubt and fear were transformed into faith and courage. His Gentile host, Cornelius,

---

29 'In Memoriam A. H. H.' (1850) by Alfred, Lord Tennyson.

30 Calvin, *Commentary on a Harmony of the Evangelists Matthew, Mark, and Luke*, p. 339.

may have echoed the words of Tennyson in the midst of his confusion of soul:

> I stretch lame hands of faith, and grope,
> And gather dust and chaff, and call
> To what I feel is Lord of all,
> And faintly trust the larger hope.

But Peter announces to him plainly and confidently that 'Jesus Christ – *he* is Lord of all.' And he presents to him the gospel hope of forgiveness and resurrection, guaranteed by the solid reality of Jesus's defeat of death. And so, in the new light of Easter, he preaches peace to both Jews and Gentiles, that they too may be one and enjoy harmony in Christ. How blessed we are to have this hope.

2nd Sunday of Easter

Exodus 14:10–31, 15:20–21 · Acts 5:27–32 · John 20:19–31 · Revelation 1:4–8 · Psalm 150

'Look, he is coming with the clouds,' and 'every eye will see him, even those who pierced him.'

The readings for this week remind us that the powerful resurrection plan of God is far greater than anything that mortals can dream up – and one day everyone will see that.

I have always been amused by what the Israelites say in Exodus 14. Confronted with Pharaoh's plan to reverse their exodus after the Passover, they forget that God has a plan too. They are terrified of Pharaoh, who is puny compared to their God, and they complain against Moses. 'We should have stayed in Egypt!' they say. They have forgotten rather quickly how terrible slavery was. When they were in it they couldn't wait to escape. Foolishly often, we look back wistfully at the past when things get tough in the present and we cannot see a way forward.

'Are there no graves in Egypt to bury us in?' the people ask – which is most ironic, since even today the one thing ancient Egypt is famous for is its graves. The pyramids of the Pharaohs stand as an enduring testimony to their death, while the people of God continue to thrive and to flourish all over the world. In the face of what they think will be imminent death, God opens up the way to new life, for their safety and his glory. Finally they believe and rejoice, though the fate of the Egyptians is publicly sealed. So as the ancient Italian bishop, Maximus of Turin (380–465) once put it, 'the one who walks calmly in faith will not fear Egypt in pursuit'.[31]

Faced by the potentially life-threatening authority of the high priest, the apostles in Acts 5 might have similarly been cowed into

[31] Joseph T. Lienhard and Ronnie J. Rombs (eds.), *Exodus, Leviticus, Numbers, Deuteronomy*, Ancient Christian Commentary on Scripture (Downers Grove, IL: InterVarsity Press, 2001), p. 72.

despondent fear and spiritual panic. Reminding them that he had given 'strict orders' that they were not to teach in Jesus's name, the high priest confronts them with evidence of their determined and brazen impertinence. But far from being silent, Peter and the others cannot help but calmly speak out (which establishment figures who have lost sight of truly spiritual imperatives have always considered to be infantile and unproductive). They must obey God, rather than any human authority – even that of the high priest – because God has acted decisively in Jesus through his death, resurrection, and exaltation. Those who repent and obey the true Leader and Saviour of Israel will receive the Holy Spirit. The authorities will not be able to deny the unpleasant evidence of their failure to get with God's programme.

The apostle John's vision of the risen and ascended Christ begins with a blessing of grace and peace from the one who has an eternal plan: he was, and is, and is to come. He has loved and freed his people by shedding his own blood, as the true Passover lamb, and faithfully witnessed to the sovereign rule of God over this world and the next through his glorious resurrection.

John testifies that Jesus will one day return. And when he does, it will not be in a corner. It will not be as a suffering servant. He will come to bring salvation for his people, but wailing and aching regret to those who reject him. 'Every eye will see him, even those who pierced him' must be one of the most devastating lines in Scripture. As the old commentator Matthew Henry (1662–1714) says, 'He shall come, to the terror of those who have pierced him and have not repented and of all who have wounded and crucified him afresh by their apostasy from him, and to the astonishment of the pagan world.'[32] Those who oppose God and his plan to save his people will, at the end, be clearly and openly defeated. Yet we are not to react with pleasure derived from someone else's misfortune (*schadenfreude*, as the Germans call it). Rather, our response today should be one of repentance and sobriety, trusting in the ultimate justice and wisdom of the one who is Alpha and Omega.

---

[32] Henry, *Matthew Henry's Commentary*, p. 2464.

3rd Sunday of Easter

Zephaniah 3:14–20 · John 21:1–19 · Acts 9:1–20 · Revelation 5:11–14 · Psalm 30

You turned my wailing into dancing; you removed my sackcloth and clothed me with joy.

This week we rejoice that God graciously chooses to use weak and feeble instruments to achieve his transformative global purposes. What a reassurance, if we are feeling weak and feeble today!

Zephaniah exhorts the people of God to shout for joy. Verse 15 lists several reasons why. God has taken away his judgment against us – whatever punishments we are due in strict justice have been passed over in mercy. God has turned away our enemies, for war is one of God's judgments, and our assailants sheath their swords against us when God himself does. God is in our midst, and no longer distant or alienated from us. Finally, we need fear no disaster, because we have such a defender.

The Lord gives victory to his weak and oppressed people, who feel like lame outcasts, ashamed and insignificant. He will turn their shame into praise, says Zephaniah, 'and renown in all the earth' – a global impact for such a seemingly unimportant group. We are to praise him for this even when, like Zephaniah's audience, we may not see the triumph with our own eyes as yet. He moves in mysterious ways, as William Cowper (1731–1800) sang, and so:

> Ye fearful saints, fresh courage take;
> the clouds ye so much dread
> are big with mercy, and shall break
> in blessings on your head.

Peter experiences transformation in the Gospel narrative. Returning to his nets, the fisherman has laboured throughout the long dark night without any joy. But this only made the miracle of the morning more startlingly clear. The presence of Jesus dramatically altered the situation, just as his advice in Luke 5:1–11 had likewise led to a huge haul of fish. On that occasion, Peter had confessed that he was a sinful man and felt he must beg Jesus to 'depart from me!' Now, though he knows his sin even more clearly, he rushes towards the bank to meet him.

The disciples count the fish so miraculously caught, and eat with Jesus, who it seems has already prepared some fresh bread and fish by himself. The fact that the number of fish caught (153) is mentioned has led to all kinds of speculation: following St Augustine (354–430) for example, might it represent the Law (the Ten Commandments) plus the Spirit (the sevenfold Spirit, e.g. Isaiah 11 or Revelation 4–5) multiplied in fruitfulness, because 1+2+3+4 all the way up to 17, equals 153? Or Gentiles (100) plus Jews (50) to the glory of the Trinity (3)? Any way you look at it, there is extraordinary fullness when Jesus is with us.

Peter is then re-commissioned and restored after his earlier treachery. His love for Christ, evident in his swift swim to the shore, is probed three times just as three times he had denied even knowing Christ. On each occasion he is told to care for God's people, and thereby demonstrate that love in future, following Christ even unto death. He is changed, from a pitiful failure to the apostolic rock for the sake of the mission to the world.

The same might be said of Saul in Acts 9. He begins by breathing out threats and murder against the disciples. At the end of our reading he declares in the synagogues that 'Jesus is the Son of God'. He is turned from a persecutor to a proclaimer. He once was spiritually blind but now he sees; yet his physical sight is taken away from him until the Lord restores it through Ananias. Saul is chosen by Christ to carry his name before Gentiles and Kings throughout the world, but his privilege is matched by his calling to suffer. On the Last Day he will rejoice at the cosmic impact of all that Jesus has achieved through him. Might we also look forward to doing the same, if we give ourselves to his service with the same fruitful faith as Zephaniah and Peter and Paul?

4th Sunday of Easter

Genesis 7:1–5, 11–18, 8:6–18, 9:8–13 · Acts 9:36–43 · John 10:22–30 · Revelation 7:9–17 · Psalm 23

Surely your goodness and love will follow me all the days of my life, and I will dwell in the house of the LORD *for ever.*

Our readings this week expound the work of Christ our Shepherd, who will keep his chosen people safe to the end. What a tremendous truth to hold on to in the midst of all life's challenges.

Acts 9 continues the story of the ascended Jesus's rule over the church. In a narrative pregnant with Gospel parallels, Jesus raises the only woman to be given the name 'disciple' in Acts – Tabitha – just as he had earlier raised the little girl – *talitha* – with a word of gentle command. This time he does it through his apostle Peter (who was there when Jesus originally performed the same miracle in Mark 5:35–43). His sheep hear his voice, and up they come. Jesus charged people not to talk about what he did on that first occasion; but word of what he did this time through Peter could not be constrained, and many believed in the Lord because of it.

Peter looks at the wailing widows and the needlework of Tabitha (who was, undoubtedly, a godly woman), and he simply puts them all outside and prays. This is not evidence that we may benefit others by our generous almsgiving, but rather points to the power of God alone, who upholds all things by his powerful word. The point is that the apostolic word has power to raise the dead, just as Jesus's word did. He continues to shepherd his people.

This is exactly what he promises in John chapter 10. To people seeking certainty and clarity, he points to his works as evidence for who he was. Yet people would not believe in him because they were not his sheep. It is fascinating that Jesus does *not* say 'You are not my sheep, because you do not believe.' The thought here is *not* that they disqualify themselves from being his sheep by failing to listen to him (which they supposedly could, if they chose to). Rather, more startlingly, Jesus is saying this: you are not mine in the first place, and that's why you don't listen. My sheep, those I have chosen, hear my voice and follow me. Whatever evidence you are confronted with, he says, you won't believe it if you are not my sheep.

Jesus claims that the Father has given certain people to him to shepherd. Indeed, they have double protection, since they are held by the hand of both the Father and the Son, and no power of hell or scheme of sinful humanity can tear them away. The salvation of those who believe is as secure as the power of God is invincible. As French commentator John Calvin (1509–64) says, 'Christ did not intend to throw this word foolishly into the air, but to give a promise which should remain deeply axed in their minds.'[33] Is this precious promise firmly etched in your brain? He will not let you go.

We see salvation achieved in Revelation 7. An innumerable multitude from around the world declares that 'Salvation belongs to our God!' They ascribe it all to him, and to the Lamb whose blood washes them clean from sin. They are sheltered by his presence. They shall never hunger, nor thirst, nor burn in the sun or in hell ('the sun will not strike them, nor *any* scorching heat'). Rather, they will be shepherded by the Lamb, guided to refreshing streams and tenderly cared for by a loving, sympathetic Father for ever. Rest in his loving arms and listen to his voice.

---

[33] Craig S. Farmer et al (eds.), *John 1–12: New Testament*, vol. IV of *Reformation Commentary on Scripture* (Downers Grove, IL: IVP Academic, 2014), p. 393.

5th Sunday of Easter

Genesis 22:1–18 · John 13:31–35 · Acts 11:1–18 · Psalm 148

So then, even to Gentiles God has granted repentance that leads to life.

The theme of our readings this week is that in his love, God has provided a way for us to be saved, so that we may glorify him and love others above ourselves. So 'Praise the LORD … kings of the earth and all nations … young men and women, old men and children' (Psalm 148:7–12).

Abraham faces his most difficult test when God asks him to offer his son Isaac as a burnt offering. As in other places in the Genesis narrative, the teaching point of the story is contained in the name given to the place where the action occurs: in this instance, Mount Moriah becomes the place where 'the LORD will provide'. Abraham trusted God to provide in some way (verse 8), either with an alternative sacrifice or by raising Isaac from the dead (note verse 5, 'I and the boy will go over there and worship and *we* will come again to you', cf. Hebrews 11:19).

The story is somewhat tense, of course, until this liberating denouement; but Abraham's faith did not waver, trusting in the fact that God had promised to give him offspring through this very child (Genesis 21:12). Later, this would be the very spot where Solomon would begin to build the Temple of the Lord (2 Chronicles 3:1): for a while at least, the sacrifice of a beloved son will not be necessary, for the Lord provides a regular substitute to take his place, until the true Lamb of God comes to take away the sin of the world (John 1:29). Abraham teaches us that faith which is willing to give up everything to please God is vindicated and rewarded when the day comes for God to keep his promises.

The Son of Man knew these things for himself when he came to be glorified and to glorify God through his death and resurrection.

He told his disciples in John 13 that they could not go where he was going, and they may have been overwhelmed by shame and despondency when they saw him dragged away to be crucified. But he reassures them beforehand that whatever ignominy he might have to suffer, that cross would ultimately bring him glory. As French commentator John Calvin (1509–64) puts it, 'in the cross of Christ, as in a magnificent theatre, the inestimable goodness of God is displayed before the whole world'.[34]

His love for us, in giving himself up in our place, is to be the pattern for our lives too. 'Just as I have loved you,' he says, 'you also are to love one another.' Like Abraham, we must be willing to trust this promise of God, that whatever we may have to forego or forfeit along the way, there is fruitfulness only in following in Christ's footsteps. This is the way which leads to glory, and by living thus we demonstrate to the watching world whose disciples we truly are.

In Acts 11, Peter explains to the critical circumcision party how God persuaded him to go to the Gentiles with the message of salvation through Jesus. The key thing to notice is that when he explains how the Holy Spirit fell on the Gentiles 'just as on us at the beginning', the circumcision party falls silent. Indeed, that critical group is said now to glorify God. Likewise, we ought all to rejoice when God grants life-giving repentance to anyone, or any group, whatever our attitude to them might have been previously. God has provided a way for anyone to be saved, so let us glorify him and love those he has chosen, whoever they may be.

---

[34] John Calvin, *Commentary on the Gospel according to John* (Bellingham, WA: Logos Bible Software, 2010), p. 73.

6th Sunday of Easter

Ezekiel 37:1–14 · Acts 16:9–15 · John 5:1–9 · Revelation 21:10, 22–22:5 · Psalm 67

Then you, my people, will know that I am the L*ORD*,
when I open your graves and bring you up from them.

In our readings this week we see the power of God's word to bring new life even in the midst of hopeless situations. There is nothing you are facing today that he cannot deal with.

Ezekiel is brought by the Spirit of the Lord to a valley full of very dry bones. It is difficult to imagine a more hopeless situation. Like the nation of Israel in exile, these bones are scattered and lifeless, seemingly without a future. The Lord confirms as much with the prophet, before he intervenes to transform the scene. The Lord works through his powerful word to command the dry bones to live – and not just to live, but to 'know that I am the LORD'. The bones obey the word. Though they were completely dried up they are changed into a vast living army.

This vision has brought comfort and hope to many who trust in the power of God's word through the ages. The Cappadocian theologian Gregory of Nyssa (335–94) said that 'Ezekiel, with prophetic spirit, has surpassed all time and space, and with his power of prediction has stood at the very moment of the resurrection.'[35] This was not just a vision to encourage the downcast in Israel, but a foretaste of the final day when all will be raised and reclothed, ready for judgment. 'We believe in the resurrection *of the body*' is a fundamental article of the creed. Yet in Ezekiel's prophecy we also see a picture

[35] Kenneth Stevenson and Michael Gluerup (eds.), *Ezekiel, Daniel*, Ancient Christian Commentary on Scripture (Downers Grove, IL: InterVarsity Press, 2008), p. 122.

of what happens when individuals are confronted in this life by the spiritual power of the word.

In John 5, the Word himself confronts a man sorely in need of that power to change. Unwell for thirty-eight years, he has been unable to access the healing waters of the pool of Bethsaida thanks to a lack of kindness from others. Yet all it takes is one command from Jesus (singling this man out from all the rest), and he is made well and walks away a changed man. Of all the lame, blind, and withered people sitting by the waters that day, it is the one who heard and obeyed the voice of God who was healed. Thus we see the efficacy of the word, quite apart from any seemingly magical cures. Even baptism, which many ancient commentators saw prefigured in the pool of Bethsaida, has no power of its own but only that which comes from the word it makes visible.

In Acts 16, Paul makes his way to Macedonia in response to another vision, that he might bring the life-giving word to Europe. He and his party (note the 'we' from verse 10 onwards) would normally have gone initially to the synagogue, to bring the good news 'first to the Jews'. But it seems there may not have been a synagogue there, so they sought out any god-fearing persons they could find, at a place of prayer outside the city gate at Philippi. They encountered Lydia, a businesswoman of some means, and 'the Lord opened her heart to listen eagerly to what was said by Paul'. The word brought life, and she and her household were baptised – the first Christian converts in Europe and, like Cornelius in Acts 10, not Jews but Gentiles. Those who once were cut off and without hope are brought near through the ministry of God's word. To which dry bones can you speak that live-giving word today?

7th Sunday of Easter (Sunday after Ascension Day)

Ezekiel 36:24–28 · Acts 16:16–34 · John 17:20–26 ·
Revelation 22:12–14, 16–17, 20–21 · Psalm 97

'I pray also for those who will believe in me through their message.'

The days after Ascension Day until Pentecost are often set as days of prayer and preparation for the celebration of the outpouring of the Holy Spirit. Our readings speak about his work of changing hearts and gathering his people, encouraging us to pray that he will open people's eyes to believe in Jesus.

Ezekiel prophesies to Israel that despite the fact they have defiled the land with their iniquity and been scattered to the nations in judgment as a result, God will gather them again. The pollution of their idolatry and sin will be cleansed through the ceremonial sprinkling of clean water. But for the restoration of covenant fellowship with God, things must go even deeper. In the Law, Moses had both urged the people to circumcise their hearts (Deuteronomy 10:16) and also promised that one day, God himself would do this for them, so that they might truly love him with all their heart and soul (Deuteronomy 30:6). Ezekiel likewise prophesies that God will perform heart surgery on the people and give them a new spirit. Lifeless, disobedient, cold hearts of stone will become living, pulsating hearts of flesh, beating in time with the drumbeat of God's will. Those filled by God's Spirit will be his covenant people; and he shall be their God.

Reflecting on these Old Testament texts, St Augustine (354–430) said that 'the grace of God is always good and brings about a good will in a person who before was possessed of an evil will'.[36] The same grace also strengthens that new will to obey God's Law, so that God

[36] Stevenson and Gluerup (eds.), *Ezekiel, Daniel*, p. 118.

can be said (with regard to the elect) to give what he commands. And we see that not just prophesied in Ezekiel 36 but demonstrated in Acts 16.

Paul and his companions meet a slave-girl in Philippi, at the same place they had previously met Lydia. She has an evil spirit and makes a fortune for her owners through trading on her biblically illicit talent for divination (see Leviticus 19:26 and Deuteronomy 18:10). Like the demons who dogged Jesus's steps in the Gospels, she quickly and correctly identifies the spiritual force ranged against her: 'These men are servants of the Most High God!' she cries out, until it drives Paul to distraction and he casts the evil spirit from her.

Her owners mean to harm him for that unwanted exorcism, rejecting the prophet who ruined their profit. Paul and Silas's subsequent imprisonment, on charges which strangely neglected to mention the commercial interest of the prosecutors, ends with another changed life. The joyful prisoners are released from their chains by an act of God, and the jailor despairs of keeping his life. But presented with the call of the gospel, he hears the word of God and believes in Jesus. As his whole family are baptised, and the wounds of the prisoners are washed, the Holy Spirit is sprinkling the hearts of his covenant people and gathering them together, even in adversity.

This is what Jesus himself prayed for in his high priestly prayer in John 17. He prayed for the apostles and those who would believe in him through their message, that they would be united together. This would be a sign to the world that Jesus truly came from God, and that the eternal intra-Trinitarian love of the Father for the Son is paralleled in his glorious love for his people. As the Philippian jailor cared for and opened his home to Paul and Silas and ate with them, the unifying and transformative power of the gospel was clear for all to see. May it also be so in our churches and communities.

PENTECOST

Whit Sunday (Pentecost)

Genesis 11:1–9 · Acts 2:1–21 · John 14:8–17, 25–27

Even on my servants, both men and women,
I will pour out my Spirit in those days.

The readings for Pentecost remind us of God's mighty deeds, particularly in the sending of his Spirit. He is the one who empowers us to serve Jesus and speak his word boldly to an unbelieving world.

In Genesis 11 we find a united humanity trying to make a name for itself, proclaiming their own mighty deeds. As Noah's descendants are filling the earth, in obedience to God's command (the process we see as a whole in Genesis 10), they pause in this flashback incident to construct a city and a tower. Stronger and bigger and higher they build, to concentrate and magnify their own greatness rather than continuing to disperse across the world as God had said. Humanity is dedicated to sin, not just individually but as a society: Genesis 11 is the logical conclusion to the sinful rebellion of Genesis 3.

Yet God is dedicated to overthrowing sin, and he makes our attempts to elevate ourselves look foolish. We cannot reach God by our efforts – however hard we try, he must still 'come down' from heaven when he comes to visit. The epitome of fruitless self-assertion is the place of primeval human confusion; 'that is why it was called Babel'.

Acts 2 sees a kind of reversal of Babel. The remnant of the disciples are all gathered in one place, and so are God-fearing Jews from every nation under heaven. It is from here that they will fan out across the world to be Jesus's witnesses and to go into the harvest as labourers for God (Acts 1:8; Matthew 9:38). As the Spirit comes down not to judge but to rest on the disciples, they begin to proclaim the wonders of God and his greatness in the native tongues of all the visitors. This is not alcoholic babbling, but Spirit-empowered boldness, the point of which is to declare that 'everyone who calls on the name of the Lord will be saved' in these last days which have now arrived.

Later, the disciples would reflect on what had happened. They would remember the upper room where Jesus said to them, 'the Advocate, the Holy Spirit whom the Father will send in my name, will teach you all things and will remind you of everything I have said to you'. He had told them in Acts 1 that they would go out and be his witnesses once the Spirit came. But he had also told them this Spirit of truth would be with them and help them. And they need all the help they can get, because the world in rebellion against God neither knows nor accepts the Spirit.

And yet, Jesus also says in the Gospel reading that with the help of this advocate they will 'do even greater things' than Jesus himself had done. Some take this as a promise of miracles, 'signs and wonders' which accompany the spread of the gospel. And indeed, the apostles do many great miracles which confirm and testify to the truth of their message. But do they do anything *greater* than raising the dead, walking on water, feeding five thousand, calming a storm and healing by a word?

They do, however, carry the gospel beyond the borders of Israel (to places Jesus has not physically been, since he is now 'with the Father' until he comes again in glory). And they preach it with clarity and openness to all the nations (whereas Jesus was sent primarily to the lost sheep of Israel, and often spoke to them in parables). How much greater than a temporary reprieve from death, such as Lazarus enjoyed, is the new birth into a living hope enjoyed by all who now trust in Christ through the apostolic gospel! So let us do the greater work of taking that gospel out, in the power and with the help of the Spirit.

ORDINARY TIME

Trinity Sunday

Proverbs 8:1–4, 22–31 · Romans 5:1–5 · John 16:12–15 · Psalm 8

And hope does not put us to shame, because God's love has been poured into our hearts through the Holy Spirit, who has been given to us.

This week's readings help us to delight in the glorious Trinity, and the peace we have with God through the eternally begotten Son who is glorified by the Spirit.

Proverbs 8 is probably the most commented on chapter in the whole of Proverbs, since verse 22 was one of the most contested passages in the early controversies about the deity of Jesus. The early heretic Arius (c. 250–336), for example, said that if it was speaking of Christ then 'The LORD created me at the beginning of his work, the first of his acts of long ago' (NRSV) clearly implied that he was a created being. Therefore, although he was an exalted and extremely important person, Christ could not be God, since there was a time when he did not exist.

St Athanasius (296–373), on the other hand, stood against the world and much of the church in his day. He affirmed that this sort of language could only apply to the incarnate Christ (whose *human nature* was created) and was not about the eternal Son as such, who is 'begotten of the Father before all worlds' (as it was eventually stated at the First Council of Constantinople in 381). This eventually became the accepted orthodox understanding, reflected in many later creeds and confessions.

On purely exegetical grounds, it is worth noting that the troublesome bit is the verb in verse 22, 'the LORD *created* me'. That is the NRSV translation (following the Greek Septuagint), but other translations render it as 'possessed me' (ESV) or 'brought me forth'

(NIV) which is a perfectly natural way to take the Hebrew and does not cause the same turmoil in our Trinitarian doctrine.

Looking more widely, this is not the only time Wisdom is personified in Proverbs, of course. Since Christ is 'the wisdom of God' it is natural for Christians to interpret these verses as being about him, and John 1:1–3 and Colossians 1:15–19 provide significant New Testament echoes of them. The main thrust of these verses, however, is that Wisdom is eternal and pre-existent, was with God in the beginning and rejoiced in the creation of the world – so Wisdom should be listened to and followed for a life of blessing.

The Trinity is not an impracticable doctrine, focusing merely on abstract questions of ontology and eternality. That is clear in the orthodox reading of Proverbs 8 as a whole but also in Romans 5, where Paul rejoices in the Trinitarian shape of salvation itself. We are justified through faith and have peace with the Father because of our Lord Jesus Christ. God's love is demonstrated by Christ's death for us, saving us from God's wrath (Romans 5:8–10). And though we, like him, must suffer in this life, our sufferings are always sweetened with hope. That hope is not some childish pie in the sky when we die by-and-by, an infantile fiction which an intelligent adult should be ashamed to cling on to. Rather, it is a glorious hope poured into our hearts through the Holy Spirit as we walk in the way of Christ – the Spirit who has been *given* to us as a gift, 'bestowed through the gratuitous goodness of God, and not conferred for our merits,' as John Calvin (1509–64) so beautifully reminds us.[37]

That same Spirit, says Jesus in John 16, made known God's word to his apostles, speaking always with a Trinitarian accent. His purpose is to glorify Christ (not grab the attention for himself) and guide us in truth (which comes from the Father and the Son). Most importantly, perhaps, he helps us overcome our inability to bear Christ's words. So let us hear what the Spirit says to the churches, and pray for his help to understand what has been revealed in his word.

---

[37] Calvin, *Commentary on the Epistle of Paul the Apostle to the Romans*, 193.

Proper 4

Sunday between 29 May and 4 June inclusive (if after Trinity Sunday)

1 Kings 18:20–39 · Galatians 1:1–12 · Luke 7:1–10 · Psalm 96

How long will you waver between two opinions? If the LORD is God, follow him; but if Baal is God, follow him.

In the three readings for Sunday we learn that there is only one true God, and only one true gospel, but that true faith in God's powerful word is sometimes astonishingly hard to find.

The confrontation between Elijah and the so-called prophets of Baal is a dramatic power encounter of the first order. Its purpose is to put a stop to the people's 'limping between two different opinions'. Should they go on worshipping Baal, the trendy and popular god of the rich and powerful establishment? Or should they follow the Lord, their 'official' national deity whose religion had been sidelined and ridiculed in their more recent public life? Elijah confronts the consumerist culture of his day, uncertain of which option to choose, with the often unpleasant and uncomfortable idea of absolute truth: If Baal is God, follow him. If the Lord is God, follow him.

This is not the test of pragmatism – which God works best for you? Which do you like the most? Which will get you preferment? Rather, the litmus test is pure existence: not which god is convenient, but which is true? Though the odds are stacked against him in worldly terms, Elijah is the one who can legitimately mock his opponents; for despite their antics, their fashionable yet brutal god is an embarrassing no-show. The true prophet then literally pours cold water on his own chances of success, not once but three times, so that the only hope for vindication could come from a living and active Lord. And come it does, in an astonishing display of power, for our God is a consuming fire; and every tongue confesses he is God.

Like Elijah, Paul also realises in Galatians 1 that 'the present evil age' is something from which we require redemption, rather than something to be embraced as our standard. He is astonished (but should he be, given the lessons of church history?) that the Galatians have so quickly deserted the one who called them by grace. They have turned not to a different god, as such, but to a different gospel (perhaps retaining the old words and familiar forms but profoundly re-interpreted so as to be more acceptable to some). No other message but salvation by grace alone truly is *good* news, so Paul warns them not to pervert the gospel into something less radically liberating. The pressure in Galatia came from influential false teachers within the church rather than a worldly establishment elite outside it, but if the pressure to compromise came even from an angel, they were to resist it. To serve the one true God means pleasing him and seeking his approval, playing to the audience of one when the pressure is on. This is not an easily marketable message in an age of comfort-seeking; yet truth always trumps convenience for the apostle whose call and message are of no merely human origin.

Finally, our Lord Jesus himself is astonished, in the Gospel reading, at finding faith in a Roman centurion. The elders appealed to Christ to help the man's slave (himself highly valued) because he was 'worthy' and had done good deeds. But in seeing Jesus more closely he knew himself more truly. He confessed he had no leverage, no merit to persuade Christ to help him. Yet despite his own unworthiness, he expressed such faith in the sheer majestic word of the Lord that the Lord was pleased in his grace to act. This precious truth that the Galatians were in danger of deserting was grasped intuitively by a Gentile seeker who discovered what glorious news it is. Will you trust in that sheer word of the Lord today, like Elijah and Paul and the centurion? If you do, he will never let you down.

Proper 5

Sunday between 5 and 11 June inclusive (if after Trinity Sunday)

1 Kings 17:8–24 · Galatians 1:11–24 · Luke 7:11–17 · Psalm 146

Do not put your trust in princes, in human beings, who cannot save.

In all three readings for Sunday we are confronted with true messengers of God who speak the truth and bring blessing to outsiders. In the face of death and of danger, this is our only hope.

The story of Elijah and the widow of Zarephath concludes when she acknowledges who Elijah is and the veracity of his words: 'Now I know that you are a man of God,' she says after receiving her son back from the dead, 'and that the word of the LORD in your mouth is truth.' She should perhaps have realised this already, since the miracles of the jar and the jug (providing her with all she needed in a time of famine) were a sign of God's favour towards this Gentile woman in her poverty. God does not fail her, 'according to the word of the LORD that he spoke by Elijah'. Elijah's words are truly God's words that this Phoenician widow and her fatherless son can cling to and trust, even in the face of death, which tests us all.

Luke frames his account of the raising of the widow of Nain's son with evocative parallels to the story of Elijah and the widow of Zarephath. They meet 'at the gate of the town,' a widow with an only son, distraught. The father, husband, provider has gone. The son is taken too. Yet in an act of compassion and mercy, the son is restored by a true messenger of God who speaks the word of truth. Jesus, like Elijah, 'gave him (back) to his mother'. The episode concludes again not just with glory being given to God, but with an acknowledgement that the one who speaks the life-giving word is an authentic servant of the living God – 'A great prophet has risen among us ... God has looked favourably on his people!'

In Psalm 146 we sing that, 'The LORD ... gives food to the hungry... he sets the prisoners free... and watches over the foreigner and sustains the fatherless and the widow, but he frustrates the ways of the wicked.' And so, from the story of a Gentile widow receiving back her son and the story of a Galilean widow released from grief, we turn to Galatians. Here we find the astonishing narrative of a zealous Pharisee who was transformed by Jesus from a persecutor to an apostle. And not just any old apostle either, but the chosen instrument of God to take the gospel of the Messiah to the Gentile world. What Paul received was new life in Christ, and the churches glorified God because of this grace shown to the chief of sinners. He is at pains to emphasise to the Galatians, who were not so quick to acknowledge the authority of his boundary-smashing message as the people of Zarephath and Nain had been to embrace the truth, that his gospel 'is not of human origin'. The true messenger of God spoke the true message of God, for the benefit of those beyond the borders of Israel, whether circumcised or not.

Our vital task today is also to speak that word of truth to a disbelieving generation, to persuade people of the inexpressible joy of knowing the barrier-free kindness of God who has rescued us from the dominion of darkness and brought us to the kingdom of his beloved Son (Colossians 1:14). Some, hungry for God, knowing their need, will ravenously gobble it up. Others, all too aware of the veil cast by death and sin over this world, will embrace it with joy. Many will be slow of heart to believe all that the prophets and apostles have taught us. But it remains our one best hope.

Proper 6

Sunday between 12 and 18 June inclusive
(if after Trinity Sunday)

1 Kings 21:1–21 · Galatians 2:15–21 · Luke 7:36–8:3 · Psalm 5:1–8

For you are not a God who is pleased with wickedness; with you, evil people are not welcome.

The psalm for today declares that God will 'destroy those who speak lies; the bloodthirsty and deceitful the Lord will abhor'. These people cannot stand in God's sight, even though they often seem to prosper in this world, unless they repent.

We see a perfect illustration and example of this truth in the confrontation between Naboth, Jezebel and Ahab in 1 Kings. Ahab is greedy and covetous; his wife is infamously bloodthirsty and deceitful. When confronted with an iniquitous demand from his earthly governor, Naboth does not slink off into a corner to hide, or cave in to his demands. He entrusted himself to him who judges justly and held fast, knowing that there was a greater king whose laws on the matter were clear: 'The Lord forbid that I should give you my ancestral inheritance.' Jezebel thrives on the power-play and asks her sulking husband, in effect, whether or not he is the real king in Israel. She knows what his power can accomplish. His sights and hers are too low, focused on the authorities of this world and the comforts of this life alone. She achieves her nefarious purpose to enrich the king and usurp the rights of the true landlord of Israel with a dodgy judicial decision from the lords and elders of the land. But the Lord sends his prophet, Elijah, to declare his own decision in the matter, and to pass sentence on the king who had sold himself to what is evil in the sight of the Lord.

Similarly, in Galatians 2:16 we see that the Lord's judgment is radically different from the ways of the world. 'A person is not justified by the works of the law' is a divine thunderbolt designed to rock the world of the religious legalists, even those who may be technically committed to salvation by grace but who effectively erect their own boundary markers around the grace of God. 'I live by faith in the Son of God' not 'I live by faith and am acceptable to God and his people through all kinds of additional rituals or shibboleths.' It is striking that the text reads 'the Son of God who *loved* me and gave himself for me' rather than 'the Son of God who *loves* me.' The love of God was expressed perfectly and beautifully on the cross of Christ, a past event. I cling to that for acceptance, and seek joy there rather than through innumerable human attempts at achieving righteousness which may look impressive in the eyes of the world.

The theme of being justified before God and what is right in his eyes continues in the Gospel reading. Jesus said 'the one to whom little is forgiven loves little'. The 'sinner' who loves Jesus is forgiven and is saved by faith. The seemingly pious Pharisee, who does not even recognise the King of Kings and Lord of Lords when he is standing right in front of him, is rebuked and humiliated. The women in this story are a wonderful contrast to the woman in the first reading from 1 Kings. Joanna, wife of King Herod's steward, stands out – a woman in the royal household, as Jezebel had been, but who knew the true king when she saw him. Rather than latching onto him for a chance of fame, fortune, and earthly glory, she spent herself and her resources to maintain the preaching of the gospel in the cities and in the villages. This, we are also called to do: to give and not to take, not for any reward we think to gain, but because we are accepted by the forgiving Saviour.

Proper 7

Sunday between 19 and 25 June inclusive
(if after Trinity Sunday)

1 Kings 19:1–15a · Galatians 3:23–29 · Luke 8:26–39 · Psalms 42–43

So in Christ Jesus you are all children of God through faith.

This Sunday's readings speak of dramatic escapes, which teach us humility before the God who rescues and continues his work. Are you overlooking how gracious he is?

Threatened with immediate death by Jezebel, in 1 Kings 19 Elijah runs to the southern border of Israel, and crosses over into the wilderness alone. He has had enough, and would rather be killed by God than keep contending with the Queen. But God sends an angel to sustain him. He needs food and rest, it is true, but also to know that God is with him and would uphold him in his weakness.

He also needed to get some perspective. So he goes back to the place where the covenant had been cut, the covenant the Israelites had broken and which he had been sent to enforce. When the word of the Lord comes to him asking 'What are you doing here, Elijah?', he recounts his woes. 'I'm the only one left, and they're trying to kill me!' he laments. So what is the point of all his strenuous effort to keep the covenant alive?

It isn't true of course: at the very least he was impetuously dismissing Obadiah and the hundred other prophets hidden away in a cave, just as he now was (see 1 Kings 18:3–4). We might also mention the 7,000 others who had not bowed the knee to Baal. When we start to see ourselves and 'our' ministries or churches as so untouchably unique and exceptional that they appear to us to be indispensable or identical to the cause of God himself, then we really do need to get out more. Even Elijah is not above the need for a divine rebuke to his narcissistic arrogance.

The Lord speaks to him, but not out of the piercing wind, not out of the earthquake. Not even out of the fire (all of which recall the frightening conditions at Sinai when Moses received the Law there). Elijah hears God's call to continue his work in a brief silenc, or low whisper – he is not active merely in the dramatic timpani and deafening trumpets, but also in the gentle violin, the sweet soprano and the pregnant pause. And so Elijah is told to anoint three others who will continue God's work for him.

The man in the Gospel reading this week does not feel alone, as Elijah felt he was. His name is Legion, and he is tormented by many demons. Living among the dead and in the wilds, he recognises Jesus as the Son of the Most High God. The demons beg him not to send them into the abyss, but into the unclean herd of pigs on the hillside. He allows them to rush down into the lake and drown, while the man is restored to his right mind, to sit at the feet of Jesus, no longer in shackles. What fills the whole countryside with fear? It isn't what happened to the pigs, but seeing the miraculous restoration of this one man to mental health. So Jesus then commissions the man to spread the good news of God's rescuing work.

Before Christ came, Legion was imprisoned by demons and bound by chains. In a similar way, the apostle Paul says the Law had us locked up and was our nanny or governess or tutor – set over us by God to care for and command us for a set period of time. But now faith in Christ has come and we escape those bonds. Just as Legion was clothed and in his right mind, so we who are right with God by faith are clothed with Christ and baptised into him. If by faith we belong to him, then we are heirs of God – our primary identity, which trumps all others.

Paul says 'unclean' Gentiles can be Abraham's offspring, not just Jews; slaves too, not just the freeborn; women also, and not just men. Like Elijah, we learn that God's promise gives us a wider perspective and pricks our sinful pride. He is far more gracious, to far more people, than we could possibly imagine.

Proper 8

Sunday between 26 June and 2 July inclusive

2 Kings 2:1–2, 6–14 · Galatians 5:1, 13–25 · Luke 9:51–62 · Psalm 77:1–2, 11–20

It is for freedom that Christ has set us free. Stand firm, then, and do not let yourselves be burdened again by a yoke of slavery.

Each of the readings this week concerns a transition. 2 Kings 2 is the very origin of one of our standard metaphors for describing transition, as Elisha literally 'takes up the mantle' of Elijah. The word translated 'mantle' is the word for a cloak (ancient Greek and Aramaic versions translated the Hebrew as 'sheepskin' or 'coarse cloak'). Elisha grabs hold of the garment which Elijah had used to part the river Jordan in a dramatic recapitulation of two similar miracles in Israel's earlier history (the crossing of the Red Sea in Exodus and the parallel crossing of the river by Joshua). Elijah had foreshadowed this passing of the mantle back in 1 Kings 19:19. But in Hebrew the word for mantle can also mean 'glory' or 'splendour', and Elisha inherits not just a cloak but a double portion of Elijah's powerful and majestic spirit. He will be the divinely vindicated prophetic voice of leadership to apostate Israel, calling them away from the burdens of false religion.

In the Gospel reading, the Lord Jesus resolutely sets his face towards Jerusalem. His earlier ministry of reaching out and gathering followers takes on a more determined aspect from this point of transition. 'The days drew near for him to be taken up' – that is, for him to go up to Jerusalem and give up his life as a ransom for many. The sons of thunder suggest that the rejection of Jesus by the Samaritans on the way should be met with signs of glorious power (shades of Elijah and Elisha). Yet they are rebuffed by the one who will show them a more excellent way and bring glory to God through his suffering and death. Likewise, those who might follow Christ are warned of the cost: proclaiming the kingdom of God is not a life of comfortable ease, or for those who cannot see it through to the end. Jesus himself knew this was to be the case for him; and those who (as the eighteenth-century hymnwriter Augustus Toplady put it) 'tread the sacred way that Jesus watered with his blood' must expect no less on the rough path their master trod.[38]

In Galatians 5, Paul speaks of several transitions, or better, transformations. In Christ we are no longer slaves to sin, but 'through love become slaves to one another'. We are to live by the Spirit, not gratifying the flesh. Indeed, the flesh has been crucified, just as we were crucified with Christ (Galatians 2:20). The fruit – note the singular! – of the Spirit, the nine-fold outworking of his powerful work in our hearts, is contrasted with the manifold corrupting works of the flesh. When the final transition comes and Jesus returns to judge the living and the dead, 'those who do such things will not inherit the kingdom of God'.

This is a sober warning that immorality and infighting as well as disordered desires and drunkenness are far more serious in the eyes of God than they often are in ours. Yet this is not a call to do the right things to go to heaven, as if Paul was suddenly forgetting his previous teaching about salvation by grace alone through faith alone. By no means! Rather, it is a reminder to be showing in our lives the practical outworking of being delivered from the present evil age (Galatians 1:4) as we keep in step with Christ and his Spirit. The Spirit gives us freedom, so why would we return to the slavery of sin?

---

[38] Toplady, *The Works of Augustus M. Toplady* (London: Edinburgh: William Baynes and Son; H. S. Baynes, 1825), 6:390–91.

Proper 9

Sunday between 3 and 9 July inclusive

2 Kings 5:1–14 · Galatians 6:1–16 · Luke 10:1–11, 16–20 · Psalm 30

May I never boast except in the cross of our Lord Jesus Christ, through which the world has been crucified to me, and I to the world.

This Sunday's readings teach us that we should not rejoice in what seems impressive to the eyes of the world and the worldly church. Should we not be more impressed by God and his ways?

Naaman is a mighty and impressive soldier, but leprous. He is healed because of the kindness of a little girl who really should have hated him for defeating her people and kidnapping her. She has an accepting, evangelistic heart which faithfully points her new master in the direction of the Lord's servant back in her homeland. He negotiates at the level of worldly magnificence: he gains the favour of his king and his visit to Israel involves international diplomacy; he takes with him a large retinue and a large fee intended for Elisha; he thinks that washing in the mighty waters of the Abana or Pharpar rivers would be more efficacious than the spluttering stream of the Jordan.

But see how wrong those at the top can be: The presumptuous king of Aram thinks the king of Israel can secure healing from a tame religious prophet who will do what he is told; the suspicious king of Israel considers a personal request for medical help to be a sneaky prelude to war; the mighty warrior is humbled and aggrieved by being told to trust in the naked word of God's prophet rather than enjoying an ostentatious display of pseudo-magical power.

The mission of the seventy in the Gospel reading has a similar focus on the word of God and mighty works of healing. The signs and wonders of Elisha's age returned with the coming of the Messiah's earthly ministry, yet it is how people hear and receive the message which is ultimately determinative. 'Whoever listens to you listens to me,' says the Lord, 'and whoever rejects you rejects me.' The word of the Lord goes out with the labourers and how people respond to that word is more important than how they respond to their healing. The seventy are delighted with the authority which being conveyers of God's kingdom word brings them. The worker is worth his wages and does have the power to do great harm to the enemy. Yet, nevertheless, their joy should not be in the extraordinary position they have, derived from their relationship to the Lord of the harvest, but in their final destiny. 'Do not rejoice that the spirits submit to you, but rejoice that your names are written in heaven.'

In the same way, Paul says in Galatians that 'if those who are nothing think they are something, they deceive themselves'. We hear again that gospel teachers must be supported out of the good things belonging to those they teach. The worker is worth his wages, though it is noteworthy that Elisha in the Old Testament reading (and also Paul himself on occasion) was sometimes willing to forgo his earthly reward as a sign to those who place too much value in the remunerations of this world. The ultimate prize is something which cannot be bought – a harvest of eternal life gained by trusting God's word, without becoming weary when the results don't seem to materialise immediately. On the other side are those who merely want to make 'a good showing in the flesh' and to boast of their converts and followers. Such things are ultimately worth nothing; what counts is a new creation and to have one's name in heaven, not to gain the whole world, or even – let the workers note – just a big, wealthy congregation. What counts in God's eyes is not the same as what people are enamoured with. Try to remember that.

Proper 10

Sunday between 10 and 16 July inclusive

Amos 7:7–17 · Colossians 1:1–14 · Luke 10:25–37 · Psalm 82

The gospel is bearing fruit and growing throughout the whole world.

Each of our readings this week, in different ways, concerns how we embrace those different to us, and what this reveals about our obedience to God's word. What do they reveal about you?

In Amos chapter 7, the rugged herdsman from the South meets the proud social elite of the North. Amos, the working-class hero, confronts Amaziah, the establishment priest of Israel's schismatic breakaway kingdom. Amos sees a plumb-line, which reveals the lop-sidedness of Amaziah's religious regime, unable to bear the weight of the prophetic word. He hears the sentence of exile and destruction against it. On hearing this condemnation of his high places and sanctuaries, Amaziah goes straight to the top and complains against Amos to the king, painting him as a subversive conspirator, a danger to the stability of the state. He also tries to banish and silence Amos himself, telling him to 'go home' and preach his unwelcome message somewhere other than in the national church where it is not wanted by the leadership of 'the king's sanctuary ... a temple of the kingdom'.

In this context, Amos, though he renounces the dignified title of 'prophet', is persistent in faithfully preaching the word he has been given by God. He keeps calm and carries on despite the threats and the vilification it brings. He reveals in the process that the religious establishment which clings too closely to the corrupt practices of the state and people it serves will itself share, perhaps rather personally, in the approaching judgment. The word of God will prove true.

The parable of the neighbourly Samaritan again touches on the raw nerve of how to embrace those different to us. As so often, it is a story which subverts the worldview of those listening, but all the more so because it is not actually a direct answer to the question the lawyer asked. Jesus teaches him how to *be* a neighbour, not how to identify who his neighbour is, which is rather more personal and pointed than perhaps the man was expecting. By using the illustration of a Samaritan loving a (presumably) Jewish victim of roadside crime, the Lord certainly challenges the accepted racial and religious prejudices of his day. By adding the priest and Levite to the story, Jesus (like Amos 7) also provides a searing critique of establishment religion, too concerned to maintain its status and privileges truly to have mercy on those suffering at the hands of a coercive, brutal, and injurious culture.

The apostle Paul had never met the predominantly Gentile Christians of Colossae, who were very different to him in background. Yet this former Pharisee shows just how powerful the grace of God in Christ can be by his response to their new-found faith in the Messiah. He thanks and praises God for it, and he puts it into global perspective: all over the world Gentiles like you are coming to know and love the Lord Jesus, he says, and expressing it in faith, hope, and love. The gospel is bearing fruit and growing, expanding across national and ethnic and racial borders. And just as it has borne fruit in your conversion, he says, I pray that it will continue to bear fruit in your good works and increasing knowledge of God. This opening section begins in a 'we-you' division, which could emphasise the distance between the Colossians and Paul (and his co-author, Timothy). But it ends in verses 13–14 with a spectacular confession of what the Father has done for 'us', Jews and Gentiles together: he rescued *us* and transferred *us* to the kingdom of his beloved Son, so that *we* together now have redemption and forgiveness. In the gospel our differences are brought into harmony, as together we seek to obey the Lord Jesus.

Proper 11

Sunday between 17 and 23 July inclusive

Amos 8:1–12 · Colossians 1:15–28 · Luke 10:38–42 · Psalm 52

He is the one we proclaim, admonishing and teaching everyone with all wisdom, so that we may present everyone fully mature in Christ.

God's word is the uniting theme in our readings this week. In Amos, a famine of the word; in Colossians, the proclamation of the word; and in Luke, listening to the word. Will you hear God's word and feed on it today?

Amos 8 begins in what some see as the same old dreary way – an oracle of doom and gloom for Israel. The songs of the Temple will become wailings, people will die; those who shove aside God's Law in an effort to make more money, who trample down the poor, will be trampled down themselves – and tremble. And though it will be 'like the mourning for an only son' when the earth goes dark in the middle of the day (an intimation of Good Friday?), there is something more terrible to come.

As in any relationship, hardships can be endured where there is communication. But if the words dry up, there is trouble indeed. So when Amos declares that there is to be 'a famine of hearing the words of the Lord', and that as a result the people will wander about and seek it in vain, we know the time is up. God's patience has run out with his wayward people. When the word of God can no longer be heard in a nation, that is indeed a cause for deep lament. In how many parts of our nations today has this famine taken hold without comment or hope of relief?

In Colossians 1 we hear about the Word incarnate, the 'image of the invisible God'. Christ is the head of all creation – heavenly and earthly – and of the new creation too, the church of those who are reconciled through the blood of his cross. Those who are reconciled to God by his death were saved in order to be holy and blameless before him, and this they shall be if they continue to hold on to the gospel word, which Paul proclaims and serves and makes fully known. By proclaiming Christ, 'warning and teaching everyone', the world is won and God's people are matured.

The result of this, of course, is that where the word of God is absent from our proclamation, or where we proclaim not Christ but culture (whether our own Christian subculture or the seemingly baptised morality of the sinful world around us), that famine of the truth will lead to stunted growth and stifled evangelism.

Martha and Mary teach us these same truths. Martha is busy with what she sees as her mission, worried and distracted by many things. Good things, no doubt they were. Seemingly necessary to the worldly eye (though the man invited for dinner could turn water into wine and feed thousands with just a few loaves, so Martha really should have been more relaxed!). She felt overloaded and wanted her sister to be part of her work. But Mary did the best thing. The best thing is listening to Jesus.

As in any relationship, nothing we do to make the other person happy will be pleasing if we don't listen to them. So it is with Christ. All our endeavours and missions and works must be put aside, and his word given priority in our diaries and desires. If we don't start by listening, we will end up deaf – like the people of Amos's day who thrust the word aside for the sake of their more worldly ambitions and the goals set by a secular agenda. Rather, let us proclaim Christ by proclaiming his word, and training ourselves to sit at his feet more avidly before we set about the tasks that *we* consider necessary. It may just be that he has better ideas.

Proper 12

Sunday between 24 and 30 July inclusive

Hosea 1:2–10 · Colossians 2:6–19 · Luke 11:1–13 · Psalm 85

If you then, though you are evil, know how to give good gifts to your children, how much more will your Father in heaven give the Holy Spirit to those who ask him!

God's relationship to his people is viewed in intimate and personal ways in today's readings. He appears both as Husband and Father to his people, just as Christ is the head united to his body, the Church. Do you know what it is to have such an intimate forgiving relationship with Christ?

Was Hosea's wife unfaithful to begin with (perhaps even a prostitute) or did she *become* so? Either way, the Lord knew, and wanted the marriage to be a picture of his own relationship to Israel, his wayward people. Sometimes marriage is used in a positive way to illustrate that relationship, such as in Ephesians 5:22–33. But here the picture is much more bleak. Hosea and Gomer's children are also part of a divine message: Jezreel is a portent of doom; Lo-Ruhamah tells the world that Israel's time is up; Lo-Ammi says the covenant of love has been broken.

Yet Hosea 1:10 enigmatically declares that the living God will somehow take back his people, his children. He will keep the promise made to Abraham that his descendants would be as numerous as the stars of heaven and the grains of sand on the seashore. How this will come to pass is not yet clear to Hosea's listeners, but the prophecy of restoration should not be allowed to dent the impact of the very real judgment being faced by the people. God will be God and keep his word; but this cannot mean we will go floating up to heaven on flowery beds of ease regardless of how we treat him.

In Jesus's teaching on prayer in Luke 11, we are taught to pray to God as Father. He is a hallowed Father, holy and different to us, yet intimately concerned for our welfare. His overarching plan to covenant to us a kingdom should be a matter for daily prayer, but he knows that we need our daily bread too and is delighted when we ask him for it. Like a friend, God hears our persistent pleas and the cries of our heart. Like a father he knows how to give good gifts to his children. This passage shows us the tenderness and kindness of God, despite our sins (for which we are instructed to ask forgiveness) and the fact that we are evil (to use Jesus's own description of us here). It is also fascinating to see all three persons of the Trinity together, as Christ prompts us to ask the Father for the Holy Spirit.

In Colossians 2, Paul urges us to continue with Christ in the way we began, and not to move away from him into deceptive philosophies. In a terrific piece of applied systematic theology, Paul interweaves various biblical themes – baptism, circumcision, incarnation, angelology, atonement – and exhorts the Colossians to hold fast to Christ because of who he is and what he's done. He is our head, our victor, our fullness. We have everything we need in him, who is the inexhaustible fountain of all good things. So much so, that if we are 'in him' it does not matter whether we are 'in' anywhere else – we cannot be disqualified or condemned by others for not being part of their groupings or cliques, nor for falling short on their unbiblical shibboleths (see Judges 12:4–6). To be led astray into a new legalism or mysticism or asceticism, or into human ways of thinking which take their lead from the surrounding culture instead of from Christ, is to flee to the shadows and away from the substance of our salvation. All we need is found in him, our head. Are you content and satisfied with that?

Proper 13

Sunday between 31 July and 6 August inclusive

Hosea 11:1–11 · Colossians 3:1–11 · Luke 12:13–21 · Psalm 107:1–9, 43

Since, then, you have been raised with Christ, set your hearts on things above, where Christ is seated at the right hand of God.

Life beyond death connects the three readings for this week. Are you living your life in the light of eternity to come?

In Hosea 11, we get a glimpse into the heart of God. In a poem full of pathos and emotion, we hear of his intense love for his children, though they are wayward and ungrateful. We must recall, of course, that God is immutable, unchangeable – not meaning that he is an insensitive tyrant, but that he is invulnerable to manipulation and is never overwhelmed and 'emotional' as we are. So his actions are the result of a settled, divine determination; yet so that we better understand both his kindness and his justice he accommodates himself to our understanding by speaking in this way. It is what the early church scholar Origen (185–253) called 'anthropopathic' language, speaking of God in terms of human emotions.[39]

His parental love is tough love, and he has resolved that since they have rejected his kindness, he will exile his people. The sword will execute his decree 'because they refused to return to me'. Yet he cannot abandon his people for ever, as he abandoned Admah and Zeboiim (verse 8), the cities that were destroyed along with Sodom

---

[39] See Origen, *Against Celsus*, 4.71–72 in *The Ante-Nicene Fathers: Volume 4* (edited by A. Roberts, J. Donaldson, and A. C. Coxe and translated by F. Crombie; Buffalo, NY: Christian Literature Company, 1885), 4:529–530; and Lee Gatiss, 'Pleasing the Impassible God' in *Foundations* 79 (Autumn 2020), pp. 3–13.

and Gomorrah (see Deuteronomy 29:23). This does not mean God is soft and judgment is cancelled, but that beyond this death and judgment there will be restoration and life. Not because they deserve it more than those wicked cities, but because 'I am God and no mortal'. Hope lies in an unchangeable God who (unlike us) does not renege on his covenant promises, rather than in our relative goodness or our supposed ability to change.

In Luke 12, Jesus warns the crowd against greed and resting their hopes and dreams on 'the abundance of possessions'. Good stewardship requires hard work, but we must not think that our security for the future is in building a good pension plan. Two brothers argue over their inheritance – this should have warned them that life is more than possessions, for their father certainly hadn't been able to take his with him! But the Lord has to remind them how foolish it is to live life for the now, without taking into account the great day of judgment we all face on the other side of death. Being 'rich towards God' and not for ourselves is what will make a difference then, when we stand before the judgment seat of Christ.

Paul has his eye on Christ at the right hand of God too. Believers have died with Christ, and been raised with him. Our hope is that when he 'is revealed', we too will be revealed in glory. So our lives in the here and now are lives of mortification, putting to death the things within us which will not survive the purging of that day, including sexual immorality (that is, biblically speaking, any sexual activity outside heterosexual marriage), evil desires and greed (which itself is idolatry, as Jesus himself just taught us in the parable).

We may have lived that way once, but should do so no longer; not because our church subculture or tradition is against it, or for any other human reason, but because of God's intense, settled, determined, implacable opposition to such lifestyles. His wrath is coming on those who are disobedient. Malice, slander, lies and racial or religious one-upmanship are all ruled out now because there'll be none of that then, when Christ returns and our renewal will be complete in the twinkling of an eye.

Proper 14

Sunday between 7 and 13 August inclusive

Isaiah 1:1, 10–20 · Hebrews 11:1–3, 8–16 · Luke 12:32–40 · Psalm 50:1–8, 22–23

Provide purses for yourselves that will not wear out, a treasure in heaven that will never fail, where no thief comes near and no moth destroys.

This Sunday we hear three challenging angles on the future for God's people. We must live now in the knowledge of what is to come.

Isaiah is our Old Testament reading for the next two weeks. His vision is addressed to the people of Judah, but in particular to their capital city, Jerusalem. It is something of a jolt, then, for him to address this major faith capital as 'Sodom' and 'Gomorrah' in verse 10. The people of faith have become as evil as those infamously degraded cities. As a result, their worship is empty and loathsome – perhaps not to them; it probably feels lavish and spectacular and appropriately dignified to them – but certainly to the God it is meant to be focused upon.

Many in our culture may think that God should be happy with whatever he can get these days. The truth is, he hides his eyes and closes his ears to those who only want to engage him superficially. The weekly Sabbath performance is not sufficient. He hates the religious mask that covers a pagan heart.

Yet even to hypocrites, the offer of forgiveness is open: their scarlet sins can be like snow. But repentance is not cheap, and Isaiah declares that only the willing and obedient will eat the good of the land and avoid the impending doom. A word to Judah, as the Assyrian comes down 'like a wolf on the fold' to devour their near-neighbour Israel.[40] A word to other cities and other churches which have become indistinguishable from Gomorrah, and as inhospitable for the faithful as Sodom. Will repentance be forthcoming? Will it be in time?

The city in view in Hebrews 11 is a far better place to hope for, with firmer foundations by far. Abraham knew it only by faith, a stranger in a foreign land most of his life. With little earthly future, it seemed, but with the promise of God in his pocket all the way. His distant homeland was a heavenly country prepared by God, for which it is worth forsaking the comforts of this life and the familiar desires of an earth-bound existence. Too often we are ashamed to admit our attachment to Jesus in a world that despises his name and pours scorn on his ways; but the issue in Hebrews 11:16 is whether *God* will be ashamed to stand by his covenant with us, not the other way around. Note that he is proud to own those who speak and act in this world as those who have fixed their desires elsewhere. Hebrews has only warnings for those whose sights are considerably lower.

It is this perspective that we hear again from the lips of the Lord himself in Luke 12. The Father delights to give the kingdom to his fearful little flock. With that reassurance and hope in place, we are free to be extreme in our generosity in this life. Those whose bank statements show that they live on the edge of eternity, and not just for the here and now, will find – don't miss the surprise in verse 37! – that the Lord Jesus Christ himself will be happy to serve them like a waiter in the feast that is to come. If that is not a humbling, almost shocking, but deeply beautiful thought for us, our bank managers will know it – and we are worryingly ill-prepared for the hour that is approaching.

---

[40] See the poem 'The Destruction of Sennacherib' (1815) by Lord Byron.

Proper 15

Sunday between 14 and 20 August inclusive

Isaiah 5:1–7 · Hebrews 11:29–12:2 · Luke 12:49–56 · Psalm 80:1–2, 8–19

Therefore, since we are surrounded by such a great cloud of witnesses, let us throw off everything that hinders and the sin that so easily entangles.

There is violence and destruction in all three readings this week, but of different kinds and for different purposes. Is it something to be afraid of, or drastic action that leads to a better end?

First, we hear in Isaiah 5 of the impending judgment on Israel and Judah, the vineyard of the Lord. The people of God begin as 'my beloved', and the song begins as a 'love song'. With fatherly affection, God cared for his people and provided for their every need. In return, he looked and longed for fruit, as any good vineyard owner would. Yet the disobedient and ungrateful people, who have experienced every blessing ('What more was there to do for my vineyard that I have not done in it?') produces only wild grapes, unusable and unpalatable.

So its protection is removed, and 'it shall be pruned', because there was no justice or righteousness in it. When Jesus applies this same image in the Gospels, the leaders of the nation realised immediately that he was talking about them (Mark 12:1–12). Does Jesus also look for such fruit from his people today, or prune and discipline us when he fails to find it? Does he remove our protection and withhold the rain?

The atmosphere of death suffuses the whole of Hebrews 11. It stalks everyone in the chapter who tries to live a life of faith in the face of it. Sometimes the faithful are saved, and the violence of God's judgment falls on those who have resisted him: the Israelites pass through the Red Sea while the Egyptians are drowned; Rahab is rescued from Jericho, while the city is razed to the ground. The catalogue of the faithful who 'conquered kingdoms ... shut the mouths of lions ... escaped the edge of the sword' is an inspiring one.

But others, no less faithful, were tortured; many were mocked and flogged and imprisoned; some were stoned to death, sawn in two (tradition says this may be Isaiah himself). They were 'destitute, persecuted, tormented'. The world was not worthy of any of them, because they met these dangers and disasters not with stoical stiff upper lips, but with a steady, unwavering faith in the promise of resurrection – the resurrection glory that Hebrews assures us they will inherit along with all those in our generation who hold fast to that same faith. Their example and witness, and that of the Lord Jesus himself, urges us on to resist our own sin and the temptation to give up, for the sake of the glory that is to come.

How anyone who has ever read the Gospels themselves can have considered the Lord Jesus an inoffensive 'meek and mild' sort of person is a mystery. His coming itself is the great dividing point for history, of course, though some people missed the disorientating significance of that auspicious time. He has come to bring fire and division he says. Not against the Romans. Not against the corrupt authorities. Not even against poverty, war, and injustice. But he came to divide families: some will follow him and others will not. The sword he wields here is not the sword of judgment on his wayward people, and it is not the refining fire of persecution which tests our faith. It is the sword which separates believer and unbeliever on the great and terrible day of the Lord. What matters then is not who we are related to by birth or marriage, but who we cling to in death.

So whether we are fruitless and faithless, or frightened and faithful, whatever the strife we face and the divisions we grieve over, Sunday's readings bring the word of God to bear on every grim and gritty situation of our lives. And only by faith can we prevail.

Proper 16

Sunday between 21 and 27 August inclusive

Jeremiah 1:4–10 · Hebrews 12:18–29 · Luke 13:10–17 · Psalm 71:1–6

If they did not escape when they refused him who warned them on earth, how much less will we, if we turn away from him who warns us from heaven?

This Sunday, our readings teach us that the world-altering word of God is not to be resisted, but rejoiced in, even if others do not like it. How do you react to the word of God?

The word of the Lord comes to Jeremiah, bringing him a commission as 'prophet to the nations'. Like Moses, Jeremiah tries to wriggle out of such a dangerous role by claiming that he has no gift for public speaking and, indeed, no experience either because he's so young. The Lord patiently reasons with Jeremiah, understanding his fears. 'You won't need experience or oratorical skill. I myself will tell you what to say. My word will be sufficient. There's no need to be afraid that people will dismiss your word because of who you are – you will speak *my* word.'

Just as in Isaiah 6, the prophet's lips are touched, though not this time by an intermediary bringing atonement but by the Lord himself in ordination. Jeremiah was right to be somewhat nervous – God's word in his mouth would uproot and destroy whole kingdoms, as well as building and planting new things – but this awesome power and responsibility could not be shirked.

The potent voice of God filled Moses and the Israelites at Sinai with such terror that they couldn't bear to hear it. But now, Hebrews tells us, we have 'a better word' through Jesus, the mediator of a new covenant. The 'one who is speaking' remains the same and is not to be refused, his voice silenced or rejected. If the word to Jeremiah was to make the nations shudder and tremble, this new word will do so even more. It will shake not only the earth but even the heavens, and result in both judgment on the unwary and an unshakeable kingdom for believers. How much more seriously, then, should we take our response to it, not snubbing the God who has always been a consuming fire, but offering a reverent sacrifice of praise and thanksgiving to him for his grace.

Luke 13 shows us Jesus, as usual, teaching the word in the synagogue. A crippled woman afflicted by a demonic spirit which prevented her standing up straight enters the scene to disturb the service. The crooked arch of her back compelled her eyes to focus constantly on her feet, as the curvature of human nature renders us unable to look to God in our own strength. Then appears the agent of change, the spoken word of God – 'Woman, you are set free!' Touched by the word, and the Word himself, she responds and rejoices.

Notice the reaction of the synagogue leader, angry at Jesus's seeming disregard for customary Sabbath observance, but not daring to actually criticise Jesus himself. His ire is directed at the people, an easier target. But he, and other unnamed opponents who sat in the synagogue that day, are put to shame by the exposure of their hypocrisy. They treat their donkeys better than they treat this woman, her long-imprisoned spirit fast-bound in sin and Satan's night. The Sabbath is not for maintenance of our comfort, but for liberty, and for revelling in 'the wonderful things' that Jesus has done, and is doing, through his word. That word brings division, as we also saw last week, both overthrowing those who resist it, and building up those who delight in its vigorous, life-giving authority. What is it doing to you?

Proper 17

Sunday between 28 August and 3 September inclusive

Jeremiah 2:4–13 · Hebrews 13:1–8, 15–16 · Luke 14:1, 7–14 · Psalm 81:1, 10–16

But my people would not listen to me; Israel would not submit to me. So I gave them over to their stubborn hearts to follow their own devices.

There are some shocking and humbling substitutions in the readings for this Sunday, as humans exchange what is good in God's eyes for temporary trinkets of their own. Beware the devices and desires of your own hearts.

Jeremiah attacks the ungratefulness of the house of Israel who have exchanged the fountain of living water for cracked and waterless cisterns of their own making. This is a personal affront to the God of the covenant: he saved them from Egypt, led them in the wilderness, gave them a fruitful homeland, and yet they have defiled it and made it 'an abomination', a hateful place, displeasing to God. The leaders, both religious and secular, forgot about the Lord and abandoned his ways, swapping the glory of the immortal God for images of false ones who could give them nothing but grief. One by one, family by family, until the whole nation was engulfed, apostasy took root and loyalty to God was eroded.

Hebrews, on the other hand, speaks of 'sacrifices pleasing to God'. These are the opposite of what the world finds attractive and normal. The world looks out for number one; but we are to show mutual love. The world chooses its friends according to usefulness; but we are to show hospitality to strangers and look out for those in prison who are persecuted or tortured because of their faith in Christ. The world thinks little of marriage as God created it; but we are to honour it and keep it special by upholding abstinence before and faithfulness within it, which the world derides or pities or cannot maintain. The world values cold hard cash, and everything revolves around economic utility and growth; we are to be content, because God will never forsake us and he is all we need. The world is chary and suspicious about leaders; but we are to think well of ours (though not naively) and imitate those whose lives and teaching reflect the character of the unchanging Saviour we worship.

In the Gospel, we note how worldliness infects the church, even among the most zealous. The Saviour is at the house of a leader of the Pharisees, a special meal no doubt, on the Sabbath itself. A careful observer of human behaviour, he quickly spots how the guests vie with one another for positions of honour at the table. Echoing the teaching of Proverbs 25:6–7, 'do not put yourself forward in the king's presence', his parable to them exposes their pride and desire for greatness. Instead, he teaches them, you should humble yourself, for only such humility is pleasing in the sight of the King who ultimately decides the fate of all.

It is as if Jesus is telling them, 'I am your King.' So when he teaches them not just to entertain their friends, but (as Hebrews also says) strangers as well – to invite those who are unable to repay the compliment – he is reminding us how he himself behaves. For in his sight we are all poor, crippled, lame, and blind, utterly unworthy and entirely unable to repay his grace and favour to us. So in all our daily affairs he urges us not to consider the polite worldly ways of the modern social contract, but the greater reward that awaits the humble at the resurrection of the righteous. Will we exchange the vaporous blessings of today's world for the way that brings glory tomorrow? Or take our eyes off the substance of eternity for the fleeting frisson of worldly respect?

Proper 18

Sunday between 4 and 10 September inclusive

Jeremiah 18:1–11 · Philemon vv1–21 · Luke 14:25–33 ·
Psalm 139:1–6, 13–18

So turn from your evil ways, each one of you,
and reform your ways and your actions.

In each of the readings today we hear a call to give something up. Are you prepared to sacrifice what God says you are to let go of?

Jeremiah is given a picture of God as the sovereign Creator and Lord of the universe, the potter who moulds things to his will. This glance at God's supreme authority is linked to Jeremiah's own purpose and call: he was called in chapter 1 and given his commission, under protest, 'to destroy and overthrow ... or build and plant' (Jeremiah 1:10). Now he must remind sinful Israel that the sovereign God can pick and choose which of these destinies they meet. But he can also respond to their response when he takes the initiative to warn them through his prophet. So as he informs them that he is devising a plan against them, he is inviting them to give up their evil way. We must remember, of course, that the eternal God is accommodating his language to our frailty and finitude here; he is not a fickle human who vacillates and changes his mind (see Numbers 23:19).

Paul is trying to persuade Philemon to give up his servant Onesimus (which means 'Useful'). It is a subtle negotiation, and the apostle does not stand on his apostolic authority to command obedience (note the absence of his apostleship in the opening greeting), but appeals on the basis of love. He appeals on many other grounds too, not least of which is the slave's new allegiance to Christ and usefulness to Paul's mission, in which Philemon considers himself a partner. What would we not give up for the sake of the gospel's advance, particularly if it was of service to one who had personally brought us the saving knowledge of the gospel? Philemon is a carefully constructed letter with immense rhetorical force, and one can only imagine that it must have had the desired effect.

The Lord Jesus confronts us with a demand to count the cost of discipleship, in the Gospel reading this week. Large crowds were following him, and with such numbers we may imagine a healthy dose of nominalism, a marginal interest in the spiritual realities of Jesus's ministry, and a significant amount of spectator religion. Jesus jolts such people into a realisation of what he is really asking them to give up, by phrasing it in stark terms: whoever does not hate his family, cannot be my disciple. So much for Christianity and family values!

The Lord goes on to explain how vital it is to be aware of the cost of following him. We must give up all our possessions. Not just our slaves, perhaps, as Philemon later learned, but anything which might be more urgently needed for the gospel than for our comfort in this life. He urges us, like a king planning a war, to sit down and think carefully about what is required; for otherwise, our initial good intentions will be quickly defeated, and come crashing down like the tower that was planned without adequate foundations. The evangelical preacher Charles Simeon (1759–1836) comments that, 'Thus it is also with a man who commences a warfare with sin and Satan without knowing how he shall make head against them: for as a hasty profession of religion exposes him to self-deception, so a hasty dereliction of it will subject him to the heavier condemnation.'[41] So as the hymnwriter Matthew Bridges (1800–1894) sang in 'My God, accept my heart this day' (1848):

> Let every thought and work and word
> To thee be ever giv'n:
> Then life shall be thy service, Lord,
> And death the gate of heaven.

[41] Charles Simeon, *Horae Homileticae: Mark–Luke* (London: Holdsworth and Ball, 1832), p. 531.

Proper 19

Sunday between 11 and 17 September inclusive

Jeremiah 4:11–12, 22–28 · 1 Timothy 1:12–17 · Luke 15:1–10 · Psalm 14

Christ Jesus came into the world to save sinners – of whom I am the worst.

Each of our readings gives us cause for thanksgiving this week, as the realities of salvation are portrayed against the blackest of backdrops. Let your heart be lifted up in gratitude.

Jeremiah foresees a time when the earth will be scorched by the hot wind of God's righteous judgment. It is directed at his wayward people themselves, who have forsaken the truth: 'For my people are foolish, they do not know me; they are stupid children, they have no understanding. They are skilled in doing evil, but do not know how to do good.' God cannot be passive in the face of such betrayal and ignorance. As he looks around after God's holy response to human sinfulness, Jeremiah sees devastation: earth, heavens, mountains, hills, birds, land – all affected and afflicted because of the rebellion of those who bore the image of God. Yet the smallest shaft of light appears at the conclusion: 'Yet I will not make a full end.' In his justice, he remembers mercy, and so there is hope.

The devoted Pharisee, Saul of Tarsus, also found God gracious and merciful. Though he was a blasphemer who raged against Christ, a persecutor who pursued God's people, and a violent man devoid of the Spirit, the grace and love of the Lord overwhelmed and transformed him. He was the chief of sinners, the epitome of religious abomination; but Christ Jesus came into the world to save exactly that sort of person. The very purpose of the incarnation, of Christmas, was to demonstrate how patient and kind God is towards such sinful, evil people.

Paul's gratitude overflows to the Saviour King who not only rescued him and forgave him, but appointed him to his royal service. He realises that this was not just for his own sake, but that Christ literally made an example out of him, so that people everywhere might know that eternal life is on offer to anyone who believes in Jesus, no matter what their past or present. He traces this divine plan back to its source and ends this passage with a doxology, giving glory to the immortal, invisible God, the 'King of the Ages'. Both judgment and salvation are ultimately for his glory and his joy.

More sinners appear in the Gospel, to prove Paul's point that Christ came for exactly such people. There is joy in heaven over even one sinner who repents, he tells the Pharisees who grumble and cannot see what he has come for ('foolish people who do not know me' as Jeremiah said). Jesus came to save sinners and bring joy to both heaven and earth. To earth as well, of course, because when the shepherd finds his lost sheep he embraces his neighbours and enfolds them into his own joy. Just as the woman who finds her lost coin spreads the good news throughout her street.

The challenge here, of course, is to have the same heart as Jesus. Note the way the Lord introduces his parables. 'Which of you...?' and 'What woman...?' This is not just, 'What kind of person would not rejoice over something that once was lost but is now found?' The scribes are grumbling for precisely that reason of course, because new people being included (even one!) is always unsettling for those who are more into religion than relationships. But Jesus also asks, 'What kind of man, what kind of woman, would you have to be to keep such good news to yourself, and not share it with your friends and neighbours?' As the evangelical preacher Charles Simeon (1759–1836) comments, 'By appealing to their own consciences he forced them to condemn themselves.'[42] How do *we* feel at hearing this challenge?

---

[42] Simeon, *Horae Homileticae: Mark–Luke*, p. 535.

Proper 20

Sunday between 18 and 24 September inclusive

Jeremiah 8:18–9:1 · 1 Timothy 2:1–7 · Luke 16:1–13 · Psalm 79:1–9

What people value highly is detestable in God's sight.

In each our passages today, we see that what we should long for most is the smile of God, which alone can lift the gloom. But what pleases us and what pleases God can often be very different.

In Jeremiah 8 the prophet weeps for apostate Zion. Though the people of God in his day had the written word of God, and boasted in its possession, they did not know it or follow it. Those responsible for teaching the word had wilfully corrupted it to suit their own desires. Because of this neglect, ominous judgment was approaching. The people are dismayed and alarmed at the imminent prospect of attack, and wonder why God, their King, will not protect them as before. Had he not promised to always do so? Why did he not smile on them now? There was indeed balm in Gilead (famous for its herbology, we might say, and medicinal cures), but human medicine would be inadequate to save these unsound, unhealthy idolaters who had provoked God by their behaviour. A sticking plaster approach cannot change God's frown. As a prophet with the heart of God, Jeremiah not only pronounces judgment and calls for repentance, but also weeps with and for the people who have not looked to God as they should.

Paul writes 1 Timothy 2–3 to help Timothy (and his church) 'know how one ought to behave in the household of God' (1 Timothy 3:15). First of all, he urges the people of God to pray. This is a letter about contending for gospel truth against false teaching (1 Timothy 1:3) and Paul says the priority in all our contending must be prayer. Many complain at the state of the church, but how few attend the prayer meetings! People are to pray all kinds of prayers says the apostle (supplications, intercessions, thanksgivings, etc.), for all kinds of people, but he especially singles out those in authority. The purpose of such prayer is not just that we pray for those in positions of power to be converted, and to be just, but so that they will govern in a way that is conducive to the well-being of the church, i.e. that whatever rulers do, Christians may be able to lead a peaceful and quiet life of dignified godliness.

All this is said to please God, whose approval we are to long for most of all, but especially because godly Christians will be reaching others with knowledge of the truth. God wants all to be saved in this way, though this verse expresses his will of command and exhortation, rather than a form of universalism (the sovereign Lord is not thwarted in his eternal decrees by the puny resistance of sinners!). In the church we have but one mediator, Jesus Christ, who gave himself not just to rescue an elite few but people out of every race, class, status and condition.

The parable in Luke 16 teaches us to use our money to make friends with eternity in mind. In a chapter devoted to the subject of our attitude to wealth, this is an exhortation not to dishonesty or to a self-interested commercial approach to friendship or spirituality, but to think about using the resources temporarily at our disposal now so that they have an eternal impact even after they're gone. One day we will be called to give an account of our management and stewardship, and we will only enjoy the warm commendation and reward of God (and the true, lasting gratitude of other people) if this eternal perspective has been uppermost in our strategy. Those who are mean or world-focused in their attitude to money will not find spiritual, heavenly riches very easy to come by; but those who are faithful with little will be given much.

Proper 21

Sunday between 25 September and 1 October inclusive

Jeremiah 32:1–3a, 6–15 · 1 Timothy 6:6–19 · Luke 16:19–31 ·
Psalm 91:1–6, 14–16

But godliness with contentment is great gain. For we brought nothing into the world, and we can take nothing out of it.

Money is a uniting factor in our readings for this Sunday. You may have riches, but they will not be enough. You may have none, and be perfectly happy. What's the secret to contentment?

Jeremiah narrates in great detail an ordinary land transaction with an extraordinary message. His prophecy to the King of Judah was that the nation and the capital city were going to fall to the King of Babylon. So shocking was this thought that the King had Jeremiah locked away for saying it out loud. Next to this announcement, the Lord also announces to Jeremiah that he is going to be offered a parcel of land to buy. We are unsurprised when this word comes true almost immediately (though this only lends credence to the bigger and more frightening prophecy of Judah's downfall). But why is the transaction here important, and why does Jeremiah make it clear that he went through with it in a legally binding way? We wait until the last verse to find out – it is because (verse 15) houses and fields shall again be bought in this land. That is, the prophesied exile has a promised end. It will not last for ever. In his anger God remembers mercy and keeps his covenant promise.

Luke 16 contrasts a rich man and a poor man. The rich man had not used his wealth wisely, so this poor man was sprawled out on the ground begging for scraps of food at the millionaire's gate. Uniquely in all of Jesus's parables, this character is given a name – Lazarus. His name means 'the one helped by God'. Two men and two destinies – one in hell, the other at Abraham's side in heaven; one in agony and torment who cannot be helped; the other, comforted. Abraham makes it clear that this is a direct reversal of their situation before death, which seals their fate once and for all. It is a grim picture for those with riches but no conscience or spiritual eyesight.

The twist in the tale here is that the rich man tries to ask a favour – in essence, 'Warn my brothers about what happens to those who have money but are not rich towards God!' (see Luke 12:21). It is an implied warning to all those hearing the parable who may fall into that category too. Abraham is stern: 'They have Bibles, don't they? They can read of the dangers for themselves, surely?' But the rich man is not so sure; he hadn't seen or heeded the warnings himself, after all. He imagines, however, that if the ghost of Lazarus appeared to his brothers, as the ghosts of Christmas appeared to Scrooge in Charles Dickens's classic Christmas heart-warmer, then they would surely repent. In fairy tales, perhaps, but not in reality. If they do not listen to the books of Moses, they won't be convinced even when Jesus himself rises from the dead. The sheer word of God has the power to convict and convince, even in the absence of further miracles and apparitions.

Paul's teaching in 1 Timothy 6 follows the same lines as Jesus's teaching on the subject of riches. We brought nothing into the world and can take nothing out of it, despite the attempt of many Egyptian Pharaohs and others to do so! The love of money is not 'the' root of 'all' evil but 'a' root of 'all kinds of evil'. This is not to water it down, of course. However, the evil Paul seems to have in mind here is not so much economic injustice and inequality as apostasy. Greed is a form of self-harm, spiritually damaging to the infected heart which should rather be seeking the kingdom that is not of this world (as Jesus confessed to Pilate, John 18:36). Our hopes should be set on the coming King and not on making ourselves as comfortable as kings, though all good things are a gift from God to be enjoyed with faith, generosity and love.

Proper 22

Sunday between 2 and 8 October inclusive

Lamentations 1:1–6 · 2 Timothy 1:1–14 · Luke 17:5–10 · Psalm 137

Do not be ashamed of the testimony about our Lord or of me his prisoner. Rather, join with me in suffering for the gospel, by the power of God.

Luke 17:5–10 is about faith and serving God. 2 Timothy 1:1–14 demands faith and loyalty to the gospel. Lamentations 1:1–6 reveal what happens when faith, service, and loyalty disappear.

In our Gospel reading, the apostles ask Jesus for increased faith. It is good that they realise faith is a gift, and that they need to go straight to the source in order to get it. It is a gift of God, something granted to us, something we must obtain: Ephesians 2:8, Philippians 1:29, and 2 Peter 1:1 are good places to look for this absolutely vital doctrine. We must remember that faith is not something we can whip up or create in ourselves or other people.

Yet Jesus corrects the error in the disciples' request, which is to think that it is the size or strength of our faith that is important. Faith the size of a mustard seed is tremendously powerful and effective, he says. The implication is that it is not the size of our faith that counts, but the object. It is what or who we trust that really counts, the power source we connect to. Our Lord's words are a challenge and a rebuke, but also a staggering promise.

Jesus insists that we cannot rack up credit in God's bank by heaping up good works over and above God's commandments. The very idea would take our eyes away from the one we are to trust, and focus instead on our own endeavours, which can never in and of themselves satisfy God in his perfection and justice. We are only ever dutiful servants, and God is not in our debt.

In his last letter, Paul calls Timothy to be faithful to their shared spiritual heritage. They both had believing families, who had communicated the faith to them. Yet heritage requires loyalty, and loyalty requires the ability to stick one's neck out. In such situations, Paul reminds both himself and his young protégé that God did not give *us* a spirit of cowardice, but of power, love and self-control. Those are the very things required in difficult pastoral circumstances: power, to endure suffering; love, especially for the most difficult people in the church; and self-discipline, so as not to fly off the handle at theological opponents, who may well deserve it, but won't be won thereby.

Paul calls Timothy to suffer with him, as the Lord Jesus himself suffered, without backing away from either Paul himself – a low-status prisoner, abandoned by a worldly church – or his teaching. The only thing which can motivate such countercultural loyalty, apart from the power of God through the Spirit of God who dwells within us, is the gospel itself (which verses 9–10 outline). Timothy can suffer the embarrassment of association with one written-off as an extremist, because it is worth it for the gospel. This is a powerful message to us in a day when many are still ashamed of Paul, whether for his teaching on marriage or sexuality or gender or judgment or compassion. Will we stand by him, or love the world as some of his followers and co-workers ended up doing (see 2 Timothy 4:10)?[43]

Lamentations is a beautiful but haunting meditation on what happens when God abandons those whose loyalty to the faith is compromised. In the opening passage, Jeremiah reflects on the emptiness of the city, once full of worshippers, and the devastation of exile and loss. He is not shy, in verse 5, of attributing the disaster which has befallen God's people to God himself. The multitude of their transgressions had finally fractured the covenant, and God's patience had run out. When faith is gone, prosperity and joy depart also as mercy gives way to justice. A sober warning next to the plea for loyalty in 2 Timothy. Will you stand firm?

---

[43] I have explored these themes from 2 Timothy in more detail in my book *Fulfil Your Ministry: 2 Timothy and Titus and the Challenges of Serving the Gospel* (Fearn: Christian Focus, 2024).

Proper 23

Sunday between 9 and 15 October inclusive

Jeremiah 29:1, 4–7 · 2 Timothy 2:8–15 · Luke 17:11–19 · Psalm 66:1–12

You let people ride over our heads; we went through fire and water, but you brought us to a place of abundance.

In each of the readings this week, the people of God are found in uncomfortable places. How do we cope outside our comfort zones? What do we do when we're there?

Jeremiah writes to the exiles of Judah who find themselves in Babylon, the enemy's capital city. His message to them is surprising: seek the welfare of the city. They are not to sit around moping or hoping that the exile will end soon. It will not. They are there for the long haul. Just as the people increased and multiplied when they were in Egypt after the days of Joseph, so now they are to increase outside the land in the days of Nebuchadnezzar. Building houses and planting gardens are both endeavours which take more than a little planning, and significant amounts of time, so the Lord's command is to settle down, not panic, and build something that will last.

The worry, of course, is that by doing this they appear to be abandoning any thought of returning home to Jerusalem, or even to be aiding and abetting the enemy. They may find themselves swallowed up or indoctrinated by an alien culture inimical to their covenant with the Lord. The challenge, as always for the people of God away from their true home, is to be a positive force for good in the place the Lord has put them, without losing sight of the impermanence of that world and their citizenship of another.

Jesus's journey to Jerusalem takes him through the almost alien territory of Samaria, in the Gospel reading this week. Yet even in this uncomfortable place, he finds the sort of faith that puts Israel to shame. Ten lepers, keeping their distance, cry out for mercy and healing. Ten lepers are healed and restored to their communities. Yet only one – and he a Samaritan – returns to say thank you. There is more than a lesson here about remember your Ps and Qs (pleases and thank yous). It is not just a story about etiquette. After all, Jesus told the others to 'go', so it may have seemed disobedient to come back! Yet the lesson is that our salvation rests on the work of God – so praise and glory are due to him. The man in the story is not the 'Good' Samaritan, but the God-glorifying Samaritan; from him we learn to prostrate ourselves at Jesus's feet for all he has done to save us. That is true faith: not to focus on ourselves and what we might contribute, but on the one who has mercy on the undeserving.

The apostle Paul is in a stinking, dirty, shameful prison cell, on trial for his life because of his public preaching of the gospel. Like the Lord Jesus himself, he suffers hardship and rejection by the world for the sake of the elect and their salvation. If we die with him, we will live with him: our lives are bound up in the death of a crucified Master who called us to follow him. Comfort is not something we should ever expect as Christians. Anyone who wants to live a godly life (as opposed to a quiet one) will be persecuted (2 Timothy 3:12). So as the evangelical preacher Charles Simeon (1759–1836) says, 'The labours of faithful ministers are, for the most part, but ill requited by a wicked and ungrateful world. But, in the midst of all the opposition they meet with, they have the consolation to know, that all efforts to stop the progress of the Gospel shall be in vain.'[44]

Timothy is told to remind his congregation of these truths, for a time is coming when he and they will be tempted to self-censorship for the sake of an easy life. In such a context, they are to put aside the unedifying word-battles which do not strengthen their faith to endure. Rather, Timothy is to handle the word of truth correctly, to aspire to be a reliable and solid worker, whose teaching builds something that will last for ever. We are called, in good times and bad, to be faithful disciples of the Suffering Servant who died and rose again.

---

[44] Charles Simeon, *Horae Homileticae: 2 Timothy to Hebrews* (London: Holdsworth and Ball, 1833), p. 26.

Proper 24

Sunday between 16 and 22 October inclusive

Jeremiah 31:27–34 · 2 Timothy 3:14–4:5 · Luke 18:1–8 ·
Psalm 119:97–104

In the presence of God and of Christ Jesus, who will judge the living and the dead, and in view of his appearing and his kingdom, I give you this charge: preach the word.

This week we are reminded by our readings that our covenant God is a righteous judge and a forgiving Lord. This is a wonderful encouragement for us to persevere in holding out the word of life to others.

Jeremiah is told of a coming day when there will be a new covenant between God and his people. This one will be unbreakable, and written on the hearts of the people, in contrast to the covenant written on tablets of stone which was smashed by their hardened hearts. God does not stop being a just and righteous judge: 'all shall die for their own sins', he says. Yet through this new covenant, the people will know the Lord and (wonder of wonders, so easily taken for granted!) be forgiven.

This long-awaited new constitution for God's people was promised in the Old Testament but finally inaugurated in the New Testament; the blood of Jesus sealed the new covenant, and gives greater blessings and privileges than anything promised by the Mosaic Law. What once was promised and anticipated is now available and open to us, who by faith enter into that covenant.

In the Gospel, Jesus compares God to a judge in his parable. The arresting thing is that God is compared to an *unrighteous* judge! The unjust judge in Luke 18 neither fears God nor respects people, yet he yields to the persistent prayers of a needy widow who continually comes to ask him for justice. The comparison is a typically Jewish one: 'if that, then how much more with God'. That is, if an unjust judge listens to determined pleas, how much more will God, who is a righteous and loving God, listen to the requests of his children. Indeed, the parable is told, Luke informs us in verse 1, to encourage us to keep praying and never lose heart.

The challenge in the parable is extended in the final sentence – when the Son of Man comes to judge the world, will he find people of faith on the earth? That is, will he find people humble enough to pray at all, never mind people who pray continually and never lose heart?

Losing heart is a key theme under the surface of Paul's second letter to Timothy. Since childhood he has known the words of the covenant God to his people, and been led by them to salvation in Christ. Paul urges him to stick closely to those life-giving, God-breathed words, not just for his personal salvation, but also for his public ministry. They are useful words, words which do things: teach, rebuke, train, correct. So he is not, as (literally) a 'man of God' (the Old Testament name for a leader is applied to Timothy also in 1 Timothy 6:11) to look elsewhere for tools with which to perform his ministry. The word of God is the all-sufficient instrument by which the man of God pastors the people of God.

The temptation for Timothy is to lose confidence in the word as other people do. Like the widow in Jesus's parable, he is urged to be persistent, whether the time is favourable or not, whatever the surrounding culture and society might think, in setting forth the gospel and commands of God. The itching ears of the elites, the tabloids and the *hoi polloi* may not like this; they will build up an impressive array of impressive people who tell them simply to go with the flow and embrace their sinful desires. But Timothy, as a good bishop, is to take the riskier path: to remain sober, endure the suffering and difficulties that come his way when he teaches truth and refutes error, and to continue to reach out with the gospel to the lost. If he does not, chapter 4 verse 1 reminds us, God is watching always, and Christ is coming to judge.

Proper 25

Sunday between 23 and 29 October inclusive

Joel 2:23–32 · 2 Timothy 4:6–8, 16–18 · Luke 18:9–14 · Psalm 65

Now there is in store for me the crown of righteousness, which the Lord, the righteous Judge, will award to me on that day – and not only to me, but also to all who have longed for his appearing.

The common thread in our readings this week is the theme of recompense or reward. Are you looking forward to getting one?

The prophet Joel had prophesied great destruction for Israel through swarms of locusts, 'like a powerful army' (Joel 2:5), consuming her fields. But afterwards, there would be rejoicing in rain (which we may dislike, but is very useful for growing the things we eat), and the supermarket shelves would be full again. 'I will repay you for the years that the swarming locust has eaten,' says the Lord, and you shall know me. Knowing God is the chief benefit of the gospel and the highest good to which we can attain.

Joel's prophecy continues, in a passage familiar to us from Acts 2 and the day of Pentecost. 'I will pour our my spirit on all flesh' is intimately related to that blessing of knowledge and friendship with God. The Spirit is not the *means* by which God makes himself known or acts in the world, for the Spirit is himself God, not some abstract power or substance through which God works. No, he is God himself, giving himself, to men and women, old and young, high and low. Through his work within us we are enabled to call upon the Lord and be saved. Whatever the state of our world might be, this very great reward is held out to those who are called by the Lord.

The Lord Jesus, whose humbling of himself to death on the cross makes possible all of these things, teaches us in the Gospel reading not to trust in ourselves or (note the double edge to the parable) to regard others with contempt. The Pharisee is far too similar to many of us today, and it would be a poor exposition which did not make us squirm at the recognition of ourselves in his description. Whatever it is that we hold to be most spiritual, most pleasing to God, most 'keen', is shown by Christ to be entirely insufficient if we lack humility.

Humility is in essence simply honesty, because all of us, like the tax collector, are sinners in need of a propitious God. The word for 'have mercy on me' (verse 13) is literally a plea for God to be propitious, to turn away his righteous, deserved, merited wrath. At this point in the Gospel, Jesus is in fact on his way to Jerusalem, to die as the propitiation for our sins himself (1 John 2:2). He says the reward for honest humility is exaltation by God; whereas exaltation of self leads only to humiliation. Though the wonder of the gospel is that we do not have to wait for the Last Day of judgment to know the verdict we will face: the humble one who trusts in a propitious God, can go home, today, *justified.*

The apostle Paul taught this truth of present justification by faith alone in Christ, very clearly, though he still looks forward (he tells Timothy) to the crown of righteousness as his reward on the Last Day. When Christ returns, all those who have longed for his appearing will receive the just reward of his grace. Meanwhile, in the dirty, unjust, angry world, they may face defeat, depression and even despair. But Paul testifies that even though all had deserted him (and his teaching), the Lord stood by him. His unshakeable confidence is that Christ will hold onto him and save him for his heavenly kingdom. No power of hell, no schemes of man, can ever pluck him from Christ's hands. Do you have that confidence in Christ for your salvation?

4th Sunday before Advent

Sunday between 30 October and 5 November inclusive

Isaiah 1:10–18 · 2 Thessalonians 1:1–12 · Luke 19:1–10 · Psalm 32:1–7

Though your sins are like scarlet, they shall be white as snow; though they are red as crimson, they shall be like wool.

This week's passages are about the forgiveness of all those who turn back to the Lord in repentance, and what happens to those who refuse to do so. Where do you find yourself in the story?

Isaiah 1 refers to God's own people as Sodom and Gomorrah. Their sins are equally abhorrent to the God who judges justly and shows no partiality. Indeed, the false veneer of piety they profess, with a multitude of sacrifices and incense, is nothing less than an abomination to the Lord. He turns his ears away from their prayers because of their sins and their refusal to repent. However, if they change their hearts, turn back to God and express this by changed actions and priorities, it need not be so. All who repent are washed clean: even the most heinous transgressions against the righteous ways of our holy God can be purged. Scarlet sins are bleached by the power of forgiveness, for all who truly turn back in sorrow and shame to our gracious God. But for those who don't, there is only the sword.

Luke 19 is a beautiful story of a repentant sinner. Zacchaeus's conversion demonstrates the power of Christ's gracious presence in an individual's life. A chief tax collector, that is, a major collaborator with the occupying Romans, wants to see Jesus. This itself is a miracle of grace in him, especially considering he has probably defrauded or cheated many people in his time and sin often makes us hide from God, not seek him out. But Jesus hurriedly responds to this small man's big act of faith in climbing a tree to even get a look at the passing Messiah. Zacchaeus's joy in being accepted by the Saviour is palpable, but others grumble, because such gracious acceptance of those on the edges of respectability in our polite circles can offend those who want to keep God to themselves. Yet that grace and acceptance transforms the man at the centre of this public outcry: he doesn't remain a 'sinner', but demonstrates his repentance immediately and generously. Jesus applies this message in a general way to teach a truth about his mission. He has come to seek and save people just like Zacchaeus, those that others might not accept but who can have their sinful lives transformed and changed by the purifying presence of Jesus.

2 Thessalonians is written to a community of such forgiven people, but a people who are being profoundly persecuted for their saving trust in Christ. The stark reality of judgment on those who will not repent and obey the call to such faith is brought to the fore in this sobering opening to the letter. On the Last Day there is eternal punishment for those who refuse the Lord Jesus. He is coming again, and as the Swiss Reformer Heinrich Bullinger (1504–75) once wrote, 'The same coming shall be to all saints very acceptable and most welcome, and to the ungodly very sour and sorrowful.'[45] The glory of the gospel is that sour punishment is not applied to those who believe. Paul prays the Thessalonians would be worthy of such a magnificent salvation and be blessed in all their endeavours for Christ's glory. The strong meat here is that he is glorified in salvation but also in his just judgments on those who oppose him and his people.

The big question for us is whether we will repent and be saved, or not.

[45] See Lee Gatiss and Bradley G. Green (eds.), *1–2 Thessalonians, 1–2 Timothy, Titus, Philemon*, Reformation Commentary on Scripture (Downers Grove, IL.: IVP Academic, 2019), p. 64.

3rd Sunday before Advent

Sunday between 6 and 12 November inclusive

Job 19:23–27a · 2 Thessalonians 2:1–5, 13–17 · Luke 20:27–38 · Psalm 17:1–9.

I know that my redeemer lives, and that in the end he will stand on the earth. And after my skin has been destroyed, yet in my flesh I will see God.

The key theme of our readings this week is the resurrection hope that we have in Christ. This is, of course, an appropriate message for a Remembrance or Veterans Sunday, but also for every day of the year.

Job 19 is a wonderful shaft of light, casting forth a sparkling testimony to the gospel from the often obscure shadows of the Old Testament. The suffering Job is convinced that one day he will have an opportunity to put his case to God. Indeed, he seems insistent that someone will stand on his side, his living Redeemer, his God. This will happen after his skin has been destroyed, that is, after his death, at the Last Day, when he will again be enfleshed. At this bodily resurrection, his eyes will see God, and he will finally be able to speak to him. He longs for that day, and his heart faints within him. As the evangelical preacher Charles Simeon (1759–1836) commented,

> Behold then the depths of divine truths which had been revealed to Job! He sees his God incarnate ... The words used by Job might be applied to the incarnation and resurrection of Christ; but they seem rather to designate his appearance in the last day to judge the

> world … He does not seem to have had any hope of restoration to temporal prosperity; but speaks in the most confident manner of his resurrection to eternal happiness. The destruction of his mortal frame by worms was not in his eyes any bar to its renovation in the last day.[1]

The Sadducees who confronted Jesus did not believe in such bodily resurrections. As the old but theologically apposite joke has it, that's why they were sad, you see. They think they have caught Jesus in a trap with a ridiculous *reductio ad absurdum* argument about a woman with seven consecutive (and related) husbands. But he is ready for such trickery and rebukes them for knowing neither the power of God nor the Scriptures. He affirms that there is indeed a resurrection hope, but not for those who 'belong to this age'. Those who will be raised are the children of God, and they are raised once and for all, never to die again. They are to be transformed in some way, and made 'like the angels', in the sense that they do not marry.

Since they had used an obscure Leviticus provision in their rather convoluted question, Jesus also responds with some astonishing exegesis of his own. They should have known that people are raised from the dead, and are all 'living' to him, because he calls himself (in a Pentateuchal text central to Sadducee theology) the God of Abraham, and of Isaac, and of Jacob. Though the patriarchs are to our eyes 'dead', God says he *is* their God still. QED as far as Jesus is concerned; but his interlocutors were no doubt left dumbfounded (as many commentators seem to be). Yet the Word incarnate knows best how to interpret the word in Scripture.

2 Thessalonians speaks emphatically and with crystal clarity of 'the coming of our Lord Jesus Christ'. On that great and awesome day, we will be gathered in Christ and to Christ. The scattered people of God, dispersed throughout the world, will finally come together.

---

[1] Charles Simeon, *Horae Homileticae: Chronicles to Job* (London: Samuel Holdsworth, 1836), pp. 405–6.

The glory of Christ is opened to those who believe the proclamation of the good news. God chose them and sanctified them by his Spirit, calling them to something purer and higher and greater. This glorious prospect is set before the Thessalonians to strengthen them in the face of temptations and dangers, and to give them 'eternal comfort and good hope'. In response, they speak good words and do good works, so that in turn it is not just they who are blessed, but others through them. The God of Abraham continues to bless the world through those who have the faith of their father, and they share in the resurrection he too will enjoy. When the saints go marching in, do you want to be in their number?

2nd Sunday before Advent

Sunday between 13 and 19 November inclusive

Malachi 4:1–2a · 2 Thessalonians 3:6–13 · Luke 21:5–19 · Psalm 98

But for you who revere my name, the sun of righteousness will rise with healing in its wings. And you will go out and frolic like well-fed calves.

Central to all three passages this week is the coming divisive judgment of God and our response to it. Will it be a joyful day, or a day of doom, for you?

Malachi's prophecy aims to convince its readers that God's covenant with his people still stands. Part of his promise is an assurance that one day evil will be destroyed and all evildoers punished. Malachi 4 warns that the day is approaching, and it will burn up arrogance and purge the world, root and branch. However, in the midst of such terrifying judgment, there is hope. Those who revere God's name, that is, who hear his word and respond with faith and generous hearts, will not face the doom of judgment. Rather, they will see the light, as the sun of righteousness rises upon them, the dawning of a new day. The sun's 'wings' will bring healing from their backsliding and the remnants of sin within, which have loaded them down with the burden of Adam's fallen race. With these chains removed, they can leap like calves released from the stall and let rip with praise to God in new and transformed lives.

2 Thessalonians began with a warning of impending judgment, which has not lifted throughout the epistle. At the end, these warnings against idleness must therefore be taken in that context of an approaching day when all must give account. The apostle's example of diligence and hard work is held up as something for all to imitate: if anyone does not work, he shall not eat.

Not that this precludes us from helping the poor and vulnerable (and children!), of course, which Paul is very clear about elsewhere. But the Christian community is not to be characterised by idleness, and full of busybodies who have nothing to do but gossip and benefit from the labour of others. More than just making a contribution to the economy, however, we are to be eager to do what is right, and not grow weary in such effort. The second coming is not to make us slack and nonchalant, in other words, but to spur us on. Hence those who are seriously lazy can have no real hope and relief on that day, and so we are not to have fellowship with them, lest such lackadaisical attitudes rub off on us too.

As well as continuing to work hard and earn our keep, Jesus urges us to watchfulness as we wait for his coming in glory. He speaks of a day, which came but forty years after his crucifixion, when the Temple in Jerusalem would be destroyed. The disciples ask him for a sign, so they will know when this is coming. What he says is that various things must happen first: false messiahs, wars, insurrections, earthquakes, famines and plagues. But worse than that, persecution of believers. Yet the word of God will be taken, at the same time, to kings and governors, who will hear the glorious gospel proclaimed.

All these things did of course happen before AD 70, as the apostles spread out across the known world and testified to who Christ was and what he had done. But Jesus also described a pattern, which has repeated ever since, of regular upheavals on the earth and in the world of humanity, where believers are persecuted but the gospel goes forth anyway. The end will one day come, but we are not to be terrified by the repeated difficulties we face. Instead, the Lord commends endurance and promises his protection. One day he will receive us, body and soul, into his new creation. The signs of the times should warn us to be ready.

Sunday next before Advent (Christ the King)

Sunday between 20 and 26 November inclusive

Jeremiah 23:1–6 · Colossians 1:11–20 · Luke 23:33–43 · Psalm 46

There was a written notice above him, which read:
THIS IS THE KING OF THE JEWS.

The readings this Sunday are reflective of the fact that it is the festival of Christ the King. They show us that Jesus is the righteous Shepherd King of both creation and new creation, who through the cross unites heaven and earth in his peaceful kingdom. What better King could we ever hope for?

Jeremiah's prophecy begins with an indictment of earthly kings and leaders who have scattered the flock they were given to shepherd and destroyed that for which they should have cared. To counter their evil ways, God himself promises to gather and to bless. He will bring his people together and they will 'be fruitful and multiply' again, a clear allusion to the creation mandate of Genesis 1, which has been overturned by the de-creation of sin.

In the days that are coming, says the Lord through Jeremiah, a righteous Davidic king will reign. In contrast to the kings in David's line who made a mess of Judah and led her astray, this one will deal wisely and execute justice fairly. Judah and Israel will be united in his days, and he will have a name – the Lord our righteousness – which may in fact imply that he is the righteous God himself, who in verse 3 promised he would himself gather and protect his people.

Luke 23 presents to us that very king, at his coronation. With his crown of thorns and attending soldiers, he is hailed as King of the Jews. Yet his throne is not of gold but the wood of a cruel cross. The earthly leaders gathered around him condemn themselves by their derision and scorn of the one who was truly born to rule. Even in this moment of apparent weakness and helplessness, amidst the injustice and barbarity, he continues the work of gathering his people, to be with him for ever in Paradise. Those who recognises him as King will reign with him in glory.

Paul's prayer and praise of Christ in Colossians 1 extols the perfection of the crucified King. The head that once was crowned with thorns is crowned with glory now, as he is lauded as King over creation and new creation. He is the firstborn of all creation, the heir, and the firstborn from the dead, the supremely exalted King. We who have been transferred into the kingdom of this beloved Son have redemption and peace through the blood of his cross, so that he is King over both heaven and earth, both unfallen angels and redeemed humanity.

Paul's rapturous praise for Christ relates back to his prayer for the Colossian believers, with which our reading begins. Paul prays that they would be strong with all the strength that comes from the glorious power of Christ – the Christ who is before all things and who holds all things together. All this power and energy Paul prays will be available to believers; but not for feats of dazzling show or miraculous demonstrations of healing, signs and wonders. The immense power of the majestic universal King is given to help us 'endure everything with patience, while joyfully giving thanks to the Father'. The perseverance of the saints is no light thing, but requires colossal spiritual resources. A thankful, joyful, trusting heart in the midst of affliction or temptation is testimony to the fact that such power is holding us together, just as it enabled Christ the Lord to hold himself to the cross.

Hymns and Songs

YEAR A

1st Sunday of Advent

Great is the darkness that covers the earth
Hark! A herald voice is calling
Christ triumphant, ever reigning
How lovely on the mountains
Hills of the north, rejoice

2nd Sunday of Advent

Thanks to God whose word was spoken
May the mind of Christ my Saviour
Rejoice, the Lord is King
In heavenly love abiding
Jesus shall reign

3rd Sunday of Advent

Be bold, be strong
Jesus, the name high over all
O for a thousand tongues to sing
Wait for the Lord
We have a gospel to proclaim

4th Sunday of Advent

All hail the power of Jesus' name
Come, thou long expected Jesus
From heaven you came
Long ago prophets knew
The advent of our King
O little town of Bethlehem

1st Sunday of Christmas

God so loved, that he gave his Son

It came upon the midnight clear
My song is love unknown
We hail thy presence glorious
Jesus, friend of sinners

2nd Sunday of Christmas
Come, ye faithful, raise the anthem
Crown him with many crowns
Come, people of the risen King
Thanks to God whose word was spoken
Of the Father's love begotten

Epiphany
Joy to the world!
At the name of Jesus
Lord, the light of your love
The Lord is my light (or Psalm 27)
We have a gospel to proclaim

1st Sunday of Epiphany
Christ, when for us you were baptised
God forgave my sin
Hail to the Lord's anointed
O thou who camest from above
The Church's one foundation

2nd Sunday of Epiphany
Called and named before your birth
From heaven you came
God of grace and God of glory
Jesus, the name high over all
Will you come and follow me

3rd Sunday of Epiphany
And can it be?

O to see the dawn (the power of the cross)
Light has dawned that ever shall blaze
The Church's one foundation
Bind us together, Lord

4th Sunday of Epiphany
Let the vain world (Contempt of the world)
May the mind of Christ my Saviour
My worth is not in what I own
O Church, arise
The perfect wisdom of our God

Presentation of Christ in the Temple
How deep the Father's love
Christ, whose glory fills the skies
Hail to the Lord who comes
Restore, O Lord
With joy we meditate the grace

Proper 1
Men of faith, rise up and sing
Thou, whose almighty word
Let us praise God together
Blest are the pure in heart
Here I am

Proper 2
A choice is set before you now
A new commandment
Forgive our sins as we forgive
Lord, when I turn my back on you
Trust and obey

Proper 3
When I needed a neighbour

Come, ye thankful people, come
Christ is all in all
All I have is Christ
Holy, holy, holy

2nd Sunday before Lent
Let the earth resound
Creation sings
Great is thy faithfulness
How great thou art
For the beauty of the earth

Sunday next before Lent (Transfiguration Sunday)
Speak, O Lord, as we come to you
How firm a foundation
Your word is a lamp unto my feet
You are the King of glory
Let the vain world applaud or frown (Contempt of the world)

1st Sunday of Lent
Praise to the Holiest in the height
And can it be?
Awake, our souls; away, our fears
From the squalor of a borrowed stable
Lord Jesus, think on me

2nd Sunday of Lent
All I once held dear
All my hope on God is founded
I'm accepted, I'm forgiven
The God of Abraham praise
To God be the glory

3rd Sunday of Lent
As the deer pants for the water

In Christ alone
Guide me, O thou great Redeemer
Holy Spirit, truth divine
The King of love my shepherd is

4th Sunday of Lent
Lord, the light of your love is shining
And can it be?
Light of the world
Open the eyes of my heart, Lord
Come, Lord, to our souls come down

5th Sunday of Lent
Great is thy faithfulness
Breathe on me, breath of God
My Lord, what love is this?
Spirit of God, light amid the darkness
Spirit divine, attend our prayers
Speak, O Lord, as we come to you

Palm Sunday
My song is love unknown
All glory, laud, and honour
O worship the King
Come, people of the risen King
Hosanna in the highest

Easter Sunday
See, what a morning
Come, people of the risen King
He is Lord, he is Lord
Light's glitt'ring morn bedecks the sky
Low in the grave he lay

2nd Sunday of Easter
Come, ye faithful, raise the strain

Lead us, heavenly Father, lead us
Come, people of the risen King
Open the eyes of my heart, Lord
All my hope on God is founded

3rd Sunday of Easter
All I once held dear
In the garden Mary lingers
We have a gospel to proclaim
We'll walk the land with hearts on fire
You met God's great fury (Hail the risen King)

4th Sunday of Easter
Let the vain world (Contempt of the world)
From heaven you came
The Church's one foundation
How sweet the name of Jesus sounds
Faithful Shepherd, feed me

5th Sunday of Easter
Christ is made the sure foundation
Thou art the way: by thee alone
Now, why this fear and unbelief?
To God be the glory!
Fullness of grace in man's human frailty

6th Sunday of Easter
O Lord of heav'n and earth and sea
All people that on earth do dwell
All my hope on God is founded
There is a Redeemer
We have a gospel to proclaim

7th Sunday of Easter
Son of God, eternal Saviour
Blessed assurance, Jesus is mine

As the deer pants for the water
Holy Spirit, living breath of God
How lovely is your dwelling-place

Whit Sunday (Pentecost)
Breathe on me, breath of God
Come down, O love divine
Filled with the Spirit's power
Spirit of the living God
There is a Redeemer

Trinity Sunday
Christians lift up your hearts!
Father of heaven, whose love profound
May the grace of Christ our Saviour
May the mind of Christ my Saviour
Holy Spirit, living breath of God

Proper 4
The wise man built his house upon the rock
Only by grace can we enter
My hope is built
Rock of ages
If it had not been for the Lord

Proper 5
By faith we see the hand of God
The God of Abraham praise
Living by faith in our Lord Jesus Christ
Now by faith
Thank you, Lord for giving yourself to us

Proper 6
In Christ alone
Hymn of the Saviour

You are our God
Good shepherd of my soul
When peace like a river

Proper 7
Above all powers
In Christ alone
From whence this fear and unbelief?
A mighty fortress is our God
Do not be afraid, for I have redeemed you

Proper 8
My hope is built on nothing less
Trust and obey
All for Jesus
There is a higher throne
Jesus, I my cross have taken

Proper 9
Come, people of the risen King
Rejoice, the Lord is King
Let the vain world (Contempt for the world)
A God who saves
Joy in the morning

Proper 10
And can it be?
A debtor to mercy alone
Praise we now the word of grace
How firm a foundation
We have a gospel to proclaim

Proper 11
Great is thy faithfulness
Come, ye thankful people, come

Only by grace can we enter
As the deer pants for the water
Jesus is Lord – the cry that echoes

Proper 12
Before the throne of God above
I'm accepted, I'm forgiven
God is working his purpose out
Come, people of the risen King
God is the giver of love

Proper 13
Beauty for brokenness
We have a gospel to proclaim
From the squalor of a borrowed stable
I, the Lord of sea and sky
Filled with compassion for all creation

Proper 14
Be still, my soul
Dear Lord and Father of mankind
O Church, arise
Speak, O Lord, as we come to you
We have a gospel to proclaim

Proper 15
All hail the power of Jesus' name
There's a wideness in God's mercy
From the sun's rising
Come, people of the risen King
Jesus shall reign where'er the sun

Proper 16
Bind us together, Lord
Holy Spirit, come, confirm us
Jesus where'er thy people meet

Tell out, my soul
The God of Abraham praise
Thou art the Christ, O Lord

Proper 17
How firm a foundation
O Church, arise
Let the vain world (Contempt of the world)
Be still, my soul
Trust and obey

Proper 18
O Lord, the clouds are gathering
Lord, for the years
When I needed a neighbour
We have a gospel to proclaim
Careless soul, why will you linger?

Proper 19
God forgave my sin in Jesus' name
Forgive our sins
Amazing Grace
There is a hope
Majesty (Here I am)

Proper 20
Only by grace can we enter
What grace is mine
Am I a soldier of the cross?
Christ's is the world in which we move
Brother, sister, let me serve you

Proper 21
From heaven you came
May the mind of Christ my Saviour
Help us to help each other, Lord

Heaven shall not wait
I will offer up my life

Proper 22
All I once held dear
And can it be?
When I survey the wondrous cross
My Lord, what love is this?
I will offer up my life

Proper 23
Lo! He comes with clouds descending
How bright these glorious spirits shine
I come with joy, a child of God
My God, and is thy table spread
There's a place where the streets shine

Proper 24
In Christ alone
Take my life
All my hope on God is founded
I will offer up my life
To God be the glory

Proper 25
We have a gospel to proclaim
A new commandment
How deep the Father's love for us
Love is his word
Let there be love

4th Sunday before Advent
O Lord, the clouds are gathering
Restore, O Lord
O church arise

How firm a foundation
Let the vain world applaud or frown

3rd Sunday before Advent
O Lord, the clouds are gathering
Awake, awake: fling off the night
Let saints on earth in concert sing
Thy hand, O God, has guided
Abide with me

2nd Sunday before Advent
O Lord, the clouds are gathering
Trust and obey
Take my life
Come, people of the risen King
I will offer up my life

Sunday next before Advent
The Lord's my Shepherd (I will trust in you alone)
You're the Lion of Judah
Meekness and majesty
My Jesus, my Saviour
O worship the King

YEAR B
1st Sunday of Advent
Creation sings the Father's song
Awake, awake: fling off the night
Come, thou long expected Jesus
Lo, he comes with clouds descending
O come, O come, Emmanuel

2nd Sunday of Advent
In Christ alone
Great is the darkness

Prepare him room
Come, thou long expected Jesus
Judge eternal, throned in splendour

3rd Sunday of Advent
King of Kings, Majesty
Love divine
You alone can rescue
God is working his purpose out
How lovely on the mountains
How beauteous are their feet

4th Sunday in Advent
At the name of Jesus
Come, thou long-expected Jesus
Long ago, prophets knew
What child is this?
Joy has dawned upon the world

1st Sunday of Christmas
Joy has dawned upon the world
Born where the shadows lie
Behold, the great Creator
Joy to the world!
Praise, my soul, the King of heaven
Thou didst leave thy throne

1st Sunday of Epiphany
Come, Holy Spirit
From the squalor of a borrowed stable
Holy Spirit, source of gladness
Day-spring of eternity
Holy Spirit, living breath of God

2nd Sunday of Epiphany
You're the Lion of Judah

Speak, O Lord, as we come to you
How firm a foundation
I will sing the wondrous story
Beautiful Saviour

3rd Sunday of Epiphany
Come, people of the risen King
O happy man, whose soul is filled
God is here! As we his people
The God of Abraham praise
Our God, our help in ages past

4th Sunday of Epiphany
How firm a foundation
By faith we see the hand of God
At the name of Jesus
How sweet the name of Jesus sounds
Thine arm, O Lord, in days of old

Proper 1
We have a gospel to proclaim
Servants of the gospel
Across the streets
Let the nations be glad
Before you I kneel (A worker's prayer)

Proper 2
May the mind of Christ my Saviour
Why do we choose what can last but an hour
Christ is all
O Church, arise
Eternal King

Proper 3
From the breaking of the dawn (Every promise)

This promise (For heartache, for sorrow)
Hear me, Lord
I will wait for you
Just as I am

2nd Sunday before Lent
Creation sings the Father's song
Jesus is Lord! Creation's voice proclaims it
All creatures of our God and king
Lord of creation, to you be all praise!
Thou, whose almighty word

Sunday next before Lent (Transfiguration Sunday)
Thine be the glory
You're the Word of God the Father
Christ, whose glory fills the skies
Meekness and majesty
We have a gospel to proclaim

1st Sunday of Lent
Let the vain world (Contempt of the world)
Be still, my soul
Forty days and forty nights
Come and see
Father, hear the prayer we offer

2nd Sunday of Lent
When I survey the wondrous cross
Take my life, and let it be
Beneath the cross of Jesus
My worth is not in what I own
The God of Abraham praise

3rd Sunday of Lent
When I survey the wondrous cross

Let the vain world applaud or frown
From heaven you came
It is finished, the Messiah dies
Who is there like you?

4th Sunday of Lent
There is a green hill
And can it be?
You children of God by faith in his Son
The Church's one foundation
O to see the dawn (the power of the cross)

5th Sunday of Lent
How deep the Father's love for us
From the breaking of the dawn
From heaven you came
Lift high the cross
With joy we meditate the grace

Palm Sunday
My song is love unknown
From the squalor of a borrow stable
How deep the Father's love for us
Tell me the story of Jesus
All glory, laud, and honour

Easter Day
See, what a morning
Crown him with many crowns
How can it be, the One who died
From the very depths of darkness
Low in the grave he lay

2nd Sunday of Easter
Before the throne of God above

Joy to the world
Let no one caught in sin remain (Christ is risen)
Mighty to save
Christ the Lord is risen today

3rd Sunday of Easter
How can it be, the One who died
How deep the Father's love for us
Crown him with many crowns
Father God, I wonder
My Lord, what love is this

4th Sunday of Easter
The Lord's my Shepherd
Look what you've done
Love divine
No other way
Saviour, like a shepherd lead us

5th Sunday of Easter
Abide in me
Speak, O Lord, as we come to you
How firm a foundation
God is love: his the care
Happy are they, they that love God

6th Sunday of Easter
Love divine
This is my commandment
As you loved me
Chosen in Jesus
Love of God, revealed in wonder

7th Sunday of Easter
Alleluia, alleluia, give thanks to the risen Lord

Christ triumphant, ever reigning
Now is eternal life
Jesus is Lord, the cry that echoes through creation
O Church, arise

Whit Sunday (Pentecost)
Breathe on me, breath of God
Christians, lift up your hearts
Come down, O Love divine
For I'm building a people of power
Holy Spirit, living breath of God

Trinity Sunday
Angel-voices ever singing
Father most holy
Holy, holy, holy, holy.
May the grace of Christ our Saviour
Join the song of the angels round the throne

Proper 4
God of grace and God of glory
Lord of all hopefulness
Meekness and majesty
O Church, arise
Before you I kneel, my Master and Maker

Proper 5
In Christ alone
Lift up your heads, you mighty gates
The Church's one foundation
The Lord is king and earth submits
All my days

Proper 6
God is working his purpose out

Lo he comes with clouds descending
The Church's one foundation
O Church, arise
Thy kingdom come, O God

Proper 7
Be still, my soul
Let the vain world (Contempt of the world)
All who would valiant be
The Church's one foundation
Will your anchor hold?

Proper 8
Lord, you were rich beyond all splendour
And can it be?
From the squalor of a borrowed stable
Blessèd be your name
Thou didst leave thy throne

Proper 9
I, The Lord of sea and sky
How deep the Father's love for us
A mighty fortress
How long?
Let your kingdom come

Proper 10
We have a gospel to proclaim
God has spoken – by the prophets
Thy hand, O God, has guided
I'm not ashamed to own my Lord
Hear the call of the kingdom

Proper 11
How firm a foundation
Speak, O Lord, as we come to you

Christ is our cornerstone
Faithful Shepherd, feed me
The Lord's my Shepherd

Proper 12
Be still, my soul
In Christ alone
Show us Christ
I heard the voice of Jesus say
To God be the glory

Proper 13
Speak, O Lord, as we come to you
Show us Christ
May the mind of Christ my Saviour
Rise and hear! The Lord is speaking
Guide me, O thou great Redeemer

Proper 14
You're the word of God the Father
I am the bread of life
Guide me, O my great Redeemer
Let all mortal flesh keep silence
My Lord, what love is this?

Proper 15
Awake, my soul, and with the sun
Be thou my guardian and my guide
The Church's one foundation
Jesus is king and I will extol him
Speak, O Lord, as we come to you

Proper 16
Stand up, stand up for Jesus
Prepare our hearts, O God
You are the King of glory

Oft in danger, often in woe
How firm a foundation

Proper 17
Purify my heart
Happy are they, they that love God
Lord, thy word abideth
Jesus pure and holy
Love divine, all love excelling

Proper 18
When I needed a neighbour
All people that on earth do dwell
Beauty for brokenness
I heard the voice of Jesus say
Praise, my soul, the King of heaven

Proper 19
At the name of Jesus
Let the vain world applaud
I'm not ashamed to own my Lord
Speak, O Lord, as we come to you
When God Almighty came to earth

Proper 20
Christ's is the world in which we move
Brother, sister, let me serve you
From heaven you came
Led like a lamb to the slaughter
Meekness and majesty

Proper 21
Loved before the dawn of time
I cannot tell
All I once held dear

Be thou my guardian and my guide
When all thy mercies, O my God

Proper 22
Crown him with many crowns
When I was lost
May the grace of Christ our Saviour
Bind us together, Lord
O Lord, my God

Proper 23
O Lord, the clouds are gathering
All I once held dear
My worth is not in what I own
I will offer up my life
Take my life

Proper 24
He was pierced for our transgressions
From heaven you came
In Christ alone
Meekness and majesty
Come and see

Proper 25
Before the throne of God above
Alleluia, sing to Jesus
Be thou my vision
I heard the voice of Jesus say
Amazing grace

4th Sunday before Advent
O love that will not let me go
Jesus loves me
My song is love unknown

Love divine
The everlasting love of God

3rd Sunday before Advent
Amazing grace
O Jesus, I have promised
We sing the praise of him who died
When I fear my faith will fail
We turn to you, O God of every nation

2nd Sunday before Advent
O God, my refuge, keep me safe
He will hold me fast
Come, thou fount of every blessing
All my hope on God is founded
Lift high the name of Jesus

Sunday next before Advent
Lo! He comes with clouds descending
See him coming
Jesus is Lord
A mighty fortress
Glorious things of thee are spoken

YEAR C
1st Sunday of Advent
Lo! He comes with clouds descending
O come, O come, Emmanuel
Restore, O Lord
The advent of our king
Joy has dawned upon the world

2nd Sunday of Advent
Purify my heart
Change my heart, O God

Long ago, prophets knew
Hark! A herald voice is calling
O Saviour of our fallen race

3rd Sunday of Advent
Lord Jesus Christ, you have come to us
O comfort my people
O day of God, draw nigh
To God be the glory
What a friend we have in Jesus

4th Sunday of Advent
For Mary, mother of our Lord
Hark, the glad sound!
O come, O come, Emmanuel
Of the Father's love begotten
You're the Word of God the Father

1st Sunday of Christmas
Lord, I lift your name on high
Once in royal David's city
Who would think that what was needed
All praise to our redeeming Lord
Holy Child who chose the hearts of men

1st Sunday of Epiphany
Christ, when for us you were baptised
Come, people of the risen King
Lead us, heavenly Father, lead us
O love, how deep, how broad, how high
When Jesus came to Jordan

2nd Sunday of Epiphany
All praise to our redeeming Lord
From heaven you came

Jesus, Lord, we look to thee
O Lord, your tenderness
Sing of the Lord's goodness

3rd Sunday of Epiphany
How firm a foundation
Speak, O Lord, as we come to you
Now in reverence and awe
God has spoken – by the prophets
We have a gospel to proclaim

4th Sunday of Epiphany
In peace and joy I now depart
Christ, whose glory fills the skies
Colours of day dawn into the mind
Jesus, joy of the highest heaven
Love of God revealed in wonder

Proper 1
See, what a morning
Come, people of the risen King
He is Lord, he is Lord
Light's glitt'ring morn bedecks the sky
Low in the grave he lay

Proper 2
See, what a morning
Christ is risen, he is risen indeed
Come, people of the risen King
Thine be the glory
Led like a lamb

Proper 3
The glory of God (We won't need the sun)
Glorious things of you are spoken

Creation awaits
For the beauty of the earth
O worship the risen Christ

2nd Sunday before Lent
Holy, holy, holy
Alleluia, sing to Jesus
Be still, my soul
Eternal Father, strong to save
Thou, whose almighty word

Sunday next before Lent (Transfiguration Sunday)
Christ, whose glory fills the skies
From glory to glory advancing
God of mercy, God of grace
Lord, the light of your love is shining
Speak, O Lord, as we come to you

1st Sunday of Lent
All who would valiant be
I bind unto myself today
Jesu, thou joy of loving hearts
O Church, arise
Your word is a lamp unto my feet

2nd Sunday of Lent
All my hope on God is founded
All you who seek a comfort sure
Do not be afraid, for I have redeemed you
Fight the good fight
The God of Abraham praise

3rd Sunday of Lent
O Church, arise
Seek ye the Lord, all ye people

Rock of ages
Repent! 'tis the voice of Jesus
All I once held dear

4th Sunday of Lent
Great God, your love has called us here
When I was lost (There is a new song)
Before the throne of God above
There is a higher throne
Amazing grace

5th Sunday of Lent
Take my life
All I once held dear
And can it be?
Beneath the cross of Jesus
To God be the glory

Palm Sunday
Rock of ages
My song is love unknown
From heaven you came
Ride on, ride on in majesty
Meekness and majesty

Easter Sunday
Come, people of the risen King
From the squalor of a borrowed stable
Christ the Lord is ris'n again
Led like a lamb to the slaughter
The strife is o'er, the battle done

2nd Sunday of Easter
Trust and obey
See him coming on the clouds of heaven

Jesus is Lord, the cry that echoes through creation
O for a thousand tongues to sing
Lo! He comes with clouds descending

3rd Sunday of Easter
Amazing grace
From all that dwell below the skies
God moves in a mysterious way
My God, I love thee
We have a gospel to proclaim

4th Sunday of Easter
In Christ alone
How firm a foundation
Salvation belongs to our God
How sweet the name of Jesus sounds
The Lord's my Shepherd (I will trust in you alone)

5th Sunday of Easter
No other name
How deep the Father's love
Let there be love
Be glorified
O for a thousand tongues

6th Sunday of Easter
Speak, O Lord, as we come to you
The Church's one foundation
Be thou my vision
Now in reverence and awe
Have faith in God, my heart

7th Sunday of Easter
Bind us together, Lord
Come, people of the risen King

Great is the darkness
Jesus shall reign where'er the sun
At the name of Jesus

Whit Sunday (Pentecost)
We have a gospel to proclaim
Holy Spirit, living breath of God
Breathe on me, breath of God
Filled with the Spirit's power
Holy Spirit, come, confirm us

Trinity Sunday
We believe in God the Father
Thou whose almighty word
May the grace of Christ our Saviour
Holy Spirit, truth divine
O Saviour of our fallen race

Proper 4
We have a gospel to proclaim
The Church's one foundation
Rejoice, the Lord is King
In Christ alone
A mighty fortress is our God

Proper 5
O for a thousand tongues to sing
Tell out my soul, the greatness of the Lord
Jesus shall reign where'er the sun
Oh, the deep, deep love of Jesus
The kingdom of God is justice and joy

Proper 6
All I once held dear
God forgave my sin in Jesus' name

I'm accepted, I'm forgiven
Praise, my soul, the King of heaven
And can it be?

Proper 7
How firm a foundation
All hail the power of Jesus' name
In Christ there is no east or west
Thanks to God whose word was spoken
To the name of our salvation

Proper 8
Let the vain world applaud (Contempt of the world)
When I survey the wondrous cross
From heaven you came, helpless babe
Lord, for the years
May we, O Holy Spirit, bear your fruit

Proper 9
When I survey the wondrous cross
A mighty fortress is our God
From the squalor of a borrowed stable
I am a new creation
When we walk with the Lord (Trust and obey)

Proper 10
O Lord, all the world belongs to you
Not far beyond the sea
O thou who camest from above
To God be the glory
God has spoken – by the prophets

Proper 11
All heaven declares
Be thou my vision

Speak, O Lord, as we come to you
May the mind of Christ my Saviour
To be in your presence

Proper 12
God of love, you freely give us
In Christ alone
Lift high the cross
What a friend we have in Jesus
Thy kingdom come, O God

Proper 13
Come, people of the risen King
Before the throne of God above
God of grace and God of glory
Purify my heart
When all thy mercies, O my God

Proper 14
How firm a foundation
Trust and obey
Speak, O Lord, as we come to you
Glorious things of thee are spoken
There's a place where the streets shine

Proper 15
May the mind of Christ my Saviour
Oft in danger, oft in woe
The head that once was crowned with thorns
Who can sound the depths of sorrow
It is not death to die

Proper 16
And can it be?
Praise, my soul, the King of heaven

Lord, we come to ask your healing
Restore, O Lord
Speak, O Lord, as we come to you

Proper 17
Glorious things of thee are spoken
Two sins have we committed
All my hope on God is founded
Maker of the heavens and earth
Everlasting God, the years go by

Proper 18
Before Jehovah's aweful throne
My God, accept my heart this day
All that I am
Take my life, and let it be
I will offer up my life

Proper 19
Immortal, invisible, God only wise
All people that on earth do dwell
Father of heaven, whose love profound
How deep the Father's love for us
Go forth and tell

Proper 20
Glorious things of thee are spoken
Great is the darkness that covers the earth
Judge eternal, throned in splendour
Restore, O Lord
Son of God, eternal Saviour

Proper 21
Restore, O Lord
Oh, the unsearchable riches of Christ

Is my name written there?
Be thou my vision
Give thanks with a grateful heart

Proper 22
Come, people of the risen King
All I once held dear
Crown him with many crowns
Rock of ages
Who can sound the depths of sorrow?

Proper 23
Come and see, come and see
Thank you for saving me
For I'm building a people of power
A mighty fortress is our God
Glorious things of thee are spoken

Proper 24
How firm a foundation
The Church's one foundation
Father, hear the prayer we offer
Father of heaven, whose love profound
Lord, thy word abideth
What a friend we have in Jesus

Proper 25
In Christ alone
Beauty for brokenness
Rock of ages
Praise, my soul, the King of heaven
Rejoice, O land, in God thy might

4th Sunday before Advent
At the name of Jesus

God forgave my sin
Lo, he comes with clouds descending
My Lord, what love is this?
Zacchaeus was a very little man

3rd Sunday before Advent
To God be the glory
There is a hope so sure
See, what a morning
Be still, my soul
The God of Abraham praise

2nd Sunday before Advent
And can it be?
Guide me, O thou great Redeemer
You are the King of glory
Do not be afraid, for I have redeemed you
Christ, whose glory fills the skies

Sunday next before Advent
Come and see, come and see
The head that once was crowned with thorns
Be bold, be strong
All hail the power of Jesus name
The Lord's my Shepherd

Index of Persons

Ambrose (339–97). Bishop of Milan and theologian.

Ambrosiaster. The name given to an unknown author of a commentary on Paul's epistles from the late fourth century.

Augustine (354–430). Bishop of Hippo Regius in Roman North Africa and theologian. (See also *Pseudo-Augustine*)

Aquinas, Thomas (1225–74). Italian Dominican friar, theologian-philosopher, and Bible commentator.

Ash, Christopher (1953–). Anglican minister and Bible commentator.

Athanasius (296–373). Patriarch of Alexandria and theologian.

Basil of Caesarea (330–378). Bishop of Caesarea Mazaca in Cappadocia, Asia Minor and theologian.

Bridges, Matthew (1800–94). British-Canadian hymnist.

Bullinger, Heinrich (1504–75). Pastor in Zürich, Switzerland and theologian.

Byron, Lord (1788–1824). Poet and British peer of the realm.

Calvin, John (1509–64). Pastor of Geneva, theologian and Bible commentator.

Carson, D.A. (1946–). Canadian-American evangelical theologian and Bible commentator.

Chrysostom, John (347–407). Archbishop of Constantinople and prolific preacher and author.

Cowper, William (1731–1800). English poet and Anglican hymnwriter.

Crossman, Samuel (1623–83). Dean of Bristol and Anglican-Puritan hymnwriter.

Cyril of Alexandria (376–444). Patriarch of Alexandria and theologian.

Denny, James (1856–1917). Scottish Presbyterian minister and theologian.

Elizabeth II (1926–2022). Illustrious Queen of the United Kingdom of Great Britain and Northern Ireland and other Commonwealth realms.

Ephrem the Syrian (306–73). Theologian of Edessa and hymnographer-poet.

Gill, John (1697–1771). English Baptist minister, theologian and Bible commentator.

Gregory of Nyssa (335–94). Bishop of Nyssa in Cappadocia and theologian.

Henry, Matthew (1662–1714). British nonconformist minister and Bible commentator.

Herbert, George (1593–1633). English poet and Anglican minister.

Hodge, Charles (1797–1878). American Presbyterian theologian from Princeton.

Horace (65–68 BC). Roman lyric poet.

Horton, Thomas (1605–73). Vice Chancellor of Cambridge University and Minister of St Helen's, Bishopsgate in London.

Leo the Great (400–61). Bishop of Rome and theologian.

Lombard, Peter (1096–1160). Italian theologian and Bishop of Paris.

Luther, Martin (1483–1536). German Protestant Reformer, Bible translator and commentator.

Maximus of Turin (380–465). Bishop of Turin and theologian.

M'Cheyne, Robert Murray (1813–43). Church of Scotland minister and writer.

Mounce, William D. (1953–). American New Testament scholar and commentator.

Newman, John Henry (1801–90). English theologian and hymnwriter.

Origen (185–253). Prolific scholar and theologian from Alexandria.

Owen, John (1616–83). Puritan minister, theologian and Vice Chancellor of Oxford University.

Packer, J. I. (1926–2020). British-Canadian Anglican theologian.

Peterson, David G. (1944–). Australian Anglican New Testament scholar and Principal of Oak Hill Theological College, London.

Prior, David. British pastor, Bible commentator and Director of the Centre for Marketplace Theology in the City of London.

Pseudo-Augustine. A name given by scholars to various works falsely attributed to Augustine of Hippo.

Robertson, O. Palmer (1937–). American Presbyterian theologian and biblical scholar.

Russell, Bertrand (1872–1970). British philosopher and public intellectual.

Ryle, J. C. (1816–1900). Bishop of Liverpool, Bible commentator and tract writer.

Simeon, Charles (1759–1836). Anglican Evangelical minister in Cambridge, England and Bible commentator.

Stott, John (1921–2011). Anglican Evangelical minister in London, England, Bible commentator and writer.

Tennyson, Lord Alfred (1809–92). Poet Laureate during the reign of Queen Victoria.

Thiselton, Anthony (1937–2023). English Anglican theologian and Bible commentator.

Toplady, Augustus Montague (1740–78). Anglican minister, historian, theologian, and hymnwriter.

Vermigli, Peter Martyr (1499–1562). Italian Reformed theologian and Bible commentator.

Whitefield, George (1714–70). Anglican evangelist and writer.

Wright, N. T. (1948–). Anglican New Testament scholar and former Bishop of Durham.

Scripture Index

OLD TESTAMENT